WITNESSES TO NUREMBERG

*An Oral History of American Participants
at the War Crimes Trials*

Twayne's
ORAL HISTORY SERIES

Donald A. Ritchie, Series Editor

PREVIOUSLY PUBLISHED

Witnesses to the Holocaust:
An Oral History
Rhoda Lewin

Homesteading Women:
An Oral History of Colorado,
1890–1950
Julie Jones-Eddy

Between Management and Labor:
Oral Histories of Arbitration
Clara H. Friedman

Building Hoover Dam:
An Oral History
of the Great Depression
Andrew J. Dunar and
Dennis McBride

From the Old Country:
An Oral History of European
Migration to America
Bruce M. Stave and John F.
Sutherland with Aldo Salerno

Married to the Foreign Service:
An Oral History of the
American Diplomatic Spouse
Jewell Fenzi with Carl L. Nelson

Her Excellency:
An Oral History of
American Women Ambassadors
Ann Miller Morin

Doing Oral History
Donald A. Ritchie

Head of the Class: An Oral History of
African American Achievement in
Higher Education and Beyond
Gabrielle Morris

A Stranger's Supper:
An Oral History of Centenarian
Women in Montenegro
Zorka Milich

"We Have Just Begun to Not Fight":
An Oral History of Conscientious
Objectors in the Civilian Public
Service during World War II
Heather T. Frazer and
John O'Sullivan

Children of Los Alamos:
An Oral History of the Town
Where the Atomic Age Began
Katrina Mason

Women in the Mines:
Stories of Life and Work
Marat Moore

Crossing Over: An Oral History of
Refugees from Hitler's Reich
Ruth E. Wolman

Those Pullman Blues:
An Oral History of the African
American Railroad Attendant
David Perata

Launching the War on Poverty:
An Oral History
Michael Gillette

Poverty, Chastity, and Change:
Lives of Contemporary
American Nuns
Carole Garibaldi Rogers

Meatpackers: An Oral History of
Black Packinghouse Workers and Their
Struggle for Racial and Economic
Equality
Rick Halpern and Roger Horowitz

Winter Soldiers: An
Oral History of
Vietam Veterans against the War
Richard Stacewicz

BRUCE M. STAVE AND MICHELE PALMER
WITH LESLIE FRANK

WITNESSES TO NUREMBERG

An Oral History of American Participants at the War Crimes Trials

TWAYNE PUBLISHERS
An Imprint of Simon & Schuster Macmillan
New York

PRENTICE HALL INTERNATIONAL
London Mexico City New Delhi Singapore Sydney Toronto

2167 7428

Twayne's Oral History Series No. 27

Witnesses to Nuremberg: An Oral History of American Participants at the War Crimes Trials
Bruce M. Stave and Michele Palmer with Leslie Frank

Copyright © 1998 by Twayne Publishers

Twayne Publishers
An Imprint of Simon & Schuster Macmillan
1633 Broadway
New York, NY 10019

Library of Congress Cataloging-in-Publication Data

Stave, Bruce M.
    Witnesses to Nuremberg : an oral history of American participants
at the war crimes trials / Bruce M. Stave and Michele Palmer, with
Leslie Frank.
        p.   cm. — (Twayne's oral history series ; no. 27)
    Includes bibliographical references and index.
    ISBN 0-8057-1628-9 (alk. paper)
    1. Nuremberg Trial of Major German War Criminals, Nuremberg,
Germany, 1945–1946.   2. War Crime trials—Germany—Nuremberg—
History—20th century—Sources.   3. Courts—Germany—Nuremberg—
Officials and employees—Interviews.   4. World War, 1939–1945—
Personal narratives, American.   I. Palmer, Michele.   II. Frank,
Leslie.   III. Title.   IV. Series.
KZ1176.S73   1998
341.6'9'0268—dc21   98-39982
                                                            CIP

This paper meets the requirements of ANSI/NISO Z3948-1992 (Permanence of Paper).

10 9 8 7 6 5 4 3 2 1

Printed in the United States of America

*To the memory of those for whom
justice was sought at Nuremberg
and to those who helped bring it about*

The defendants at the International Military Tribunal sit in the dock: front row, left to right: Göring, Hess, Ribbentrop, Keitel, Kaltenbrunner, Rosenberg, Frank, Frick, Streicher, Funk, Schact; second row, left to right: Dönitz, Raeder, Schirach, Sauckel, Jodl, Papen, Seyss-Inquart, Speer, Neurath, Fritzsche.

"I was there when they all pleaded innocent, not guilty. I couldn't believe my ears."
—Harry Fiss

Contents

Foreword

A cataclysmic event on the scale of World War II directly affected millions of people around the world. By contrast, the Nuremberg Trials, where the leaders of Nazi Germany were tried for war crimes, involved only a small number of direct participants. The trials drew international attention in 1945 and 1946, and were captured on newsreels, but they seemed distant and peripheral in the postwar era when most people were preoccupied with rebuilding shattered lives, communities, and economies. In 1961, Hollywood focused renewed attention on the trials in the dramatic film *Judgment at Nuremberg*. By the 1990s, as the world confronted new cases of wartime atrocities, the Nuremberg Trials resurfaced as models for those seeking international justice. Since a half a century had elapsed since the trials, the need to interview surviving participants became imperative. The director and staff of the Center for Oral History at the Thomas J. Dodd Research Center of the University of Connecticut believed that oral history interviews would ensure the preservation of individual recollections along with the more formal documentation of the trials. The interviews from their collection contained in this volume record the stories of not only the prosecutors, but the jailers, interrogators, and translators involved in the trials, the journalists who covered the proceedings, and even the architect who designed the courtroom. Each testimony offers a distinctly personal view, recalling impressions of the atmosphere, details, and personalities of the trials. They re-create a historic reckoning that the world can ill afford to forget.

Oral history may well be the twentieth century's substitute for the written memoir. In exchange for the immediacy of diaries or correspondence, a retrospective interview offers a dialogue between the participant and the informed interviewer. Having prepared sufficient preliminary research, interviewers can direct the discussion into areas long since "forgotten," or no longer considered consequential. "I haven't thought about that in years" is a common response, just before an interviewee begins a surprisingly detailed description of some past incident. The quality of the interview—its candidness and depth—generally depends as much on the interviewer as on the interviewee, and the confidence and rapport between the two adds a special dimension to the spoken memoir.

Interviewers represent a variety of disciplines and work either as part of a collective effort or individually. Regardless of their different interests or the variety of their subjects, all interviewers have a common imperative: to collect memories while they are still available. Most oral historians feel an additional responsibility to make their interviews accessible for use beyond their own research needs. Still, important collections of vital, vibrant interviews like those scattered in archives throughout every state, are undiscovered or simply not used.

Twayne's Oral History Series seeks to identify those resources and to pub-lish selections of the best materials. The series lets people speak for them-selves, from their own unique perspectives on other people, places, and events. But in order to be more than a babble of voices, each volume orga-nizes its interviews around particular situations and events and ties them together with interpretive essays that place individuals in a larger historical context. The styles and format of each individual volume vary with the mate-rial from which they are drawn, demonstrating again the diversity of oral his-tory and its methodology.

Whenever oral historians gather in conference, they enjoy retelling their experiences: inspiring individuals they have met, unexpected information they have elicited, and unforgettable reminiscences that would otherwise never have been recorded. This invariably reminds listeners of others who deserve to be interviewed, provides them with models of interviewing techniques, and inspires them to make their own contribution to the field. I trust that the oral historians in this series—as interviewers, as editors, and as interpreters—will have a similar effect on their readers.

DONALD A. RITCHIE
Series Editor, Senate Historical Office

Acknowledgments

We wish to express our deep appreciation to all the participants in the *Witnesses to Nuremberg* oral history project: Harold Burson, Burton Carlow, Benjamin Ferencz, Gertrude Ferencz, Harry Fiss, William Glenny, Whitney Harris, Manfred Isserman, William Jackson, Annette Jacobsohn, Peter Jacobsohn, Dan Kiley, Henry King Jr., Robert King, George Krevit, Andy Logan, Joseph Maier, Mark Natlacen-Malec, Palmer McGee, Raymond McMahon Jr., Seymour Peyser, Edwin Rettig, Aino Rockler, Walter Rockler, Howard K. Smith, Richard P. Smith, Drexel Sprecher, Herbert Wechsler, Belle Mayer Zeck, and William Zeck.

Space limitations, and, in some cases, lack of final permissions, made it impossible to include all of their interviews in this book. However, their transcripts are on file in the Center for Oral History Collection, Archives and Special Collections Department, Thomas J. Dodd Research Center, University of Connecticut Libraries.

We also are grateful to Leslie Frank, who began as our research assistant on the *Witnesses to Nuremberg* oral history project and proved so helpful we wished to give her further recognition by including her among the authors.

Steven Park, a graduate assistant at the Center for Oral History, gave unstintingly of his expert computer support during the entire project, including the preparation of the charts in the Appendix.

Phil Samponaro and Joan Miller, also history graduate students, helped with the unending task of proofreading the transcripts.

Jeff Bass, a graduate assistant for the Thomas J. Dodd Papers, gave us a very useful overview of that collection and helped us find whatever we needed in the Dodd papers.

The entire staff of the Archives and Special Collections Department at the Thomas J. Dodd Research Center was also of invaluable help to us, including Director Thomas Wilsted, Bruce Stark, Terri Goldich, Tara Hurt, William Uricchio, and Rudy Witthus, as was the staff of the Homer Babbidge Library.

Other University of Connecticut colleagues we wish to thank include Alex

Bothell, for his help with reproducing the photographs; Arnold Dashefsky, Director, Center for Judaic Studies and Contemporary Jewish Life; Henry Krisch, who headed the Academic Committee for the Dodd Year; Judith Meyer, then Associate Provost, who found resources for the project when it first began; Linda Perrone, who directed the Dodd Program; our colleagues in the history department; and Jeffrey Diefendorf of the University of New Hampshire, who commented on papers based on the project presented at the 1996 Annual Meeting of the Oral History Association in Philadelphia.

Dara Hall, Martha McCormick, and Barbara Connor did their usual excellent job of transcribing.

General Editor Donald Ritchie, and Mark Zadrozny, then of Twayne Publishers, were supportive of the project from its inception. We particularly thank Don for his thoughtful editing. Others helpful at Twayne were Jill Lectka, Michele Kovacs, Jennifer Farthing, and Kim Brophy. Impressions Book and Journal Services assisted greatly in bringing this book to final form.

Finally, we give our thanks to our spouses, Sondra Astor Stave and Michael Palmer, for their encouragement, and to Michael, for his computer, as well as moral, support. Channing M-L and Sara Schloss Stave offered similar encouragement, as did Dara and Bill Hall and Rachel and Jim Schaeffer.

Photographs and Credits

The defendants at the International Military Tribunal sit in the dock. From the Thomas J. Dodd Papers, Archives and Special Collections Department, Thomas J. Dodd Research Center, University of Connecticut Libraries. Used with permission. Page vi

Dan Kiley. Photo by Bruce M. Stave. Page 15

The exterior of the Palace of Justice. From the Thomas J. Dodd Papers, Archives and Special Collections Department, Thomas J. Dodd Research Center, University of Connecticut Libraries. Used with permission. Page 22

The courtroom in the Palace of Justice during renovations. From the Thomas J. Dodd Papers, Archives and Special Collections Department, Thomas J. Dodd Research Center, University of Connecticut Libraries. Used with permission. Page 25

The finished courtroom at the Palace of Justice (shown during the Medical Case). Photo courtesy of George Krevit. Page 30

William H. Glenny. Photo courtesy of William H. Glenny. Page 39

Guards covering the prison wing were assigned to a cell, two hours on, four hours off. From the Thomas J. Dodd Papers, Archives and Special Collections Department, Thomas J. Dodd Research Center, University of Connecticut Libraries. Used with permission. Page 53

Burton Carlow. Photo by Bruce M. Stave. Page 55

Following the suicide of Robert Ley, one guard was assigned to each cell. From the Thomas J. Dodd Papers, Archives and Special Collections Department, Thomas J. Dodd Research Center, University of Connecticut Libraries. Used with permission. Page 59

George Krevit. Photo courtesy of George Krevit. Page 71

Corporal George Krevit presents Alfried Krupp with papers for his indictment. Photo courtesy of George Krevit. Page 73

Harry Fiss. Photo by Bruce M. Stave. Page 87

A chart and photos of the concentration camps and other evidence shown at the war crimes trials. From the Thomas J. Dodd Papers, Archives and

Special Collections Department, Thomas J. Dodd Research Center, University of Connecticut Libraries. Page 104

Joseph Maier. Photo by Michael Palmer. Page 108

Hermann Göring was the highest-ranking Nazi to stand trial at Nuremberg. From the Thomas J. Dodd Papers, Archives and Special Collections Department, Thomas J. Dodd Research Center, University of Connecticut Libraries. Used with permission. Page 116

Seymour Peyser. Photo by Bruce M. Stave. Page 127

The Grand Hotel housed the bulk of the legal staff during the trials. From the Thomas J. Dodd Papers, Archives and Special Collections Department, Thomas J. Dodd Research Center, University of Connecticut Libraries. Used with permission. Page 134

Seymour Peyser poses with two young German boys and two American colleagues. Photo courtesy of Seymour Peyser. Page 136

Nazi Labor Minister Robert Ley was one of the original defendants at the IMT at Nuremberg. From the Thomas J. Dodd Papers, Archives and Special Collections Department, Thomas J. Dodd Research Center, University of Connecticut Libraries. Used with permission. Page 140

Robert King. Photo by Bruce M. Stave. Page 150

U.S. chief prosecutor Robert Jackson's opening remarks at the IMT were inspiring. From the Thomas J. Dodd Papers, Archives and Special Collections Department, Thomas J. Dodd Research Center, University of Connecticut Libraries. Used with permission. Page 152

Robert King listens to an English translation during the closing arguments of the Justice Case. From the Robert King Papers, Archives and Special Collections Department, Thomas J. Dodd Research Center, University of Connecticut Libraries. Used with permission. Page 158

Henry King Jr. Photo courtesy of Henry King Jr. Page 167

Albert Speer served a prison sentence of 20 years for war crimes and crimes against humanity. From the Thomas J. Dodd Papers, Archives and Special Collections Department, Thomas J. Dodd Research Center, University of Connecticut Libraries. Used with permission. Page 171

Harold Burson. Photo by Bruce M. Stave. Page 179

The old city of Nuremberg was almost completely destroyed during the war. From the Thomas J. Dodd Papers, Archives and Special Collections Department, Thomas J. Dodd Research Center, University of Connecticut Libraries. Used with permission. Page 183

Andy Logan. Photo by Bruce M. Stave. Page 193

Personnel organize the 4,000 tons of documents used in the trials. From the Thomas J. Dodd Papers, Archives and Special Collections Department, Thomas J. Dodd Research Center, University of Connecticut Libraries. Used with permission. Page 202

The liberation of Dachau concentration camp. Photo courtesy of Richard P. Smith. Page 204

Introduction

Writing on Christmas Eve, 1945, to one of the American prosecutors at the Nuremberg War Crimes Trials, a former concentration camp inmate had no doubt about the guilt of the defendants. "There is no verdict which could even partially atone for these crimes, since even these men have only one head," proclaimed the aggrieved writer, who thought that one hanging per defendant was not enough. Another anonymous correspondent pointed out that "even if some individuals should have committed an injustice, this does not concern the entire, *descent* [*sic*] German people." Both, along with the entire world, expressed concern about justice after World War II.[1]

What was justice in light of the heinous crimes committed during the Holocaust and had there been any "*descent* German people" during the war? Such questions still resonate more than a half-century since the war, particularly after the 1996 publication of Daniel Jonah Goldhagen's *Hitler's Willing Executioners: Ordinary Germans and the Holocaust,* a book that questions the complicity of ordinary Germans in the Holocaust and demonstrates their involvement, and the impact of Steven Spielberg's acclaimed film *Schindler's List* which tells the story of Oscar Schindler, a German industrialist who saved the lives of many of his workers while simultaneously benefiting from their free forced labor.[2]

In 1945, however, American officials desired to avoid the assessment of collective guilt and the appearance of revenge without due process. Major Nazi leaders were indicted on four counts—conspiracy, crimes against peace, war crimes, and crimes against humanity—and tried by an International Military Tribunal (IMT) made up of Americans, British, French, and Russians. Twelve subsequent trials under solely American auspices followed and brought to judgment Nazi doctors, lawyers, industrialists, concentration camp administrators, and others. The IMT trial began in the fall of 1945 and concluded less than a year later; the final subsequent trial, the Ministries Case, lasted until mid-April 1949.[3] The idea of establishing an international court to judge those accused of violating international law was not new and received consideration during World War I. Some among the Allies in World War I urged that the German military and its leadership, especially Kaiser Wilhelm II, be

1

placed on trial and punished as war criminals. The quest for justice, despite the Allies' own infractions of international law, primarily stemmed from Germany's ruthless invasion of neutral Belgium. Allied propaganda exploiting German atrocities increasingly stoked the public's ire for revenge. However, for a complex set of reasons, the first attempt at international war crimes punishment failed.[4]

Some believed that such failure to assign individual accountability in World War I paved the way, at least in part, for the atrocities of World War II. Reports of Germany's treatment of the Jews and others in the years immediately prior to the outbreak of World War II shocked other nations. However, nothing was done to intervene, perhaps because the actions seemed unbelievable, nations felt constrained to interfere with the "internal affairs" of another, or because of indifference and prejudice. Nor did other nations prevent Hitler's seizure of territory such as Czechoslovakia. Relative silence marked the era of appeasement. Once war broke out, however, the Nazi atrocities no longer avoided accountability. For instance, in January 1942, nine Allied powers issued the St. James Declaration establishing as a war aim the punishment of those guilty of war crimes. At the Moscow Conference in November 1943, the United States, Great Britain, and the U.S.S.R. laid the foundation for what was to become the international Nuremberg Trials. And, in August 1945, at the Conference of London, the Allied powers established the Charter of the International Military Tribunal, which detailed the crimes to be tried and the procedures to be followed. Those crimes, which included the establishment of concentration camps, the "final solution" that attempted to wipe out the Jewish people; the additional killing of Catholics, gypsies, homosexuals, political dissenters, and others deemed "undesirable"; horrific medical experimentation; and the general imposition of totalitarian terror, indeed marked the Nazis as very special criminals.[5]

In such a context, not all parties easily agreed to trials, which attempted to abide by due process. British Prime Minister Winston Churchill remembered the failed efforts after World War I, as did his countrymen. To simplify matters and to exact deserved revenge for Nazi atrocities, they called for summary executions of captured Nazi leaders. In the United States, Secretary of the Treasury Henry Morgenthau, a Jew, agreed. He developed a plan to reduce Germany from an industrial giant to a pastoral nation. Because Nazis had treated others so horrendously, it would be fitting for them to suffer equally. Low-level officials should be impressed into forced labor in order to repair the damage Hitler's Germany imposed on the rest of Europe. War criminals, under the Morgenthau Plan, would be shipped back for trial to the countries where they committed their crimes. Major criminals, once identified to Allied forces, would be summarily shot.[6]

Official American policy moved in other directions. President Franklin D. Roosevelt and other policy makers such as Secretary of War Henry Stimson— perhaps haunted by the fact that the United States avoided international responsibility in the eyes of some when it did not join the League of Nations after World War I, along with a desire for postwar stability encouraged by rule of law and a recognition of the advent of a Cold War with the Soviet Union and Germany's role in it—advocated an internationalist foreign policy after World War II. This included organizing the United Nations and participating in the IMT. As Stimson wrote to President Roosevelt on September 9, 1944, "the very punishment of these men in a dignified manner consistent with the advance of civilization will have the greater effect on posterity. . . . I am disposed to believe that, at least as to the chief Nazi officials, we should participate in an international tribunal constituted to try them."[7]

At the trials, the masters of the Third Reich convicted themselves. The cases were based primarily on documentation. "Thanks to the nature of the German people, they recorded just about everything they did," noted an American attorney who participated in the prosecution of Nazi lawyers. This may be an understatement when one considers that the documents at the IMT trial included over 700 million mimeographed pages, "the paper weighing more than 4,000 tons and, stacked flat, reach[ed] 47.4 miles in height. There were 2,296,958 photostats, 640,000 off-set prints, and 950,000 stencils." The attorney advised, "When you confront somebody with a document with his signature on it, it's very difficult for him to deny that it happened or that he said it." While the defendants in the dock did attempt to deny their guilt, their own records made it hard to do so convincingly.[8]

Those charged constituted a roster of leading Nazis still alive at that time, but key players in the German tragedy such as Adolf Hitler, Heinrich Himmler, and Josef Goebbels were no longer around to be judged by humanity. Hitler's henchman, Martin Bormann, received judgment in absentia. The head of the German Labor Front, Robert Ley, escaped the gallows by committing suicide before the trial. According to one of his prison interrogators, questioners confronted Ley in an attempt to reconstruct the Nazi organizational structure. The interrogator described how Ley, ill with a cold, distracted, and smoking cigarettes offered to him by Americans, spent hours answering questions. As an American Jew, Seymour Peyser had read some of Ley's writing and noted, "I hated the SOB." However, by the end of their meeting, Peyser admitted, "I realized he was a human being." The actual trial brought out the human frailty of other defendants. They ranged from the key figure Hermann Göring, who also committed suicide, to Admiral Karl Dönitz, who received a 10-year sentence, to Franz von Papen, one of only three acquitted defendants.[9]

The notorious celebrity of the defendants confused their treatment by American captors. A former prison guard, who was 18 years old at the time of his service in the army, seemed impressed enough by those he guarded to the point of breaking rules and getting their autographs, apparently not an uncommon practice in the prison area. On the other hand, he expressed disgust with their deeds. "The whole world was screaming for revenge. . . .These men got what they deserved," he concluded.[10]

Not everyone at the trials shared the same goals. The Americans had squelched the Morgenthau Plan earlier and expressed concern about restoring a respect for the rule of law and de-Nazifying Germany. The British reluctantly consented, but the Russians, who suffered greatly during World War II, sought revenge. Even before the IMT trial, visiting Russian politician Andrei Y. Vyshinsky led a toast to the speedy conviction and execution of the defendants. When three of the 22 defendants were acquitted, those who sought "fairness" believed it had been achieved. A young Jewish refugee from Austria, who emigrated to America, joined the U.S. Army, and attended the IMT trial as a translator, did not share such satisfaction. "I was there when they all pleaded innocent, not guilty. I couldn't believe my ears." He felt that all of the defendants should have been hung. The concept of conspiracy, which cast the widest net in bringing Nazis to trial, had roots in Anglo-American law; this concept appeared foreign to the French and Russians, as did the proceedings generally. The early stages of the Cold War did not enhance trust between east and west. The trials played out against a backdrop of changing diplomacy and the onset of a new world stage.[11]

More noticeably, however, they played out against the destroyed city of Nuremberg. When the Americans arrived for the trials, most were struck by the devastation wreaked on the war-ravaged city. Germans spoke of *Trümmer*—rubble—and lived a life amidst the rubble. In Nuremberg, there were 10.7 million cubic meters of rubble or 23.5 cubic meters per inhabitant; almost 50 percent of its total housing had been lost. A young American lawyer recalled, "It was a staggering sight to roll into the city and see nothing but rubble. . . . It took a while to get used to that." Another American remembered that the Germans "were living in homes that were destroyed." It was a "bleak, cold winter. . . . it was really a very tragic sight to behold." A Special Services soldier described his quarters across the street from the Palace of Justice, site of the trials: "Most of the roof was gone. The top floor was uninhabitable. The second floor had holes in the wall. Each [room] had a coal stove. I'd get up at 5:30 and start the fire, because it was freezing."[12]

Even at the city's Grand Hotel, which was residence for a number of high-ranking Americans and served as a watering hole and social center, all was not free of problems. A female attorney at one of the trials subsequent to the IMT remembered her room as very impressive, with tasteful furniture and beautiful floor-to-ceiling drapes. But it was chilly on her first night there, and when she went to close the window and pulled the beautiful drapes aside, she discovered that the entire wall was missing, which left her staring down at the street below! The Palace of Justice was one of the few buildings that had been mostly preserved. That twist of fate, plus the intention to hold the trials in the city that served as the center of Nazi ceremony and the origin of the notorious Nuremberg Laws, provided the site for the trials.[13]

For the lawyers, translators, interpreters, secretaries, prison guards, minor functionaries, journalists, and members of the military, coming to Nuremberg was a rendezvous with history. In a more prosaic sense, it meant participating in a community of Americans abroad, sharing the joys of camaraderie as victors in an occupied land, while living among those suffering the trials and tribulations of defeat. For many, involvement in the trials was a defining experience that welded lifelong friendships, encouraged matrimony, and shaped their worldview and sense of justice.

The trials brought to the bombed-out city a combination of American celebrities and anonymous participants. Among the former, Robert H. Jackson, Francis Biddle, Thomas J. Dodd, and Telford Taylor stand out. Robert Jackson, on leave from the U.S. Supreme Court, became the chief U.S. prosecutor at the IMT. His introductory statement at the trial has been praised for its eloquence and goes down in the history of international jurisprudence as a major document. He began:

> The privilege of opening the first trial in history for crimes against the peace of the world imposes a grave responsibility. The wrongs that we seek to condemn and punish have been so calculated, so malignant, and so devastating, that civilization cannot tolerate their being ignored, because it cannot survive their being repeated. That four great nations, flushed with victory and stung with injury stay the hand of vengeance and voluntarily submit their captive enemies to the judgment of the law is one of the most significant tributes that Power has ever paid to Reason.

Jackson went on to place Nazi actions within the framework of a conspiratorial plan. While he won worldwide plaudits for this opening, he was faulted later for his cross-examination of Nazi leader Hermann Göring, whom many believed bested Jackson in a battle of wits.[14]

Francis Biddle pulled no punches when he wrote to his wife, "Jackson's cross-examination, on the whole, has been futile and weak. [Göring] listens to every question, takes his time, answers well. Bob doesn't listen to the answers, depends on his notes, always a sign of weakness. He hasn't *absorbed* his case." Biddle, a Philadelphia aristocrat who had succeeded Jackson as U.S. Attorney General and then was fired by President Harry S Truman, received some solace when the president appointed him a judge at the IMT trial. Jackson, however, thought Biddle was undistinguished and unfit for the bench at Nuremberg. His appointment, according to the chief prosecutor, diminished the occasion. Moreover, Jackson, the U.S. Supreme Court Justice turned Nuremberg prosecutor, had to plead his case before Biddle, the attorney transformed into one of the four IMT judges. Needless to say, personal conflicts, internal politics, and infighting shaped in the courtrooms and political arenas of the United States did not stop at ocean's edge.[15]

Conversely, participation at Nuremberg paid political dividends at home as some claimed was the case for Connecticut's Thomas J. Dodd. Dodd, a Yale Law School graduate, joined the FBI in 1934 and as a special agent became involved in cases leading to the capture of "public enemies" John Dillinger and "Babyface" Nelson. He then served as a New Deal state administrator for the National Youth Administration, and in 1938 joined the U.S. Department of Justice as a special assistant to the attorney general. During World War II, Dodd handled espionage and sabotage cases, which led to the conviction of several spies. At the war's end, Robert Jackson asked Dodd to join his IMT team and Dodd served as Executive Trial Counsel, which made him the second-ranking U.S. lawyer at the IMT and manager of daily operations for the prosecutors. He cross-examined many of the Nazi defendants in an attempt to prove the charge of conspiracy to wage aggressive war. Dodd's flair for the dramatic (in one instance, display of a shrunken head of a concentration camp inmate as evidence of Nazi atrocities) earned him the reputation among some colleagues as a grandstander. On the other hand, on return home, his Nuremberg participation won him presidential praise and the Medal of Freedom. It did nothing to discourage his later victories for Congress and the Senate.[16]

Telford Taylor, a star of the trials subsequent to the IMT case, had less success in establishing a post-Nuremberg political career but went on to a distinguished career as an attorney, teacher, and writer. Many thought he was intellectually the best mind among the prosecutors. Holding the rank of colonel, Taylor served as prosecutor of the German High Command during the IMT trial, a case that initially went begging for an American lawyer. Taylor's incentive to take it on was a promise that he would replace Robert Jackson as chief prosecutor at the subsequent trials. He also won appointment as a general, which did not sit well with some senior military personnel who envied his success. Taylor has been described as "a Renaissance man: tennis player, pianist, clarinetist, composer, writer, bridge expert, dancer," but somewhat standoffish and not possessing the common touch. No one, however, questioned his legal acuity, which, along with his Renaissance airs, made him the star of the trials in their final years. The lessons of Nuremberg resonated for Taylor during the Vietnam War when he compared the two experiences and began a book with a quote from Robert Jackson's opening statement: "While this law is first applied against German aggressors, if it is to serve any useful purpose it must condemn aggression by any other nations, including those who sit here now in judgment." The Nuremberg experience surely had a long-term impact.[17]

It is this "Nuremberg experience" that the interviews published in this book attempt to capture. From arrival in the bombed-out city, to the reconstructing of the courtroom, to the trials themselves, to the everyday social life of the participants, those interviewed remember back to more than a half-century ago. In evaluating this oral history, readers must recognize that these are memories that have been filtered by the passage of time. Some of our interviewees have told their stories numerous times. Others have read or seen documentaries or filmed fictionalized accounts about the events they have lived.

In 1961, the Hollywood film *Judgment at Nuremberg* not only earned an Academy Award for Maximilian Schell as best actor but shaped the public's consciousness about the trials. Books have done the same. As one Nuremberg attorney told us, "I don't remember how much of this I got from Telford Taylor's book. . . . Memory is a strange thing when you go back 50 years." In this context, noted psychiatrist W. Walter Menninger suggests, "It is significant that, no matter how accurately an event may be perceived and stored, when it is remembered it is not simply replayed as on a videotape; it is reconstructed."[18]

Such "reconstructions" serve as valuable sources for historians who use them wisely in collaboration with other sources and understand their limitations as well as the opportunities they represent for constructing the past. Taken together, the interviews amount to a portion of the collective memory of those Americans who participated in the Nuremberg Trials. For readers of this volume, the conversations offer something else. They humanize history, permitting individuals to personalize events and make them accessible to a wide audience. This was not lost on the same attorney, who remarked, "You asked generally for human stories. I guess that is one of the reasons for the oral history process."[19]

The "human stories" we collected include those of the architect who redesigned the famous courtroom. He explained how he sought a chamber that was "unified, orderly and dignified and reflected the scales of justice." He revealed how he planned to increase the defendants' discomfort by building backless benches for the dock but ultimately had to relent. How did he compare his work to Hitler's architect, Albert Speer, one of the defendants? We couldn't resist asking that question and were instructed that Speer's was "not a design for democracy." Some might argue that because German POWs were impressed as laborers to complete the necessary work on the courtroom, we dropped the ball as interviewers by not asking about the comparison to Speer's use of slave labor.[20]

That question might disturb those who see an ethical chasm between innocents pressed into work because of their religion, nationality, politics, or sexual orientation and soldiers who fought for the triumph of genocide, prejudice, and totalitarian injustice. Whatever one's response to these polarities, it is clear that in oral history it is important to know which questions have been asked and how they have been posed. That is because oral history is an interactive process and the interview is shaped by the give and take between interviewer and interviewee. Consequently, although the transcripts of our interviews have been edited for publication in this volume, we have included some of our most significant questions as well as responses. In this manner, it is hoped that readers will get a sense of the shaping of each interview.[21]

Full interviews, along with others not published herein because of the limitation of space or the lack of final permission, are available in the Center for Oral History collection at the Thomas J. Dodd Research Center, University of Connecticut. It was in conjunction with the opening of the Dodd Center, inaugurated by President Clinton in October 1995, that this project began. Tom Dodd, a former U.S. Senator from Connecticut, served as a prosecutor at the IMT Trial, a fact that encouraged the university to devote the first year after the Research Center's inauguration to reflection on the trials and human rights.

Identifying potential interviewees is an early and often difficult task when formulating an oral history project. The existence of name lists of those who attended reunions of Nuremberg personnel had been collected by the university in anticipation of the Dodd Research Center opening; these lists offered us a base for selection of interviewees who could reconstruct the Nuremberg experience. Resources limited our choices for visits primarily to those who resided in the New York–New England region, although our scope was broadened when a number of attorneys and their wives participated in a conference in Storrs, Connecticut, where we are located. Five of the conversations in this volume were undertaken by a single interviewer. In some instances, two of us participated as interviewers, and on relatively few occasions, three of us did. In all, we conducted 30 interviews in what we believed to be an original project. This volume, which includes 11 of those interviews, is divided into five parts related to the functions of individuals at the trials: the courtroom's architect; prison and security guards; interrogators and translators; attorneys; and journalists. The conclusion is a conversation among the authors in which we discuss the making of this book, its purpose, and the value of oral history for this project. One appendix lists the defendants with the charges against them, the verdicts, and sentences, and the other is a transcript of an early broadcast on the eve of the IMT trial on Armed Forces Radio.

While a number of projects have been devoted to Holocaust survivors (the most ambitious evolving from Steven Spielberg's Survivors of the Shoah Foundation), when we began work we knew of none devoted exclusively to the Nuremberg War Crimes Trials. It was not until we were well along in our interviewing and already had chosen a name for our project that Hilary Gaskin's *Eyewitnesses at Nuremberg* came to our attention. First published in Great Britain and hard to come by in the United States, the book, which is organized differently and does not include questions along with the statements of its 24 participants, covers similar material and should be read as a companion volume by anyone interested in published first-person accounts of the Nuremberg experience.[22]

Our oral history accounts offer life stories as well as personal recollections of the Nuremberg experience. All interviewees were asked about their early background and events and decisions that led them to Nuremberg. Some had European Jewish backgrounds and suffered from Nazi persecution but were fortunate to leave their native nations prior to the Holocaust and returned as part of the U.S. Army. One came to the trials because it offered an interesting first job to a young attorney. Another became a translator because the job provided him a ticket back to Germany where he could ask for his future wife's hand in marriage from her parents, who had survived the war there. A U.S. lawyer, who became a prosecutor at the subsequent trials, was so inspired by chief American prosecutor Robert H. Jackson's opening statement at the IMT that he felt compelled to join the proceedings. He recalled, "The eloquence of the speech was just overpowering to me."[23]

The interviews relate tragic tales of the liberated concentration camps; provide portraits of Nazi prisoners, particularly the infamous but apparently highly intelligent and perversely charming Hermann Göring; describe living conditions of the American trial community; consider the growing tension and distrust but occasional camaraderie between western and Soviet participants; and discuss the reactions of Americans at home to those who returned from Nuremberg, which often amounted to indifference.

Such immediate indifference pales in the long view of history. The importance of the trials as a paramount historical event of the twentieth century, if not of all time, leaves little to question. Their lasting legal significance may be less certain. As William E. Jackson, who assisted his father, America's chief prosecutor, at the trial, remarked, "Nuremberg made clear once and for all that crimes against peace are international crimes. . . . The law has been clear. What is lacking, of course, is enforcement." Other interviewees agreed that the principles of the Nuremberg Trials have not been applied to the perpetrators of aggression and atrocity in the half-century that followed the judicial conclusion to World War II.[24]

However, almost exactly 50 years after the execution of the IMT defendants, a newspaper headline proclaimed, "Bosnian Serb draws first war crimes sentence since WW II." Drazen Erdemovic, age 25, a Croat who served with the Bosnian Serb army, admitted being part of an eight-man execution squad that gunned down unarmed civilians in 1995. His defense contended that he only carried out orders to shoot because he feared for his life, but a United Nations Court sentenced him to 10 years in prison for his role in the massacre of 1,200 Muslims. Subsequently, 41-year-old Dusan Tadic, a Bosnian Serb convicted of five war crimes and six crimes against humanity, was sentenced to 20 years in prison for torturing and killing his neighbors. Between 1993 and 1997 the tribunal publicly indicted 77 people, including the two main leaders, Radovan Karadzic and General Ratko Mladic, both of whom were charged with genocide. Neither was in custody, although pressure built to bring them to justice. Clearly, while the concept of Nuremberg lived, the tribunal did not apply it to the main players in the "ethnic cleansing" that ravaged the former Yugoslavia during the 1990s.[25]

As a new millennium approached, however, Nazi war criminals suffered the possibility of capture a half-century after Nuremberg. Isolated instances of the unearthing of a Nazi past appeared intermittently in American newspapers during the 1990s. This results in part from the U.S. Justice Department's Office of Special Investigations (OSI), which includes lawyers and historians who still hunt for Nazis and their collaborators in the United States. The office didn't get started until 1979—34 years after the beginning of the Nuremberg Trials. Congressional pressure forced its creation after authorities determined that through neglect or bungling, the U.S. Immigration and Naturalization Service had denaturalized only one Nazi between 1945 and 1979. OSI can sue to revoke the citizenship of immigrants who concealed their Nazi war records to obtain admission to the United States. Between 1979 and 1997, the office filed civil suits to revoke the citizenship of over 100 defendants; 60 had been denaturalized and 48 were deported or left voluntarily. Thomas Dodd's son, Christopher, who succeeded his father as a senator from Connecticut, said in 1997 that Congress would not tolerate disbanding OSI while anyone implicated in the Holocaust remained alive. "If we declare the search is over, we are saying, 'To those of you involved in this, sleep well tonight. Enjoy your meals. Relax. It's over,' " Dodd said. For him, the legacy of Nuremberg made that unacceptable.[26]

That legacy lingers. The memories of American participants at Nuremberg hold the experience in high regard. Many would agree with one spectator at the trials that those who sat in judgment at Nuremberg acted as the "conscience of the world." Those who witnessed this conscience at work experienced a very special part of history. For several, the idealism of their youth had not disappeared even after 50 years. The defining experience of Nuremberg left a lasting imprint. As one attorney exclaimed, "If you wanted to see the stars, you had to climb the mountains. At Nuremberg, I got a sense of the blueprint of the world, the future, the way it ought to look, and I became an idealist because I had the vision. . . . I had the time to see the stars, and have the same vision myself, and I try and work for the achievement of the goal, with a sense of mission."[27]

As night had descended on the planet during the Holocaust and World War II, with the trials that ended that trauma their starlight began to illuminate a new postwar era that would have its own examples of human tragedy and triumph. American witnesses to Nuremberg give testimony to that historic transformation in the pages that follow.

Notes

1. Phil Oberbuchner to Colonel [Robert] Storey, December 24, 1945, and undated letter signed "One for all" in the Thomas J. Dodd Papers (387:8575), Archives and Special Collections Department, Thomas J. Dodd Research Center, University of Connecticut Libraries, used with permission.

2. Daniel Jonah Goldhagen, *Hitler's Willing Executioners: Ordinary Germans and the Holocaust* (New York: Knopf, 1996); *Schindler's List* won the Academy Award for Best Picture in 1993.

3. Norman E. Tutorow, *War Crimes, War Criminals, and War Crimes Trials: An Annotated Bibliography and Source Book* (Westport, Conn.: Greenwood Press, 1986), appendices 5 and 8.

4. James F. Willis, *Prologue to Nuremberg: The Politics and Diplomacy of Punishing War Criminals of the First World War* (Westport, Conn.: Greenwood Press, 1982), 3–4, xi–xii.

5. John Alan Appleman, *Military Tribunals and International Crimes* (Westport, Conn.: Greenwood Press, 1971), vii–viii.

6. Ann Tusa and John Tusa, *The Nuremberg Trial* (New York: Atheneum, 1984), 50–52.

7. Willis, *Prologue to Nuremberg*, 173–75.

8. Interview with Robert King herein; statistics from Appleman, *Military Tribunals and International Crimes*, ix.

9. For a description of defendants and the counts on which they were charged, the verdicts determined, and sentences they received, see Tusa and Tusa, *The Nuremberg Trial*, 494–504; also see appendix 1 herein; portrait of Robert Ley from interview with Seymour Peyser herein.

10. Interview with William Glenny herein.

11. Robert E. Conot, *Justice at Nuremberg* (New York: Harper & Row, 1983); interview with Seymour Peyser herein; Tusa and Tusa, *The Nuremberg Trial* , 232; Joseph E. Persico, *Nuremberg: Infamy on Trial* (New York: Penguin Books, 1994), 123–34; interview with Harry Fiss herein.

12. Jeffrey M. Diefendorf, *In the Wake of War: The Reconstruction of German Cities after World War II* (New York: Oxford University Press, 1993), 13–15, 126; interviews with Raymond McMahon, WTNCOH, and Harold Burson and Burt Carlow, herein. Original transcripts on file in Center for Oral History Collection, Thomas J. Dodd Research Center, University of Connecticut, Storrs, Connecticut (WTNCOH). WTNCOH refers to interviews in the Center for Oral History Collection that are not included in this book.

13. Interview Z, WTNCOH. Identity of interviewee withheld because permission not final.

14. Quote from Robert H. Jackson, "Opening Address for the United States, November 21, 1945," in Michael R. Marrus, *The Nuremberg War Crimes Trial, 1945–46* (Boston: Bedford Books, 1997), 79–85; for the full text, see International Military Tribunal, *Trial of the Major War Criminals before the International Military Tribunal, Nuremberg, 14 November 1945–1 October 1946*, 42 vols. (Nuremberg: International Military Tribunal, 1947), vol. 2.

15. Persico, *Nuremberg: Infamy on Trial*, 61, 280–81.

16. For a useful sketch of Dodd's career, see the introduction by Jeffrey D. Bass to the finding aid for the Thomas J. Dodd Papers, University of Connecticut Libraries Archives and Special Collections, Storrs, Connecticut, December 1996. Also, see Jeffrey D. Bass, "Wellspring of a Connecticut Crusader: Thomas J. Dodd and the Nuremberg Trial," *Connecticut History* 37, no. 1 (Spring 1996): 31–45.

17. Persico, *Nuremberg: Infamy on Trial*, 204–6, 309–10; Telford Taylor, *Nuremberg and Vietnam: An American Tragedy* (Chicago: Quadrangle Books, 1970),

11–12; for Taylor's story of the trials, see Telford Taylor, *The Anatomy of the Nuremberg Trials: A Personal Memoir* (New York: Knopf, 1992).

18. Interview with Seymour Peyser herein; the film *Judgment at Nuremberg* dealt with the "Justice Trial," one of the proceedings subsequent to the IMT, which specifically concerned lawyers and judges—those who administered (or perverted) justice—under Hitler's Third Reich. Peyser was a consultant to the film; Robert King, whose interview appears herein, served as an attorney on the case. Also, see Taylor, *Anatomy of the Nuremberg Trials*; W. Walter Menninger, "Memory and History: What Can You Believe?," *Journal of the Midwest Archives Conference* 21, no. 2 (1996): 100.

19. For considerations of memory and history, see Michael Frisch, *A Shared Authority: Essays on the Craft of Oral and Public History* (Albany: SUNY Press, 1990); the special issue "Memory and American History," *Journal of American History* (ed. David Thelen) 75 (March 1989); and Tracy E. K'Meyer, " 'What Koinonia Was All About': The Role of Memory in a Changing Community," *Oral History Review* 24, no. 1 (Summer 1997): 1–22; interview with Seymour Peyser herein.

20. Interview with Dan Kiley herein.

21. For a discussion of the interactive nature of oral history, see Valerie Yow, " 'Do I Like Them Too Much?': Effects of the Oral History Interview on the Interviewer and Vice Versa," *Oral History Review* 24, no. 1 (Summer 1997): 55–79. Space considerations, as well as the desire to avoid repetition and to maintain the flow of the interview, prompted us to eliminate the inclusion of all questions.

22. Hilary Gaskin, *Eyewitnesses at Nuremberg* (London: Arms & Armour Press, 1990). We wish to thank Alexander Krulic, then a Yale University undergraduate writing his senior thesis, for bringing this volume to our attention.

23. See interviews with Harry Fiss and Robert King, herein. Also see interviews with Raymond McMahon and Peter Jacobsohn in WTNCOH. For an accessible excerpt of Robert H. Jackson's opening address to the IMT, see Marrus, *The Nuremberg War Crime Trial*, 79–85.

24. Interview with William E. Jackson, WTNCOH.

25. *Journal Inquirer* (Manchester, Connecticut), November 30, 1996, 3; July 11, 1997, 5; July 14, 1997, 5; *Willimantic* (Connecticut) *Chronicle*, July 14, 1997, 1; *Hartford Courant*, August 10, 1997, A1.

26. *Hartford Courant*, August 7, 1997, A1, A12.

27. Interview with Richard P. Smith, WTNCOH; interview with Henry King herein.

THE COURTROOM'S ARCHITECT

DAN KILEY

Architect of Palace of Justice Renovations

Drafted into the U.S. Army, Dan Kiley worked his way into the Presentation Branch of the Office of Strategic Services (OSS), eventually taking charge as Chief of Design after the departure of Eero Saarinen. Kiley was given secret orders to find and renovate a location for the German War Crimes Trial. Eventually, the Justice Department selected Nuremberg as the site, and Kiley went to work renovating the Palace of Justice. "Unified, orderly, and dignified, that's what the courtroom should be—and it should reflect the scales of justice." Kiley went on to become an internationally renowned landscape architect.

I was born in Boston on September 2, 1912. That's the year the Red Sox won the pennant. My father was in construction, and we weren't very well-off. But it was a very nice childhood. Actually, I was born in Roxbury Highlands, which is part of Boston, and is now pretty much of a slum, but it was a beautiful place. In 1912 it was pretty nice; it was overlooking Boston Harbor, across Dorchester. I went to grammar school there. Then we moved to West Roxbury, about 10 years later. That was the next step up in economic terms. I went to Jamaica Plain High School. When I graduated in 1930 it was the height of the Depression, and it was very difficult to find jobs, so I wrote to all the landscape architects in Boston—and planners—and was offered a job without pay with this very nice man, Warren H. Manning, one of the great practitioners of early landscape architecture. He was an associate of Frederick

Law Olmsted Sr., and he gave me a free hand. I was a kid. He thought I could do everything. [laughs] It was a wonderful opportunity; that's how I really started.

Did you go to college?

No. Number one, I was too poor to go to college. I had to get a job out of high school. And probably I wasn't that bright. It would have taken me a year or two of prep school to get in. It was just as well, though. I was lucky in a way that I wasn't too serious. I just liked to have fun, you know? I liked girls and fun. [laughs] I was working for Manning. I started as an apprentice in September 1932. He's quite well known, even now. Mr. Manning gave me two pieces of advice. Number one was don't join the American Society of Landscape Architects. He was the founder of it and a past president. And the second advice was don't go to Harvard. [laughs] Well, I didn't disobey the first one. I never joined it. But I did disobey the second one. It took me two years to find out I didn't want to go anymore, so I quit and opened my own office. So I didn't have a degree; I didn't have anything. I quit after two years, but my best course was Music I. Nothing to do with architecture. [laughs]

How did you get involved in the army and Nuremberg?

After Mr. Manning died, I had my own office. He died in 1938, and so I quit Harvard the same year. In 1940, I met my wife, Anne Lothrop Sturges, in Franconia, New Hampshire, and we got married there in 1942, just before I went into the army. We were ski instructors up in Cannon Mountain, Franconia, New Hampshire. I decided I wanted to enlist in the mountain troops, so Anne and I drove up with our dog and our skis to Fort Lewis, where the mountain troops were stationed, and I was about to go in the next day, and I got a telegram from Lou Kahn. He's a very famous architect—one of the great architects of the world. He died a few years ago. I worked with him before he was known that well. Later he was thought of as *the* best architect in America. I got a telegram asking if I could come back and work on a war housing project in Detroit. I was sort of broke, and I decided to go back. I left Anne out there; she had to drive back home.

Then I went back and I worked on a couple of housing projects in the East, and then I got drafted into the field artillery, down in Texas. I was motivated in the field artillery to live off the post so Anne could join me. I hated the whole deal. I didn't try to become advanced in rank because of any ambition for that, but more to get off the post. So the first month I became a corporal. The second month I became a technical sergeant, and the third, a staff sergeant, so I could live off the post. So Anne and I lived off the post. I got appointed to the [U.S. Army] Corps of Engineers in Fort Belvoir, Virginia—outside of Washington—and got my second lieutenant commission. But while I was there my friend Eero Saarinen [called]. Eero was Chief of Design of the Presentation Branch of OSS. General "Wild Bill" Donovan was the head, you know? Eero said to me, "Dan, you should get my job. I'm leaving as a civilian." And so he arranged it, and I got secret orders. When nobody could leave because they needed engineers—officers—I got secret orders to go to Washington, to OSS. My colonel didn't even know about it. [laughs] I mentioned it to him and he said, "Oh, you're crazy. You can't." He didn't even know, and I left.

I became the Chief of Design of the Presentation Branch, which was like having a big private job. You know, my own office. I had a hundred artists—some of the most famous artists. And we did visual graphic studies for the conduct of the war, working with the Pentagon, the Joint Chiefs of Staff, and the Combined Chiefs of Staff. We made different strategic studies, like, how do you shorten the Japanese war? Do you bomb an airplane, or do you bomb a gas tank, or do you bomb a tube in the radio, or do you bomb a filament? And it turned out that the filament was the most important thing. I did a study showing how that came about.

But anyway, how I really [got] to Nuremberg was that my boss was a wonderful guy named Hugh Barton. He's dead now, but he was a fantastic guy. In those days, you know, everything was organized and tight. But he ran his office as part of OSS. Very open. Every time he had a meeting, he invited all the office, all the clerks, typists, and everybody into the meeting, so everybody knew what was going on. Our office got the task to set up the thing for the San Francisco Conference, which was the start of the U.N. I didn't go out on that. We had to stage the whole setting. Hugh Barton knew I was disappointed so about a few months later he came in and he said, "How would you like to go to Nuremberg?" Bill Donovan asked us to do graphic work to show the Nazi trials, the organization, and all the atrocities. Also, somebody had to find the place for the Nuremberg Trials, and, once found, to arrange it so it would work for a world spectacle trial. This was 1945. He came to me in June of 1945 and he said, "Can you leave in a week or two weeks?" I said, "Sure." So I had to get my shots and so forth. I've forgotten what day in June it was, but it was towards the end of June, and we all met on General Donovan's plane. It was a four-motor C-4 constellation type of plane. He was there. Incidentally, while I was at OSS working on different things, I got to know Donovan quite well because he asked us for certain information. We had to do big, 40 by 40 charts that he'd have to [show] to Congress on [Capitol] Hill, and explain if he wanted this or wanted that. One of them was universal military service, and to sell that idea. But I used to go to his house in Georgetown—a beautiful house he had—late at night, and brief him on all this stuff. He always gave me a drink. He was a very fatherly type.

17

Anyway, we went over in the plane, and in the plane was Allen Dulles; Gordon Dean, who was later Atomic Energy [Commission] Director; the head of the European Air Forces—Hap Arnold or some[one]; Ben Baldwin, who was a lawyer from Detroit; and two or three other people. We had to land up in Labrador, at Goose Bay. We stopped for a couple of hours and each one had a bedroom, and about 18 different whiskey bottles on the bureau. [laughs] Then we took off again and went to London. I was traveling in class and style then. These English WAFS [Women's Air Force Services]—the drivers of little taxis—they drove us to the Claridge Hotel, where Bill Donovan always stayed. We went there, but after that meeting I was on my own. I wasn't in [a] high class anymore. I was just a second lieutenant, and I had to get a billet. I went over to the billeting officer and I said I needed a room, and he gave me a place to go in Knightsbridge in London. I went there, and I didn't like it very much, and so I came back. I said, "Hey, I didn't like that." [laughs] He said, "Who are you to not like it?" [laughs]

We had a little office, a beautiful office right on Grosvenor Square. My branch of OSS had a little office on the top floor—it was like a penthouse—with a deck, beautiful rooms with fireplaces. I said, "To hell with the army." There were three boys who were head of the office there, but they were living off the post. I said, "Hey, why do you live off the post? You could save seven dollars a day if you'd just go to the depot and get a bunk, and you could live here." So I took them over to the depot and we all got bunks and stuff, and sheets, and came back and set up house there. I lived there for over a month and saved seven dollars a day. So that worked beautifully. Nobody was telling me what to do. I had private orders—secret orders. I said, "Look, I'm sitting here. Shouldn't I go to Germany or something?" [laughs] He said, "Oh, you'd better wait until somebody tells you something." This is Gordon Dean, later head of the Atomic Energy Commission. So I waited another couple of days and I said, "The hell with that." I didn't tell him. I went down and got the orders made out. I dictated my orders.

I was transferred from OSS to the Office of U.S. Chief of Counsel, which was the organization in charge of the Nuremberg Trials, and Colonel Gill was in the office in Paris, so I got orders to go to Paris. I went to Paris, talked to Colonel Gill. I said, "I'm ready to go and find a place for the trials." He was Justice Jackson's executive officer. I said, "Is there any program? How many offices do you need? What do you need? Tell me what's the program. What do you need?" He kind of brushed it off and he just said, "Oh, we just need a few offices. Just a few. I'm a planner and I know about the future." I said, "Nobody gave me directions, so I'm going to go over to Germany," and I was on my own with my own orders. I arranged to fly to Frankfurt. We had our headquarters in a champagne factory in Wiesbaden, which is near Frankfurt. I went there, and checked in, and we had all the free champagne you could drink. [laughs] It was quite a temptation.

Then I arranged to get a Jeep and driver, and this is what I was doing all on my own. Colonel Gill didn't even know what I was doing. I decided I'm going to see where there are some good places. I made some inquiries and so forth, and there was a place called Bad Kissingen, one of the Bads. There was, of course, Nuremberg and Munich and a couple of other places. So we drove all through Germany like this, in a Jeep; we had our feet up. We were out of uniform completely, and overseas captains are supposed to wear helmet liners. We went to Bad Kissingen and different places. I took pictures. I made plans of each place. I wanted it in Munich because it was close to the skiing. [laughs] That's a real motivation, I guess. So I looked at the Munich Opera House, measured it all up and drew it.

But then there was a beautiful museum in Munich—Deutsche Museum. It had big, broad steps going up to it. My Jeep driver and I, we drove up to it. Before I could say anything, the driver drove right up the steps of this building and parked in the front. I went inside. Do you know what it turned out to be? General Patton's Officers' Club, I found out later. I went in. Nobody was in the whole thing, this beautiful place. I made a measured drawing of it. But then, as I was going out, this lieutenant accosted me. He said, "What are you doing here?" And I didn't want to let him know what I was doing. I said, "I'm an architectural student," and so forth. And then do you know what he said to me? He said, "Do you know who is here? This is General Patton's Officers' Club." He said, "Patton left here just before you arrived. If he caught you he would have either shot you or court-martialed you." So I got out of that one. [laughs] That was really close.

And also, you know, Patton had general officers—generals out on the road—to catch people out of uniform. So what made it even worse [was] I had an overseas cap and not a helmet liner, and I didn't have polished parachute boots, like they all had to wear. I had low shoes. And my driver, too. We were completely out of uniform. He would have been furious because he was terrible at details like that. I went back to London, from Germany. I was drawing up these plans. It was late one night. I was making these big drawings, 40 by 40 panels, which we always did. It must have been around eleven o'clock at night. I don't know whether it was Colonel Gill or somebody else said, "Can you go to Nuremberg tomorrow morning?" Justice Jackson, Donovan, Judge Falco, Hartley Shawcross, and all these people were all going on the plane the next morning. So I worked feverishly to finish all the drawings and get them done for the next morning.

I said, "Yes," I could go with them the next morning to Nuremberg. And we all flew over. I have pictures of the flight, even the cloud formations and stuff. I have it in slides. I was trying to sell them on Munich, not on Nuremberg. I sat next to Judge Falco from the French [delegation], and I told him what a great place the Munich Opera House would be to have the trials in. You could hang out and take photographs. Anyway, it was in the works to have [it in] Nuremberg.

Whose idea was Nuremberg?

I guess it was the Justice Department. I mean, it's documented in all those books. General Donovan had a finger in it. He was a great trial lawyer, and he wanted a big part in it. But he finally had a little disagreement with Justice Jackson and they parted ways, so he never carried through on it.

Nuremberg—that's where the Nazis had all their rallies. But Munich was a cradle of Nazism, which was even better, from my point of view. Anyway, we all flew over there, and now I was in good company again. We had the best then. I remember landing in Frankfurt, and we drove along the streets—it was like a parade. All the people lined up, and I had two generals on each side of me. We're saluting the people going by, like heroes. [laughs] Then when we got to Nuremberg, there was the Grand Hotel, which we had a big meeting in. That had been bombed out, too. The Russian prosecutor was there, too. I think his name was [Lieutenant General Roman] Rudenko.

They asked me to speak. You know, it was a big meeting with all these high people. [They wanted me] to tell how the courtroom could be. So I mumbled some things and said we had a fine dinner.

What did you tell them?

I told them that I thought it was going to be a world spectacle, and it wasn't just an ordinary trial. I felt that we had to have a beautiful courtroom. We had to have it arranged so that commentators could speak and could talk to the radio, in soundproof booths. We had to have good lighting. We had to have the proper furniture, and all of that, which I got later.

I remember one incident. I was so excited about the project. I was going up to look at the courtroom—an old courtroom, big flights of stairs—and I started running up in front of everybody, and Colonel Gill kept saying, "Be to the rear and the right of the general." [laughs] And here I was, five steps ahead of everybody. I remember it was General Bull, who was one of the leading generals in the war, that I jumped ahead of.

The thing about the whole trial—this whole experience—was that I really didn't have to report to anybody except Colonel Gill. I was just on my own. I made all my own decisions for the whole damn thing, all the way through. I decided what I had to do, when it had to be done, where I'm going to get the materials. I even got the rug. I had to go to Paris a week before the trials opened because I wanted a gray-green rug. [The courtroom] had gray-green drapes on the walls. I found in the black market [that] I could buy the rug that I wanted for $40,000. I lost my courage then and I decided I'd better call. I acted like I was Humphrey Bogart. I had a trench coat and I went down to the black market. It was raining and everything. I didn't smoke, but I was acting like a big gun here. [laughs] So I called Colonel Gill and I said, "Look, I can get this rug for $40,000, but we shouldn't buy this rug." He said, "Forget it. Buy it. The Germans will pay for it."

So then I had to get it back to Nuremberg. How do you get it back from Paris to Nuremberg? We had a very short time before the trial. The army ran express service. It was called the Red Ball Express, these big trucks that take stuff. So we loaded all these in a truck, and they rolled it over, and it got there before I got back, even. When I went over from Nuremberg to Paris, I had a staff car, and I had a driver, and I was in back, like a general. [laughs] We drove all night through the Black Forest, and it started to snow, and I was afraid we might not make it. The snow got deeper and deeper and deeper, but we finally got through and we came through Strasbourg about four or five in the morning, and we got to Paris. So then I had to go back to Nuremberg, and I was told to go ahead and arrange the facilities for the trial.

I was the first one over there. Tom Dodd came. He was the first lawyer I met, and he came during that week, I think. Tom and I had a lot of fun together. Incidentally, he was the first, but they ended up having a thousand lawyers, from all the different countries.

So Tom and I used to go on weekend trips throughout Bavaria and different places, together. I have two or three pictures of him on one of these trips, on the beautiful mountainside. He was great company, and it helped me very much having a friend like that in Nuremberg.

We were mostly just looking at the mountains, and looking at little villages and mountains, and seeing the wonderful scenery of Bavaria. I remember there was another fellow who used to go with us; I've forgotten who it was. But I remember Tom Dodd because he had sort of silverish hair.

Did you see him at all in the courtroom once he was acting as an attorney?

I only stayed three days for the trial. I was so sick of trials by then, that I got Justice Jackson to make me a courier so I wouldn't get bumped on the plane by a general and get back to Washington. Because if I got back at a certain time, I could get out of the army without points. I would have been in another year. I got back and got out.

Let's go back to the design of the place. What concept did you have?

Well, the concept was like what I do now. I'm looking at seeing what the problem is and trying to solve the problem in the best way I can, and in the most economical way, and the fastest way. I started really to design the [Nuremberg Trials site] in July, and it opened in November, and it involved five or six million dollars' worth of work. We had very little time to do it. In America, it usually takes two years to do something like that, by the time you do the drawings and bid it out. Also, it was in [Germany], and I had a local

German architect to carry out my orders to the workmen and so forth. We had to work in meters instead of feet and inches. So I had a foot and inch tape and a meter tape in my hand. But anyway, I didn't have any staff, you see, to begin with. I asked Washington to send certain people over to help me. It took a long time for them to come. I did pick up a local draftsman through the Army Corps of Engineers. I got all the supplies from the Depot of Supply for drawing and all that sort of thing. Then I finally got a fellow named Jim Johnson, who graduated [from] MIT as an architect, and then I started to fill out my staff.

Besides designing the facilities, OSS Presentation Branch had to document Nazi organizations by way of charts, document the atrocities by way of film, etc. Budd Schulberg, [who] wrote the books *What Makes Sammy Run?* and *The Harder They Fall,* was in charge of that unit. John Ford was in charge of the photography unit of OSS. We had the top people in the country. One of my jobs was to arrange housing for them, and also office space. I had 10

The exterior of the Palace of Justice. Besides the courtroom, architect Dan Kiley designed offices, restaurants, dental and medical clinics, and a PX in the building.

"[It was] like a little town." —Dan Kiley

offices, myself. I gave out offices to all the different people. I asked Colonel Gill. I said, "How many offices do you need?" He said, "Only a few." Well, it was like planning a whole town. I made a plan of the whole building. There were 650 offices in the building, on several stories. I still have plans of the whole thing. I had an entrance, kind of a vestibule, a big reception area for people coming in to find out about it. And then we had to have restaurants. We had a PX—that's army stores. We had to have dental and medical clinics. We had all those kind of facilities like a little town—over two thousand people, really.

The one thing I did, that my planning background helped on was that I knew if I designed the thing all tight and with the number of people that were going to occupy the office now, it would be tight. There wouldn't be any way to expand. So what I did, I made satellites like this. The French, the British, and the Russians. And also, we had it made for the Germans. I made little satellites with vacant office space around there. So that as they grew, they expanded in the office, and we didn't lose the communication network. Luckily it happened because every office was taken. Instead of Colonel Gill's few offices, 650 offices were occupied. The building was bombed in five places. I had to repair the building, break down through to the basement, put in trunk telephones, electricity. I had to restore all the offices, paint them, and arrange [them] depending on what rank you were. I had to do it for the judges and all that.

How many people worked with you, ultimately?

Well, here's how it worked. I had my own staff for designing and doing the drawing. Oh, this is an amusing incident [about] Colonel Corley. He was colonel of an engineering battalion of the First Army, the Red Division. They'd gone through everything. They were very famous. I remember I was in my office. He was assigned to service our operation, and he came in. He was this tough Irishman. I was standing at the desk. I looked at him in the eye and I said, "You know, Colonel, in this job, rank doesn't mean anything." I expected him to swat me. Instead, do you know what he did? He saluted me. [He was] a man who had been through the whole war and everything [and here was] this little jerk—the architect—telling him what to do. Anyway, he was wonderful, and he helped me so much.

We had a battalion of engineers to work, and then we had 500 Germans. Two hundred and fifty SS troopers, and 250 German civilians. The battalion of engineers supervised them. We had to take brick and stone, passed [from] hand to hand, all the way up to the roof. I had to staff factories for the tile, factories for the glass, factories for beautiful old plywood. I designed all the furniture, and used old plywood to do it. It was very simple, modern kind of furniture.

Did you have much first-hand contact with the Germans?

They presented a little problem every once in a while. But also, the discipline wasn't too good in the place. I remember one day I walked into this office, and the office was all SS troopers, and the guard with a big gun [was] sound asleep. I kept writing memos every time I found something like that. But then, another time I was walking down the corridor and there was this GI with one of the Nazis, making him hold his hands up, making him stand, never letting his hands go down. I mean, [he was] disciplining him, but not doing what he was supposed to do. So we had both going on.

I didn't discipline them. The [U.S.] Army did that. I had primary contact with a German architect, who was quite a nice man. But I didn't have any direct contact with the Germans other than that.

Whose idea was it to have the SS work on this?

I suppose it was the army. I don't know whether it was from Jackson. We had priority to take whatever we wanted. I had a letter from President Truman, after Roosevelt died, authorizing me to take anything I wanted in the whole war zone, which was wonderful. I remember I went down to one of the German towns, and I went to this theater, and there were a lot of wonderful theater seats, all red plush. I said, "Boy, they're beautiful. Just what I need for the courtroom." The general wouldn't let me take them. So I flashed my letter, and I got them. I had a letter also from General Eisenhower, both from Truman and Eisenhower, giving me authority because this was a first priority to get the trial done in time. So that made it easy.

Almost every weekend, we used to drive down and go skiing in Garmisch Partenkirchen, in Bavaria. I got a lot of skiing in despite [the work]. We actually opened a mountain. This friend of mine happened to be the director of the recreation in Garmisch. Anyway, they arranged a big party. The mountain hadn't been opened, you see? The news went out all over Germany, and even in France, that they were going to open the mountain, and all the old skiers—some of them—flew in. One of the guys I knew was in the Air Force. He flew his plane over. It was a beautiful, big mountain, and you'd go up on a railroad, all the way up and around, and you go through the mountain, and you end in the lobby of the hotel. On the other side, the glacier drops down like this, and you can ski right down there. We took Red Cross girls, and a German band. We had a fantastic party up there. Then the next day I skied with the German Olympic team, which happened to be around. We practiced slalom with the German team, on the slopes.

Aside from the colonel, did anyone else give you resistance, in terms of taking material away?

No, no. Everything went in order, and I got everything I needed. We had to open factories and we had to make tiles to put on the roof, and glass. I'll show you pictures of the furniture we did. I was there [in] July; we worked through August, September, and October, and it was November 21st the trial opened. We opened exactly on time [because of] the cooperation of the army and the help I got. There was a wonderful Captain Meadows assigned to me, that Colonel Corley assigned. I couldn't praise Captain Meadows and Colonel Corley more because they were so cooperative. They never asked questions. For instance, if I wanted something done, like opening the glass factory, they didn't say, "How do you do it?" They opened it. They didn't say, "Well, how do you do that?" or "What do you do?" Anything I asked them—no questions; they did it. But then later—to show you the difference—towards the end of the trial, we got GIs who had never been in the war. When they came over, if I asked them to do something they'd say, "How do you do that?"

The courtroom in the Palace of Justice during renovations. Kiley designed all of the seating, including the dock for the defendants (not shown).

"I thought it would be good to make it hard for [the defendants], so [at first the benches] didn't have any backs on them. But a person can't sit all day without a back, and so we had to add backs to them." —Dan Kiley

This was before the trials. Colonel Corley and his people were able to leave, so maybe it was a month or two weeks before. But then the help I got—you couldn't do anything. It was just ridiculous. Anyway, there were lots of episodes. We had a very nice house to live in. We had to commandeer German houses from a little way off.

It was sort of a big German, kind of country-looking house. It had lots of rooms. Besides my architectural staff, I had the Presentation Branch staff, who were separate. They were some of the research and analysis people, and editors and economists. They came over, too, and so I provided them with this big house, and we all lived in that house together.

The design of the courtroom itself—the way it was set up with where the judges were sitting, and where the prosecutors were, and the defendants—was this your design?

I arranged it, but also getting all that furniture, too. I built the lectern, for instance, that Justice Jackson and they all spoke from. I had a gray velvet panel, so his papers wouldn't slip off. And I designed the prisoners' benches. I thought it would be good to make it hard for them, so they didn't have any backs on them. But a person can't sit all day long without a back, and so we had to add backs to them. [laughs] Then I had to design the translators' [booths]. There was a quadrilingual translation system. Earphones, and so forth. I have pictures of myself, during one of the practice trials, before the trials, showing that ... I designed the judges' seats and everything ... I had to design the walkway [from the prison], to go into the elevator, up to the courtroom. I had to take a wall out and put this balcony in because it wasn't big enough. The courtroom was not that big. We had to have a dock for the prisoners. We had to have a wall to show charts and movies of atrocities, and so forth.

I didn't have any direction. I had to do it myself. But our office in Washington—OSS—had a directive report that outlined what the purpose of the trial was. It's the document that got me started. Well, let me just quickly read part of it. "Presentation Branch Work on War Crimes Project. June 14, 1945." I left about a week after that. Here's the outline. "Work of the Presentation Branch has five main parts. (1) Participation and collection of evidence." Our OSS people were on the road. As a matter of fact, I met two. They were like G-men, gangsters; you know, mobster-types. I met them in Paris, and they had captured these films. They had guns on both sides. [laughs] They were neat. They were little, kind of rubber-soled people, you know, like Edward G. Robinson. "(2) Preparation of materials, especially charts for inclusion in trial briefs. (3) Preparation of materials, charts, exhibits, etc. for trial. First for the trial briefs and then for the trial. (4) Planning and layout of courtroom, its facilities and its mechanical operation. (5) Production of public relations material and consultation on public relations program." The floor below the court-room was the press room, and I designed all the tables and stuff. They had to have lots of layout tables because documents were released, and the different newsmen picked up their documents and so forth there. "Responsibility for collection of visual evidence has been assigned to the Field Photographic Branch, but the established machinery of Presentation Branch has been coor-dinated into this effort, and also into the work of the War Crimes Office, JAG [Judge Advocate General]. Presentation Branch is using its established con-tacts with newsreel company libraries the foreign information services and the Signal Corps in Astoria, as well as its European agent ... Motion picture film when located ..."—they talk about picking up all that stuff. "Material from R&A ..."—that's Research & Analysis Department of OSS. That's how I got started. Here it is right here. I have a copy. [showing photos] That's during construction of the balcony. On the morning of the trial—this is the dock here—I was leaning against it. Oh, another funny thing that happened. My wife hardly ever goes to the movies, but one night—this is in Littleton, New Hampshire, because we lived in Franconia—she went to the movies, and they had Pathé News, and she screamed because my head filled the screen. [laughs] It was the funniest thing.

This is the prisoners' dock. I was leaning here the morning of the trial. Some German woman worked all night sewing carpets down; [they] finished the morning of the trial. Göring came in first, sat, then Hess, and the whole busi-ness lined up, while I was leaning against here. And I was that close to Göring.

I knew through Colonel Gill how many prisoners there were. Our office made the charts showing the Nazi organization and the culprits and every-thing. [showing photos] I had charts up on here, and movie screens. That's a screen that goes up, and then there's a place where I could pull several charts out and show them from there. You see, that's the prisoners there, and that's where I was leaning against.

The courtroom is sort of like this [sketches]. There's a balcony like this above. This is where the charts were shown. The prisoners' dock. Interpreters were here, the prisoners' dock was here, and there's a door here. And then the lectern was here. The witness box was here, and the judges were here, like this. Francis Biddle was one of them.

I had beautiful green drapes along the windows, like this. I wanted a neutral kind of soft color. It wasn't jazzy, but it was nice. Then, up above there was an attic, and William L. Shirer was here, Kaltenbaum was here, and I made sealed glass windows, so they could do radio from there. And there were photogra-phers; also, there were more here—writers—and Associated Press, and all that.

Then the defense counsel were here. It was very tight. And our back-up staff and counsel were here. So that's the diagram of the whole courtroom right there, you see. We made a model of it. You see, this is the balcony here. This is for VIPs. This is for most of the staff, and all the different lawyers involved were here. And then these were tables for our staff, and this was the benches for judges, and this is the lectern, and this is the defense staff, and right here is the prisoners' dock.

I showed [the model] to Justice Jackson and Colonel Gill and a lot of the other lawyers who were involved in it. Tom Dodd and [other] people.

What was their reaction?

Well, they seemed to have liked it very much. [laughs] They didn't have any criticism at all. I was very lucky. It's not like working here, where—especially if you work for the government—you have to justify every step. Meanwhile, they wouldn't hire the people who were talking to you. But anyway, it was a great experience. I was privileged, also, to go to some interrogations. I had all lawyer friends by then. We'd been there for four months together.

What happened at the interrogations?

I was just a listener, sitting at the side. The interrogator was asking questions, and they were trying to answer them. But the other thing was that [Robert] Ley committed suicide. And also Göring. And I remember Colonel [Burton C.] Andrus was in charge of security, and it's rather amusing—or tragic, really—he kept telling me, "No one is going to escape this." And the next day Ley committed suicide. And before Göring committed suicide, [Andrus] said the same thing to me.

What was your reaction to the defendants?

I treated them objectively. I can remember when Göring came in. I was very close. He had a neatly pressed summer uniform, and he looked quite nice and pleasant and so forth. Hess looked a little crazy. He had deep-set eyes, like this. The head of the army and the navy were all kind of so-called "gentlemen." [laughs] And Hjalmar Schacht, the financier was a proper businessman. But they didn't look that good, really, as a group of men. [laughs] They looked pretty lethal. And, of course, the architect Albert Speer, too.

As an architect yourself, or a designer, landscape architect, did you get to know Speer at all?

No. I didn't try to. I had a job to do, and I just concentrated on it. It was very creative, and it had to get done, and I had to get it on the road and so forth, and I had to chase material, make sure it got there. You know, everybody was depending on me to produce a finished courtroom for the trials, and if it wasn't done, I'd be in trouble. [laughs]

Did you have any sense of empathy [for Speer] as an architect?

No, no, I didn't. I hated it. I have two books—nobody has these books. I got them out of the library. I was the first one there. I found two ten million deutsche marks in them, too. They were worthless afterwards. I still have the books. They're rare copies—the big books showing all of the Nazi buildings that they did in Germany, all during the Third Reich. I went to the Nuremberg rally place, where they had the great big Nazi rallies. I walked all over, up in the benches and so forth.

It was just a big, dictatorship spectacle, where the chief gets up and harangues people. It's like any dictatorship. It's not a design for democracy at all. Democracy would be more in the round where people were involved. But this was for spectacle, you know? And I guess [Benito] Mussolini, too—when you went to his room in Italy, he did it very dramatic. He was in the back, and there were big windows, and all the light came in. You had to walk down this long room to approach him, and he was in silhouette. One other thing that happened—this is in the beginning. Because I wanted to find out about how the trials might run—the [Philippe] Pétain trial was on in Paris, and so I went over.

Incidentally, I kept a hotel room in Paris all the time. I used to go there every other weekend, every three or four weekends. I kept my bag there. I got an ice ax. I was a rock climber and a skier, and I got a big rope from the German army that I took back with me. I went to the [Pétain] trials. I didn't learn very much. It was chaos. There were people all over the courtroom; it wasn't organized very well. So I looked at it. Francis Hekking—he was a lawyer on the staff from the French [delegation]—he got me into the trials.

Did those trials give you a feeling that you didn't want to have that happen at Nuremberg?

Yes, it was chaotic, and I didn't learn much from it. There were even people standing behind the judge's bench. What I was trying to do was have a unified and orderly and dignified [courtroom]—that's what the courtroom should be, and it should reflect the scales of justice, you might say, too. We had a logo that one of the boys in my branch designed, and it shows the typical woman with the scales of justice. And we had shoulder patches with those on them.

If you go back to your activity now, and choice of materials, and the motto— overall, were you satisfied with what you had put together?

Yes. I was satisfied. I was very satisfied because I was able to do what I wanted. There wasn't enough light for photography so one of these pictures shows one of the GIs. You see these lights? I designed these big lights. And

The finished courtroom at the Palace of Justice, shown during the Medical Case against the Nazi doctors. The defendants sit in the dock at the left, with their lawyers in front of them, facing the judges (not shown). Prosecutors are at tables in the foreground; translators are in the glass booths in the background.

"What I was trying to do was have [the courtroom] unified and orderly and dignified.... that's what the courtroom should be and it should reflect the scales of justice." —Dan Kiley

one of the boys that worked for me installed them. He was a nice guy, and so when I left I wrote a note to Justice Jackson. I recommended that they keep him as a civilian so he'd get out of the army because he knew all about electrical layouts and so forth. And so they did. Oh, this is a mistake. This is a newspaper article when I went back to New Hampshire. I gave a talk before the Lions Club, and it says here, "A graduate of Harvard Law School." [laughs] I never had a degree.

The furniture was a nice thing to design, and afterwards, I was interested in the design of furniture, and I designed this table here. It's beautiful. It's birch and black walnut. An old furniture company put that table out as production. So I like designing furniture. So everything that went into that room, we drew. And then the room below was the press room, and the room on the first floor was the cafe. We had a café restaurant on the first floor so that during the trial they could eat. But one of the things that I was worried about during the trials was the security. For instance, [there was] this attic all around the courtroom, like this. I would go up there, and I'd find German prisoners alone up there, and I said, "Jesus, they could easily plant a bomb or something." So to protect myself, I kept writing memoranda to Colonel Corley's staff and saying that I'm worried about the security, because I found Germans without a guard above the courtroom. "Is that good?" [laughs] The security wasn't good during the preparation. Once the trial started, the tanks came in, and everything was very rigid. But there could have been a bomb ticking away in there. [laughs]

I never got any reaction from them. I used to send memos to paint Room 116 this way, put [in] furniture, this kind of furniture. Besides doing this, at the same time I was arranging 650 offices. I designed some tables in the reception area that were kind of going back like this, and I designed a wood screen . . . I did all those kinds of things.

What was your reaction to the city of Nuremberg, when you had gotten there?

Oh, well, that was devastating, almost in rubble. And it's amazing how quickly the Germans had it neat looking. Everything was piled neatly around. There's a church—Hitler Platze, it was named afterwards—but the church facing it—all it was was a facade of a beautiful gothic church. It was pretty devastating. And also other towns. When I drove around looking for the trial sites, there was a town called Pforzheim, and there was nothing; it was just down to the sill line, gone completely. Interestingly, in Nuremberg and other towns and cities, in the bombing, the only things that stood were the chimneys. Do you know why? Because it's a circle. It's an arch, and the concussion makes it stronger. It's like trying to break an egg. A circle is a stronger structure, in a glass concussion type of thing, where you're getting impact, concentrated loads.

Did you have any desire to rebuild the city?

Well, nobody gave me the chance. I would have liked to. The Regnitz River ran through it, right back of the jail and the courtroom. And I did remodel the Grand Hotel. When I first went there, it was amusing. I got Hitler's suite. Hitler had a suite in the Grand Hotel, and all his henchmen had rooms. So I asked about the hotel, and I said that I wanted to see Hitler's suite. So I got that—it's in one of the articles. I remember impressing one of the fellows who was a skier, and who worked at the tram up in Franconia, New Hampshire. He's the one who was head of the Recreation Department in Garmisch. He told the people back home, "Oh, you should see Kiley. I came into his room, and there were two generals in there, and Dan kicked the generals out so he could talk to me." [laughs] But there were millions of other episodes that I could relate.

For me, it was a great education, fascinating education because in a way, I was going out on a limb because I wasn't trained as an architect even. At that time I was going to the Harvard Graduate School. I had a couple of problems from Gropius. I gave a talk at the Rockefeller University just after the war. David Rockefeller was there, and President Pusey of Harvard, and all these different people. I gave a short talk. Dr. Brock was the head of Rockefeller University at that time. On the way, as I'm talking along, I said, "You know, in life you cannot be safe. You have to go out on a limb. You have to take chances." I said, "I was fortunate in this case because under the limb was David Rockefeller." [laughs] I'm still that way. You can't be safe. You can't be secure. The only thing that you can do is be self-reliant, like Emerson said. And if you're self-reliant, you can take care of yourself, wherever you are.

My unit was being transferred to the State Department, the OSS Unit of the Presentation Branch. And once transferred—it was a civilian agency—I wouldn't be in the army anymore. I had 10 days to get back. That was another anecdote that probably the army if they knew about it then, they would have been mad. Colonel Gill—he knew that all the general officers in the war were trying to get back to the United States. They kept bumping lower-ranked people off the planes, so they'd get back. So Justice Jackson made me a courier, with a package and a .45 pistol that I had to take back. He said, "So you don't get bumped." He was very nice, letting me go and everything. I wrote a note saying that I really finished everything at the trial, and was in control, and it was going well. And he was very nice to relieve me. I had to get back fast, so I went to Paris, and I had to take a medical exam to go out of the country, and had to get influenza shots. I had a cold, and the doctor wouldn't give me an influenza shot. And so you know what I did? I signed the doctor's name. I signed my own name. [laughs] I signed my initials. And so I didn't get bumped. I remember I flew back—it was bucket seats—and it was furious as you passed getting near Bermuda. We landed in Bermuda. A big electrical storm, and boy, the thing was rolling all over the place. Lightning flashing. Then I got home.

We got into Washington at midnight, and I called Hugh Baton, my boss. He had a very nice young wife who is a great lady. He said, "Tell him to sleep at our apartment." And so I came and I slept. The next day I went through the process of getting out of the army, and they interrogated me and everything, and I finally got out. I had orders from the theater of war in Europe—I didn't have time to get the proper orders. The orders were only to come to the United States, but I had to return in 10 days. So meanwhile, I got out of the army, and I went back to New Hampshire, and I wrote a letter in military verbiage about one, two, three. I'm out of the army now and all this. I sent it to the post where I was supposed to report. They sent me a letter from there—from Washington, from the Air Transportation Command. I said, "I'm out of the army," and I never heard from them again.

But then, afterwards, I was surprised and delighted. I got a notification from the army that they're going to present the Legion of Merit to me for doing the trial, which is the fifth highest award. If I had gotten the next highest, I would have gotten a pension out of it. [laughs] They said they would make a formal presentation with troops and everything, if I wanted to come to this certain place. I said, "No, no. Send it out to me." [laughs] I still have the medal they sent out to me. This [picture] was a practice session of the quadrilingual system before the trial started, and that's me listening to [it]. IBM developed that.

One of the other things that happened in the trial—you know, there was bad publicity about it when I was working on the trials. Of course, the engineers were supervising everything, and they had gotten a whole bunch of debris to make the balcony, and they piled it up at the end of the courtroom, underneath the balcony out there. It was about eight feet high, and it collapsed. It collapsed the ceiling. It went all the way down to the bottom. Ian Hunter—he's a Hollywood writer—and he wrote in the *Stars and Stripes* that it was going to delay the trials. I said, "Well, it saved me two days. We would have had to cart all this stuff out, from three floors up." We saved two days by dropping down to the basement. [laughs]

You were in the United States when the trials finished?

Yes. Frankly, I was so fed up. I had been there with all those lawyers for all those many months, that I just wasn't interested in them too much. Telford Taylor, who came over, was a very good prosecutor. I liked him very much. I had a young lady who worked for me in OSS named Cornelia Dodge, and she got to know him very well. She worked with me over there, and she stayed there and worked with him, too. I'm always trying to picture the courtroom and the Palace of Justice in my mind because it just seemed like a dream when I was there. I kept thinking about going back for a long time.

After dreaming so much about it, I was quite curious to see what it really looked like. I was on a business trip, and I took the train up—I've forgotten where it was from—Munich or someplace—and I went there and it was great. I stayed at the Grand Hotel. Everything was wonderful. I had dinner there. I had many, many dinners there, with Tom Dodd and all these different people. Colonel Aman. I also got friendly with Justice Jackson, and his son, Bill Jackson. We used to play volleyball together. My house and their house were back to back.

I used to dream about my experience at Nuremberg. I had many dreams about it because it seemed in a dream anyway. In the dreams, I was sort of going through the corridors and the courtroom and so forth. I finally went back in 1974, and I stayed at the Grand Hotel, which I had restored, and the next day I went to look at the building to see what had happened to it. It looked very official when I got there, and I decided I better not ask questions, because if you ask questions they always say, "No," and make it difficult for you, having been in the OSS. So I just went in as if I was doing business. I just walked in. I knew where I was going. I walked the line—the corridor—went up to the second floor of the wing, and I went up to my room on the second floor. I knocked on the door, and a man said to come in and I went in. There was a German in there—well, of course, they're all Germans. I said, "You know, you're in my office."

I said, "I was the architect who designed the Nuremberg courtroom and the trials," and he started to laugh. I said, "I'd love to see the courtroom. Is there any chance?" He said, "Well, they're having a session in there right now, but I can take you in the side door." And so he took me down. We had to cross the length, over to the courtroom building. And I went inside. I was a little disappointed because they changed [it]. I had it very simple and very austere, and they seemed to decorate it a lot with Victorian jazz or something. [laughs] Of course, they had new, big chandeliers, and those were good because they needed those.

Why did you dream about going back?

I was very curious. After I had done that whole thing, and I hadn't seen it afterwards, it was wonderful to go back and see a big construction job I did. And, of course, Nuremberg had changed, and it was almost normal then, you know? It was something I had dreamed about doing and doing, and I finally did it.

What did you look for when you went back into the courtroom?

I was just trying to see if there were any vestiges of my work left. And there weren't. I didn't go through the whole Palace of Justice. You know, that is a big building. I was mostly concerned with the courtroom. But, of course, they've been using it ever since, and changed everything to how they worked and how they operated. So there was really nothing much to see, you know, of what I had done.

How valuable in your career was working on the Nuremberg courtroom?

Oh, it was very valuable. It was my architectural education. I was doing it and learning at the same time. I started my office in 1940, and I worked with Lou Kahn, the famous architect, and Eero Saarinen. But I did a lot of private jobs. My first job was for John Collier. His father was the Indian Commissioner in Washington, John Collier. I did John Collier's place, too. Those were my first two jobs. And I lived with Charles Collier and his wife, and they gave me an automobile, and I did all the work right on the grounds—like Nuremberg. I got the bulldozers and did everything ... I did a study for the city of Concord in 1938. "Wild Bill" Donovan's wife was Mrs. William S. Donovan. She lived in Berryville, Virginia, in 1940, but she was separated from Bill Donovan, so we didn't even talk about him. But I did her place afterwards, which is quite a coincidence. These are all private ones. I did several housing projects for Lou Kahn in Philadelphia and the Washington area. In 1943, I designed the camouflage demonstration area. Here's a joke. I said I also camouflaged an air field where you land in Pennsylvania, and I made it look like a farm pattern going right across. [laughs] The joke was the pilots couldn't find it. [laughs]

And then in 1944, I was loaned to the Air Transport Command and International Airport. I did work there. Quito, Ecuador, is the name of it. And then in 1945, Nuremberg Courthouse ... [Nuremberg] gave me an uninhibited chance to design something from scratch and get it built immediately. It was a great experience. The credit should go equally to the people who helped me. The engineers, the First Army, the Corps of Engineers, the First Battalion, Colonel Corley, and Captain Meadows. These are the people who implemented it and made it possible because they knew what they were doing.

Did you ever build any other courtrooms, subsequently?

No, I didn't, strangely enough. And also, I'm a registered architect, and I started doing private houses and things. The biggest job I did was in 1970. I designed the four highest buildings in Calgary, Alberta, in Canada: Mobil Oil, the Royal Bank of Canada, and two twin towers. But the reason I got away from pure architecture was my friends all were the best architects in the world that I've worked with, and I still do. Now I am working in England. I'm working with Sir Richard Rogers, and we're working on the Court of the Human Rights for the E.C. countries in Europe [in] Strasbourg, and I've been over there a couple of times.

People say, "When are you going to retire?" And I say, "What? Retire from what I love to do? You're crazy." [laughs]

What are the principles that you espouse today, as far as architecture is concerned?

Principles? Well, number one, integrity. Number one, ethical. You don't have to pass a law on ethics. It won't work. You have to be personally ethical for what you do, and professionally. And so I don't do work for money. Money is a side benefit from it. It's a result of what I do, for my work. I'm trying to make environment, places for people to live—either singly or hundreds of people. I'm trying to give them a place where they can become aware of themselves in the world and the land, and to enhance and fulfill their life, enriching their life. That's what I'm trying to do in my work.

My approach to it is I don't have any ideas in my head. I have no preconceived ideas. I call it the *tabula rasa*, clean slate. I don't want to have ideas. I want to study the problem, see what's there, work very closely with the clients—this is an interchange—and keep up with the latest technology and solve the problem. If the problem is a house or a park or a campus, solve the problems for what the program is and [for] the people. The client is very important in the interchange. I don't think of myself as design or as art, or anything like that.

I think of myself as somebody who is living, and it's a life problem and it's a life process. It isn't some little field called "art" or "design" or architecture or landscape. I'm inspired not just by artists and designers, but I'm inspired by broad-thinking philosophers in the world, like Carl Jung. And other philosophers and writers. There's a wonderful man in England named Laurens van der Post. He wrote some beautiful books on Africa and so forth, where he was born. But I'm inspired by everything, and I feel your body is important in life. It affects what you do. To ski well you have to listen to the mountain. I mean, [I] don't ski the mountain; the mountain skis me. And what I'm trying to do is just let it go, you see? Let the poetry of motion and gravity do everything. It's like a dance, you see? And the same thing in design. Design is a dance. I had an exhibition in London last fall, and the title of the exhibition was "Dance, Design and Architecture." It's closed now, but it's circulating in Europe right now. But I've been very fortunate in my life. I've had fantastic projects. I've had just about the best projects you can get.

PRISON AND
SECURITY GUARDS

WILLIAM H. GLENNY

Cell and Escort Guard for Major War Criminals

Drafted into the U.S. Army in 1945, William Glenny went overseas in February 1946. It was his first stay away from home. Glenny was impressed by "the big shots" he guarded. "I was just a stupid 18-year-old kid who knew I was in history at the time.... I met the biggest men in the world." Glenny became a machinist; retired now, he is able to pursue a lifelong interest in music.

I was born in Holyoke, Massachusetts, and I grew up in Holyoke, Massachusetts, and my father was a tool maker. I first went to parochial school, Precious Blood, and I went to trade school, graduated, and I worked in some of the paper mills in Holyoke. I was drafted in 1945.

I turned 18 on September 21, 1945. I was drafted into the military and I was overseas in February 1946. The war was over. I landed in Europe at Le Havre, France, and then I was stationed in Nuremberg.

I didn't go to the Nuremberg Trials right away. I stayed at a place on the outskirts of Nuremberg which, I imagine, was used as a concentration camp at one time. We had close to 20,000 SS prisoners that we guarded at the Stalag D-13; they called it Lang Wassen. At that time, according to the Geneva Convention, you couldn't hold a prisoner of war any longer than one year. So we were getting rid of these SS men 1,500 at a time. We put them in box cars and we would run them up to Hamburg. We never went into the Russian zone of occupation.

Did you have much sense of what was happening in Germany in terms of the Holocaust?

Well, no. Nothing was proven, but the Germans were bad guys and, of course, I was growing up and I heard quite a bit about Hermann Göring. [Göring] was a big name at the time. Of course, Hitler was the biggest. There were a few names that I remembered before I got to the Nuremberg Trials. One was, naturally, Rudolf Hess. I remember seeing [in the newsreels] what a terrible, frightful man Julius Streicher was. The reason he stayed on my mind was because he had a bald head and when he spoke, he'd sweat. I kept thinking of a spotlight. He looked brutal; a very emotional person.

So, I got there—I think it's on my pass—in May before this was made out; I got a temporary pass. [It is dated June 15, 1946. It says 26th Infantry Regimen[t] Company B First Battalion. "Is authorized to enter the area of the Palace of Justice," signed by a security guard.] I turned 18 on September 21, 1945. I went in about a month or two months later, whatever it was. I can remember I didn't come home for Christmas, that holiday. We just went through basic training and that was it, I went overseas. We stopped at this placement camp, and I stayed there for about a week and then we were all to find out where we were going. I got picked. I was either going to go to the Nuremberg Trials at that time, or this prisoner of war camp. It was a good size one, like I said; it held close to 20,000 SS persons, mostly from the Russian front. So that was my first assignment. I got over to this camp with the 26th Infantry Division and stayed there.

The reason I know most of them fought on the Russian front is that I used to collect medals at that time. We wheeled and dealed. So, I wheeled and dealed.

I can still remember the first medal I ever got when I was in a camp here. It was like a regular concentration camp. They had two fences with barbed wire in the middle. There was a road that cut the camp right in half [with] one barbed wire fence. So I was walking there. This was my job, just walking back and forth. So, I was walking and I noticed this SS man, he was sort of following me. He couldn't speak English, but he showed me this Iron Cross that he had, an Iron Cross, First Class. I went over and I knew a couple of words in German and I looked at him and he had just the lobe of his right ear, that's why I never forgot him. I didn't know what happened to the rest of his ear. Probably shot off or something. So I was looking at him and I felt a little sorry for him at that time.

So he shows me this Iron Cross. I grabbed it and looked at it and I said, "How much?" in German. I knew a few German words. He mentioned something about three or four cigarettes. I did not smoke at the time but I had some cigarettes on me and I pulled out a handful and gave them to him. And that's when I started collecting some of these medals that I have.

I wanted to go overseas real bad. Well, I was taking clarinet lessons, I was a musician, and my instructor said, "Bill how would you like to play at Westover Field?" So, he sent this warrant officer to interview me. The warrant officer came over. I was living in Holyoke then, in an apartment; of course, my mother wasn't there. I said, "What's the sense of going in the service if I'm going to go work in Westover Field?" He said, "You could come back any time you would like." You know, at night. Just commute back and forth. I said, "What's the sense of going in?" I wanted to go overseas to Europe. So anyway, he said, "I think I know what you mean." So I told my mother that I didn't make it. And the tears were coming down. Oh my God, I was feeling a little guilty after that.

I finally went to a basic training at Fort McClellan, Alabama, and I came back and I was going to go overseas and just when the boat is taking off, I get another call saying [I was] wanted some other place. I went back in and I'm trying out for the band again. Second time. I listed on my application that I played the clarinet. So, first thing you know I'm in line and I said, "Geez, there's my boat, I'm all set to go." And this I did deliberately. So the warrant officer who was there with this first sergeant, he said, "Play this bar." I said, "I can't; the reed is too stiff." He said, "What do you mean, the reed is too stiff?" I just tweaked it a little. He hands it to the first sergeant. He said, "Nothing's wrong with that." He hands it back and I said, "I can't blow it." Oh, next. So I get aboard the boat and I went overseas and I was happy. And the first place we landed was—(I never told my folks. That was years ago. That was my secret.)—at Le Havre, France. We went across in the USS Anderson. It was a fairly large ship. It wasn't like a victory ship. There were ships that were sunk and you could still see some of the masts sticking up out of the water. You could see half-bombed buildings just standing up and it was something that I had never seen. This was something to see.

We got aboard trucks, we were going all over the place. We landed at this camp, don't ask me what it was. There we got our orders. Then I went to Nuremberg from there and I went to this Lang Wassen that I believe is the name of the prison camp. I stayed there, oh, several months; well, probably until the end of May, approximately two months. Then I got to Nuremberg— it had to be the 28th, because this card was issued two or three weeks [later]. They check on you, your fingerprints and everything. But, meanwhile I had access to go in there.

When I first went to the Palace of Justice we were ordered to go in this room. There were about seven of us. We were going to be cell guards. We were going to take care of these prisoners. So, we were all sitting in this room, reading papers, magazines. We were told to relax. "The colonel will come in and interview you personally." Anybody who goes on the cells is interviewed personally by the commandant of the prison, who is Colonel Andrus.

A young lieutenant comes in the room, like he's running and he went off to the side and at the top of his lungs he yells, "Attention," like a cannon going off. I almost went over backwards. A couple of guys did, chairs tumbling over; it was a racket.

This colonel comes in. He had a highly polished green helmet. He carried a riding crop, and had a little mustache. Right away he mentions, "At ease, at ease." He says, "You men are going to be on the cells, two hours on, and four hours off, for a period of 24 hours. You will be on duty for 24 hours and you will be off for 24 hours." On for one day and off for one day. Two hours on duty, and four hours off. When the white helmet guards come in, say nine o'clock or whatever time they come in, then we are relieved until they come back from the courtroom and bring the prisoners back to their cells.

Now the first time I went into the cells, I can still remember. Just one long wing. Just one wing was held just for major war criminals. There were 21 major war criminals, representing the whole of the German war regime. The military men were represented by [Major General] Wilhelm Keitel and General [Alfred] Jodl, who were both found guilty and were hung. The navy was represented by two navy men; the Commander and Chief of the German navy was Erich Raeder and the other one who replaced him in 1943 was Karl Dönitz. He was also the founder of the U-boat flotillas.

Ernst Kaltenbrunner was a big, tall guy, about six foot seven. He had huge hands. I got his autograph. I took a look at this man; he had scars on his face. In prison, he looked terrible. Here's a person you'd hate to meet in an alley. Picture a murderer or a killer. This is the type of guy he looked like, believe me. [Yet] he was the biggest crybaby in the prison. He would sit at this little table in the cell; he would sit there, and all of a sudden he'd start crying. He was the biggest crybaby in the prison.

The first night, the first man I guarded was a guy by the name of [German vice chancellor] Franz von Papen. I'd seen a nameplate over cell number five: Hermann Göring. Geez, I'd been reading about him in the paper when I was going to school; he was a big man. I stopped because I had to see him, so I looked in the cell, and I was looking in there and I told the guard, "So that's Hermann Göring," I said. "He doesn't look like such a big man in prison." He was smoking a Meerschaum pipe.

The guard pulls me aside and says, "Göring can understand English. If he turns you in, you could get court-martialed because they are very strict. So be careful what you are saying." I said, "Okay." So I went over to von Papen— von Papen at the time was in his 60s, 67. He spoke excellent English. Beautiful English.

Let's just step back to when we were being interviewed by the colonel. He said, "These prisoners will be in your charge for two hours and there won't be anybody falling asleep or you'll be court-martialed. If you are by a door and you are leaning on a wall, you are off your post and you will be court-martialed." That's why you see these guards always standing straight. "So," he says, "the prisoners are not allowed to turn their backs on you for any amount of time. If they do, you yell at them to turn around. When the prisoners sleep, they are not allowed to put their hands underneath the blanket. You hook up this light so they are not allowed to turn. They sleep towards the light. No hands under the blanket. And you don't take your eyes off the prisoners more than two seconds at a time." All these rules. I'm looking at the colonel and I'm saying [to myself], "This man's out of his mind." But, you have to take orders.

I went over to von Papen. He seems like a nice old man. So at ten o'clock, I believe, was the curfew; the lights are dimmed. In the cell there was a cot bolted to the wall. There was one chair that comes out at seven o'clock. There was a table that is collapsible under 60 pounds so you can't really put too much weight on it. They use this as a desk, and that is about it. They had one change of clothes. They do not use any knives or forks to eat; all they had was a spoon. No belts. No shoelaces. Security was really tight.

It was time to set up this light. It was the first time that I did this, so I'm shining the light, way over in the side of the cell and von Papen is watching. In perfect English he says—and some things you never forget, as long as you live—"Would you mind shining the light on the other side of the wall? Otherwise the glare from the light will keep me awake all night."

It sounded reasonable, I was so surprised that he spoke so well, I said, "Certainly." I was going to move the light over. He must have known that I was new. He says to me, "Do you mind if I give you a hand." I said, "No, that's fine." So he is helping me with the light. I said, "How's that?" He looked and he said, "That's fine. Thank you." He was a real gentleman. He went to bed.

As I look back on it now, and I'm looking at him and I'm saying what a nice old man. What's this guy going to do? He is 67, and I'm looking at him and I'm 18 years old and I am saying to myself, "He could be my grandfather." I'm a grandfather now; I have two grandchildren. He was just seeing what he could get away with, breaking these rules.

So he gets in bed and he is laying flat down with his hand out. He was laying there about five minutes. He started a precedent with me. After him telling me what to do with the light, how to put it over and shine it on the other side of the wall. I did that to all the other prisoners, because they used to say, "How could you sleep with the light shining in your face?" Somebody asked me, "What was the power of this light? Did you know?" I remember asking that myself. It was either [a] 40- or 60-watt bulb. [What was I going to mention here?] Oh, so he is laying flat on his back and all of a sudden one hand goes under the blanket. He is breaking the rules. I'm looking and I'm saying, "What am I going to do, wake this guy up all night?"

Then I see the other hand go under. So, now it's getting a little deeper. He was just conning me into this. I did not know it at the time. But that was what he was doing. Then the first thing you know, about another minute later, he turns over towards the wall, away from the light. Let him sleep. So, I broke all those rules which I said were impossible to follow. And, I'm sure I am not the only one who did that.

Before [Robert] Ley committed suicide there wasn't one guard for each cell. There was probably one guard for every four to six prisoners or something like that. When he did commit suicide then they put one guard for each prisoner. They were watched 24 hours a day. Dr. [Gustav M.] Gilbert used to go in there and he used to talk to the prisoners. I'm outside saying, "Well, why can't I do this?" I was a draftee. You know, things like that did not make too much sense to me at times. Why should this man be able to do this?

How did you get autographs from the ones who didn't speak English?

Most of them, believe it or not, spoke English. Julius Streicher did not speak English. Ernst Kaltenbrunner; I don't know if he did. All you had to do was take a sheet of paper like this, and I really cut mine big if you noticed. I want those autographs large, not small. I had these papers already cut out. I had a pen and paper. It was like a little routine. I just handed it in.

[Hjalmar] Schacht was a financier, a big man. He's got his little table like a desk, facing the door. If you come in, it was like coming into his office. He was the only one who did that. I said, "Schacht, autograph, autograph." He says, "Nein." He spoke with a strong German accent. "Ein autograph, ein cig-arette." So, I had to give him a cigarette for the autograph.

Julius Streicher wanted chewing gum. Every morning he would get up and he would chew gum. When I went over to get his autograph, he said, "Kow-gummy." I said, "Next time, next time." So he signed it. He never got the gum.

Was this autograph collecting well known to those outside of the guards? Did your superiors have a sense?

I do not know, to tell you the truth. I just started with my buddy, Andy. I said, "Come on and we'll get some autographs," and he said, "That's a good idea, Glenny." I wanted to get [Karl] von Rundstedt's autograph. He was a typical Prussian field marshal, except he was not arrogant. He was a nice guy. We spoke about ten minutes with von Rundstedt. The prison was in back. The Palace of Justice was in the front. There was a huge wall surrounding the prison, and basically there were four wings to the prison. What do they call them today? There were four cell blocks. The first cell block housed just the major war criminals. It was sealed up on both ends by guards; you couldn't get in unless you had your pass. The second wing was for the witnesses who came in to testify at the trials. The third floor housed all of the generals; the rest were for colonels who were to testify at the trials. The third cell block was [for the guards]. We had this section up here where if you were, let's say, on the first shift, you would stay on the first floor, the second would stay on the second floor, third on the third floor. The last cell block was used for storage and a game room. We used to play the radio, or pool, or something like that.

There was only one time when I went into the major war criminals section that we had seven women there. They only stayed in there about two weeks. These were the women who were going up to trial themselves because they were the wardens in concentration camps. I guarded them one night when I was up there. Of course, it was not like the men. The women, they had these little peepholes, and we allowed them a little privacy. That was the easiest job I had. As soon as I checked once, I went over to the little office (it was just a cell, but we used it [as] an office), and I put my feet on the cot and I went to sleep. I didn't get up until I heard the footsteps of the guards coming through.

We wanted to see von Rundstedt. He was on the third tier and the second cell block. I said, "Come on, Andy, let's go over and get von Rundstedt's autograph. We will just knock on the door and tell the guard that we are going to deliver a message to von Rundstedt." It was very daring at that time. We went up and pounded on the door and said we had a message to deliver to von Rundstedt. "Okay, he's on the third tier." We went up these winding stairs and we got up to the top and I spotted von Rundstedt. He was talking to this other German officer. He was a very impressive man. They flew him in from England to testify at the trials. When I first saw him he had to come through our area to go to the courtroom. As he was coming through, he looked like he owned the place. The guard in the back of him was at a distance. He was not in the front; he was in the back. Von Rundstedt would come to a door and wait. He would be about six or eight feet from a door and he would stop. The guard would come over and open the door. Von Rundstedt took about eight steps, turns around, waits for a guard to close the door and then as soon as the guard is set, he takes off again. It was very impressive to see him, as straight as a board. He was 69 or 70 years old at the time. He is talking to this other general. We waited there until he finished. Then the other general sort of bowed, and in German, I guess, he excused himself and von Rundstedt turned right to us and in perfect English he said, "What can I do for you, gentlemen?" Of course, I had a routine by then. I had the paper and pen all ready. I said that we had come up to get his autograph. He said, "What, only two?" So he is signing and asking us where we are from and how long we had been in the military. I told him I was from Boston; nobody ever knew where Holyoke was. My buddy said New York. Then he asked us how "the fat one" was. "Oh, Göring is fine." These guys, von Rundstedt or Prussians, can give you a look like that—like it is a slap in the face.

So I told him, I said, "Oh, Göring is fine. He is going to hang like a man." I should not have said [that]. He gives me one of those looks, you know, like "Geez." As soon as he looked, I knew it was too late to change my blunder. So, I said, "That's what everybody seems to think." And I started squirming and I looked at my buddy, Andy, and I said, "Andy, is that right?" Then von Rundstedt looked at my buddy and he took his eyes off me and it [was] just something that I should not have said. I knew it when it was too late. He just gave me a dirty look. He let me fumble, so I threw him onto Andy DeVito. Then he looked at DeVito and DeVito sort of said, "Well, that is what they seem to think." We got out of it like that. He was a gentleman, a very, very interesting person.

Did you get into conversations with the defendants?

Oh, you could not speak to the prisoners; it had to be brief. This was according to Colonel Andrus when we were being interviewed. He said nothing to be exchanged among prisoners. You cannot lend them anything. You cannot exchange anything. No lengthy conversations are allowed. The only time you can speak back to them is if they ask you what time it is, you can tell them. But it has to be brief.

One prisoner, Hans Frank—the Governor-General of Poland, also known as the Butcher of Poland—I watched him during the night. He read continuously. All of a sudden he would get up and he would pace back and forth in his cell. He would talk to himself. So, I inquired; I asked what the heck he is doing. One of the guards told me. He said he is reading the Bible. Imagine that. He was reading the Bible. I thought these guys were all atheists and devils. These were the biggest murderers in the world. I'm looking at [Göring] and he is a human being. If I took a gun and shot him, he would bleed red just like anybody else. The man is a human being. Von Papen is a human being. I was saying to myself, "Gee, we could solve the problem if these guys had horns sticking out of their heads and they bled green; then we could say, these guys are evil." But they were human beings that did all of these crimes, all these murders. It was a terrible time.

Did you rotate, or stay with the same prisoner?

We did not have the same prisoner. If we were there for one day, we would have the prisoner all day. If I had Göring, I'd have Göring all day. Then we were off for 24 hours. When we would come back, we would not know who we were going to get or where we were going to be. Or are we going to be in the prison? I was dying to get into that courtroom. My buddy, DeVito had the courtroom. I was just an extra guard in case somebody got sick. I told DeVito, "I am just hanging around doing nothing. Let me take your place; I want to go to the courtroom. I just want to see the courtroom." First thing you know, he said, "Go ahead, Glenny. Take my place in the courtroom."

If one of the major war prisoners is going to the courtroom, you would not see that prisoner from the time he left the prison until the time he stepped into the prisoners' dock. You would not see him. There was an elevator that went down and then you had catwalks that went right back to the prison. In other words, very rarely do you see pictures of this. We were not allowed to take cameras in there either. I got a chance to go up and down the elevator and into the judges' chambers. I saw the black robes. Of course, there wasn't anyone there at two o'clock in the morning. I had the whole place to myself. I was fooling around with a Russian camera. I hope I did not do damage because I was inside one of the booths that they had in there. I was just playing around the whole place. I sat down in Göring's seat and mostly all of the other prisoners' places. It was really hard. They did not have any cushions; it was just a plain bench. The interpreters were just over to the side. The courtroom itself was not a huge courtroom. If you take a look at a picture like that you could probably get the idea that it was huge. It was not; it was relatively small.

How long did you remain as a guard at the trials?

The night they hung was October 15th and 16th. I was not there. Right after they came up with the verdicts. They called every prisoner one at a time. They mentioned whether they were guilty—death by hanging. But just before that we took some of these people, judges, secretaries and that, and we went to a little town—Zurndorf. We guarded the secretaries, the judges. They were put in a little place where nobody knew where it was. When I learned that Göring committed suicide, the first thing that entered my mind was, "What is going to happen to the poor guard?" As it turned out, nothing happened to him. As a matter of fact, I spoke with Ben Swearingen, about the book that he wrote. He said to me, "Bill, do you know a Lieutenant [Jack] "Tex" Wheelis?" I said, "Yes, he was a big, tall fellow." He was over six feet. He was a very easy-going guy. We didn't salute in the prison. As a matter of fact, we used to play ping-pong in the little day room. He was very friendly.

"Tex" Wheelis used to stop by Göring's cell and talk to Göring. There was nothing to search in Göring's cell. I'm looking inside the toilet bowl. There's no cover, just porcelain. I'm looking and you could see right down into the bowl, there was a little ridge that goes around the bowl. I stuck my hand in there and I said, "Hey, sergeant, look, I'm not going to put my hand around this ridge, but I can't see under there." He told me to do the best that I can. So, I stuck my head down and I looked in. There was this [cartridge] which he used to commit suicide. I saw the [cartridge]. It was about two inches long. It was a shell with a cap on it. I had a picture; I'll show you. It is a little shell with a cap and inside is a glass vial of cyanide and that is what Göring used to commit suicide.

Two cells were used to store luggage. Göring had three or four bags. He had luggage in there. The last night, Ben Swearingen asked me and I said, "Look, if Göring committed suicide and he had a capsule, he had to get that capsule. He couldn't have hid it for two weeks." As for hiding it for almost a whole year, throughout the whole trial, there was always a possibility that it could have been done, but not probable. The night before Göring committed suicide, Tex Wheelis was in charge. Göring was the type of guy that could be the friendliest guy in the world. He used to walk up and down—I used to watch him in the exercise yard. They were not allowed to talk while they were in the exercise yard. Hess used to walk very, very fast. I am watching these guys and all of a sudden Göring is going fast and he turned around and walked with Hess. And then he would get him to slow down a little and then all of a sudden Hess would start talking. I do not know what they were saying in German. All of a sudden you would hear Göring laugh, going, "Ha, ha, ha." He must have gotten Hess off on something. Then, first thing you know, Keitel would come over and they were having like a little party and laughing and I think it was at Hess's expense—it is very simple for Wheelis to—he did not exactly have to give him the pill.

But, Göring kept bragging that [he] would never hang. He made that statement more than once. He was not going to hang. He said that the firing squad he could accept any time. When the two military men, Keitel and Jodl, received the sentence, death by hanging, the only thing that they wanted is the method of execution changed. They just wanted the method of execution changed to be shot rather than hanged. I could never figure that out. It took me quite a while to figure that out. As a matter of fact, for years after I got out I could not understand. You know why?

Because, especially to a Prussian officer, to hang is a disgrace. To be shot is an honorable death. They wanted to be shot, not hung. The court denied that. But, it was a disgrace to hang. It is honorable to be shot—Wheelis could have easily opened the door, let Göring in. He did not have to be there. Göring could have said just to leave him. He got that friendly. Göring, believe me, could move you. He was the most dominating man in there. Anybody there would tell you the same thing. He could have easily told Wheelis to just unlock the door and not be involved or anything.

That was the only way. How else was he going to get the pill? Wheelis could have just opened the door and turned his back and let Göring go in there. In other words, they found [that] Göring had three capsules. One they found on him and he had two others. One that was inside his jar of face cream. As a matter of fact, when they checked his baggage again, sure enough, it was still there. It was very simple for Tex Wheelis, who had the key that night, to unlock the door, let Göring in there to retrieve the cyanide capsule. The capsule was a very small capsule. They found it on him.

Did you have much to do with the German public when you weren't on duty guarding?

In Nuremberg, they told us not to walk out by ourselves. They did not allow us to carry guns. The tension was still there. When we went out, we did not go out alone. You went out in twos or more. As a matter of fact, in Nuremberg there was a Czech SS man who went around murdering GIs. When I left he was up to 26 or 36. Every weekend, this guy was killing American soldiers. It was dangerous. The Germans hated us, especially those 16-year-old Hitler youth. They were brutal. We took a couple of them and we used to put them in our barracks and just sort of de-Nazify them. Stubborn little sons-of-guns. Stubborn. They must have taken this "master race" [idea] seriously. Even von Rundstedt when he was in the courtroom—that is why I admired this guy—and they questioned him how he felt about a master race, he said, "We officers of the German general staff have never believed in the theory of a master race." The man thought clearly. Hitler, on the other hand, is doing this but those little devils, those Hitler Youths, sons-of-guns. We used to have them up there and you could tell the tension of those kids. They were superior.

This was a fair and just trial. These men deserved what they got. I'm not a lawyer. I'm not a judge. I was not an interpreter. I did not even know how to speak German when I went over there. I was a stupid 18-year-old kid who knew that I was in history at the time. I never thought I would be interviewed or anything like this. It was just that I met the biggest men in the world. These men impressed me. The same thing with von Rundstedt. As much as that man impressed me, I looked at him as a great military man. After the hangings and the IMT trial was over, I was transferred to the army band. I played with the First Division Army Band. I was happy. No more riding in trucks. We had the best of everything. We would stay in hotels and we would always go to the Nuremberg stadiums. Oh, it was a fair and just trial. These men deserved this, like I said. At that time, the whole world was screaming for revenge. They wanted somebody to pay for these atrocities and the murders that were committed in the concentration camps. You could not let this go by. And regardless of how the laws are twisted and whatever comes out a hundred years from now, this had to be done. Because, like I said, you could not let this go by, with all those millions of people and everybody screaming for revenge. These men deserved what they got.

When you left the army and you went to work, did you pay much attention to Nuremberg?

No, but it was constantly brought up in front of me. I did not think of it. Even now, when I watch television, all of a sudden they will come up with these documentaries. You should never train a soldier so well that he is only going to take orders and not turn around and say, "Wait a minute, let's think this over." They just take orders and follow orders and carry them right through. We should never train people like this. You train them so well that they will do anything that you want.

I would turn around and say, "Look, this is not right." I did not blame the colonel because he did not have any choice himself. But he is pawning this onto us. I am the little guy at the end of this. I am right at the bottom. I am a private. How much lower can you get? I had the most boring job you had in there. It was like wasting your time on those cells. It was a very boring job just watching these men. I took advantage of that. I turned it the other way. I was going to get autographs and I was going to make something out of this, which I did. To throw orders on a guy saying that the prisoners are not allowed to do this. You do it. See if you can do it. You cannot do that in the service. You take orders. This is why I do not like the military. Even to this day I do not like the military. If a guy says to me that this is a direct order, go up and blow up them—what do you mean blow them up? How do you know what's there, who is there? Maybe there are people there. You are going to take an order like that? Or else, blow up this building; there are people in it. You can't say, "What, are you crazy?" See what I mean?

Was there a particular defendant that you either enjoyed guarding or that made an impression on you?

Speer was a gentleman. He was always easygoing. Not that I talked to him that much. He did do little drawings for some of the people. Somebody told me he was an architect. I said, "What's an architect doing in here?"

What did you think of the film Judgment at Nuremberg?

Terrible. It is not the way this was done in the courtroom. I'm not a lawyer; I am just a layman. But, at Nuremberg to give you an example, when Göring went up, they just asked, "How do you plead: Guilty or not guilty to this indictment?" In *Judgment at Nuremberg,* they would be rattling off, rattling off, rattling off, on and on forever. Something like the O. J. Simpson trial. [laughs] Ridiculous. The only difference here was that they had tons of evidence. They had these men here. They were so guilty that none of the lawyers had ever even thought of objecting to these murders, because it was ridiculous. They had so much proof. Then you got judges there that know what they are talking about. It was not just that they could fool them or something like this. It is not just some idiot that you can turn around and say, "Look, this is not the right shoe."

We had our own problems downstairs. There was one guard by the name of Angelo. What he did when we were guarding I will never forget. I am sitting down with Andy DeVito and Angelo comes over and he had a big separation between his teeth. He took a regular little string and he made a noose out of it. He put it in front of the light in the cell. If you put it in front of the light on the wall it looks huge. He did that to one of the prisoners. I do not remember who the heck it was, but he did that. Made a noose from some string, and placed it in front of the light so it would shine on the other side of the wall. You are going to hang and you get up and you see a big noose on the light on the wall on the other side. So, he was screaming. He was trying to turn the guard in. Nothing happened.

As far as the day-to-day accounts of what went on in the courtroom, how did you hear about them?

To tell you the truth, 90 percent of the time I did not even know what was going on up there. The escort guards went upstairs and brought them back and we took care of them and that was it. We did not pay that much attention to what was going on up there. We just did our own little job downstairs. Now and then we would hear little things that would pop up. Most of the stuff I learned, more or less, was after I got out. Did you ever read about this Rudolf Höss? At Nuremberg he mentioned that he created—that was the term he used—the greatest murder camp in the world [Auschwitz]. He took credit, at that time, for two and a half million [deaths]. The prosecuting attorney asked him, "How do you feel about sending people into these gas chambers and murdering them?" He said that he never gave it a thought. He said that he had a job to do and he was doing his job to the best of his ability. They said, "Didn't you stop to think that someday you may have to pay for these crimes?" He said, "Yes, I did think of that." "When did you think of this?" He said, "When we started losing the war." How's that? Isn't that terrible? Like I say, I look at these men and it would be so simple to me if they were monsters and if you shoot or stab them, the ooze coming out would be green. Then I could say that these guys are not human; that they were monsters, not human beings.

Did you think about your own disliking of taking orders in terms of the trials and the excuse that people were just taking orders?

No. I went in and knew that I had to take orders. I was taking orders and doing the best I could. I was not smart. I was 18. I was just doing more or less what an 18-year-old would do—stupid things. When I got out of the service, I started analyzing and seeing that this was not right and I may have done things wrong, but I never killed anybody. I didn't steal. I never did anything real bad. I probably was a little cocky and I felt a lot of freedom and I felt that what I was doing was right at the time. Who was I hurting if I got an autograph at the time? Who was I hurting? It was against all the regulations, but was I shooting somebody? It was nothing. It was nothing. Of course, at the time I could have been court-martialed.

Being 18 at the time, what did you understand about "the master race?"

I could not understand what was meant by German blood. But, the main point is my father is Scottish, my grandfather had come in through Canada. He [was] a Canadian and came down here. My mother is French. So I have no "pure blood," if you want to call it that. My mother is French; my father is Scottish. I think everybody has a mixture of blood. You cannot say you have one German blood, one French blood, or one British blood. It's mixed eventually. Is an Englishman smarter than I am? Are you smarter than I am? I don't think so. And you cannot go by a master race. What Hitler was trying to do was breed people like you do racehorses. You want a good breed of horse, you get the top horses and breed them. He wanted to do the same thing with human beings.

I was not brilliant enough to figure this out or even think about it. I just thought that this is wrong and I knew right and wrong and that is about it. I thought this was wrong and I did not really stop to think about it.

After I left the Nuremberg Trials, this made such an impression on me that I started saying after I saw some of these people, I asked, "Why did they hang?" Like Keitel, he seemed like a good military man taking orders. Why did they hang this man if he was doing his job? But there is such a thing as going above and beyond your orders. There comes a time when your conscience has to come in there and you say, "Wait a minute. This is wrong." Not just orders, you can't let that be an excuse, that if I carry out these orders I am vindicated from all crimes. No, you are not. Your conscience comes in there somewhere. It has got to come in there. Or you are going to say that I can't do this because something is telling me not to do this. It took me a little while to figure this out. Yet, I could have been in their position and I could have been that man up there. I could probably, if I was that age, been the man that hung up there. The only thing I would wish was that I had enough courage to say, "Yes, I realize my mistake. I deserve to hang."

Do you think any of them did realize their mistakes?

Speer. I am still not sure of Speer, but he made a good showing. He said that the Nazis were wrong, and he got off with 20 years [in prison]. He could have hung, too. This might have had an effect on the way he turned around and got his defense going in the other way. He wasn't really such a bad guy.

Fritz Sauckel hung. Fritz Sauckel was the labor chief. Speer was actually his boss. The boss got away with it. Fritz Sauckel hung. Even on the gallows, he was screaming that he was dying an innocent man.

Hans Frank, the guy that read the Bible, turned completely around. When he got up to hang he made a statement: "I am thankful for the kind treatment I have received while in prison. I ask God to accept me with mercy." It was his own diary that more or less put the rope around his neck.

Today people say that this did not happen. It is hard to believe. You have to laugh at this. What are they going to say 200 years from now?

Did you have any contact with Thomas Dodd?

He was the second in command under [Robert] Jackson. I just saw them from a distance. I never spoke to Dodd. I was only a private. I was right at the bottom. My God. We used to see the Russians. They used to come in with their uniforms. Russians were the only ones who wore uniforms when the judges were up there. They should have put on dark robes or whatever. They had big bars on their shoulders. I did not know whether to salute them or not. I never saluted them. Everybody is walking around. I used to see that they were all over there and I used to sneak out. That's it. I'm gone.

Did you meet any of the foreign soldiers?

Yes, the Russians. As a matter of fact, we used to get on the bus with the Russians. We learned a little song. I never knew what the words were. We used to have vodka. The Russians always drank their vodka. They would sit in the back of the bus and they would drink vodka. They could not speak English;

Guards covering the prison wing were assigned to a cell, two hours on, and four hours off, for a period of 24 hours, every other day.

"At times we felt like we were part of them. The only thing was that we could open a door and go out where they could not do this." —William Glenny

53

we couldn't speak Russian. They would pass the bottle. Very friendly. The war was over. We would drink the bottle and sing this song and I got to memorize the words. I could say the words but I did not know what they meant. It is [singing]. Then the middle part goes [singing]. Then the guy reminded me to think of smoking. This other American that knew the words said to think of smoking. I never had any trouble with the Russians at that time. They were friendly, the ones that were at Nuremberg. We never had any problem with them. But, the Cold War was just beginning then.

It was all American guards—an international military trial held in the U.S. zone. Then after the trials they put them into an international prison where the four nations—French, Russians, English, and Americans—every month they would change the guard. First the French one month, then the Russians one month, etc.

What did you do on your day off?

I used to go to the Nuremberg stadiums. They fascinated me. I walked down there where Hitler used to put a wreath for the unknown soldier, and I saw all these names on these columns. They were all the people who died during the First World War in Nuremberg. It had a population of over 300,000 at the time.

I never learned to speak [German]. Just a few words: *eine, zwei, drei, kaput*, stuff like that. I never learned the language. I went to Soldier's Field, where Hitler made all his big speeches. I often wanted to go back, to find out. My boy went over there and he came back and he said, "Dad, you know Adolf Hitler's Soldier's Field? It's gone." Hitler said that his Reich would last for a thousand years and Speer also said that. Well, it did not last that long. In 50 years the thing was gone. Everything is gone. It is completely changed. The whole city is rebuilt.

You must have identified with the defendants to some extent. You must have felt imprisoned in some way yourself.

Yes. At times we felt like we were part of them. The only thing was that we could open a door and go out where they could not do this.

BURTON CARLOW

Special Services for Prison and Court Facilities at Nuremberg

Burton Carlow enlisted in the Army Specialized Training Program at age 17 to provide himself with the means to go to college. After the Battle of the Bulge, Carlow was pulled from school to be a rifleman in General George Patton's "Rat Race to the Rhine." Afterwards, Carlow's commander detailed him to Special Services at Nuremberg. "Being 18 years old, I didn't know if it was a traffic court ... but I knew it had something to do with law." Carlow's division was a collection of people, including the hangman, who took care of specific miscellaneous tasks at the IMT. Carlow's task was to supply recreational materials such as books, stationery, and films to the guards and prisoners. Since much of the work consisted of showing films at night, Carlow was able to witness much of the IMT trial. Carlow's job provided him with access to the prison, where he collected autographs and gained a sense that, "I don't think anybody respected [the defendants, but] I do feel that most people didn't hate them."

I was born in New Haven, Connecticut, April 23, 1926. The oldest of three brothers. My father was a tailor. [He] passed away the year I got out of service, actually very young. He had always told me he came from Poland. I had to get, for some reason, an original copy of my birth certificate in New Haven. I've always had photostats of just the facts. In reading it over, I found that it said "Father's Name," which I knew. And it said, "Nationality: Russian." And I said, "No way. He was never Russian. He was Polish." When he was born, there was no Poland. I didn't know that. The part of Poland he was born in was part of Russia. And it took me all my life to find out that my father wasn't born technically in Poland. He was born in Russia. But yes, he came over. He was a tailor, first in Florida, and then in New Haven. As I say, he died the year after I got out of service.

I went to grammar school in New Haven, junior high school and Hillhouse High School, which, at that time was the academic high school in New Haven. People who went there generally went on to college, or hoped to. I could not afford to go to college in those days, so I enlisted in the army at 17, with my parents' permission to get into this, and I'm pointing to the patch of the Army Specialized Training Program—ASTP—which meant that any person who enlisted before age 18 would be sent to college, and that turning 18, would then go into active service, and possibly be sent back to college later. But meanwhile, you'd be accumulating college credits. I was selected [and] sent to Norwich University in Northfield, Vermont.

At 18 I went to Fort McClellan, Alabama, as an infantry private. I was sent to Ohio State University after that, and during the Battle of the Bulge I was pulled out and sent to Europe to replace people who were killed, captured, or injured. I was 18 years old. I stayed in Europe until—was I 19 or 20? Just 20 when I got out, and spent 18 months in Europe, and was assigned to the War Crimes Trials just prior to the beginning of the trials, which was in November [1945]. I got there in October, and stayed until the following June, when I came home.

What kinds of things were you involved in before you got to Nuremberg?

I was an infantry rifleman in the 94th Infantry Division. I was actually in combat. Our division was involved in what was referred to as the "Rat Race to the Rhine." We were in General Patton's Third Army, and this was when the Germans were retreating pretty rapidly. We were chasing them pretty rapidly, and the only thing we ever needed was fuel for the tanks. I mean, Patton just said "go" and everybody went. We took the cities that we had to, stopped at the Rhine, and were in that general area when the war ended a few months later. So I was actually a rifleman in the 94th Infantry Division, up to that point.

When the war ended, my captain was a gentleman named George Buck. George Buck was—and his son today is—a golf pro at the Long Shore Country Club in Westport, Connecticut. George Buck Sr. And I think it's George Buck Jr. who may still have that job. Again, he was older. He was in his mid-30s. I was 18 at that time. He knew they were going to send most of us to the Pacific, [those who] did not have enough time to be sent home, and I was scheduled. He didn't want me to go to the Pacific because of our Connecticut relationship. In his spare time, he was giving the general of our division golf lessons. Now, this was during the war. I think he asked him as a favor to kind of help him get me out of this thing. The next thing I knew, I was assigned to Special Services, not to be confused with Special Forces. Special Forces kill people. Special Services are worried about books. So it's a totally different connotation.

And he did that, and I was stationed with Special Services in Munich for a very short period of time, and they assigned me then to the Nuremberg Trials. Being 18 years old, I didn't know if it was a traffic court. I had no idea. But I knew it [had] something to do with law. And I did go to Nuremberg, at which point I was presented with the two patches I showed you earlier.

The official designation of [the] unit that I was attached to is 6850th Internal Security Detachment of the International Military Tribunal. In other words, 6850ISDIMT. That's what it referred to. I can't believe that there were 6,849 other units like this. But anyway, as such, we wore the patch. This patch depicted the internal security of the Nuremberg courthouse and prison. The external was provided by the four conquering powers—Russia, France, Great Britain, and United States, on a rotating basis. One week the Americans would have the whole exterior security. The next week [we] would be replaced by Russia. Each country presented its finest, handsomest, tallest, most picturesque military people, because this was the world looking in. So they were all hand-picked. Internally, they couldn't have cared less. So we had all kinds of people in the internal security segment. It was our people who guarded the actual war criminals in their cells on a 24-hour basis, after [Robert Ley] committed suicide. And shortly after he did, a General Wolfe from the SS, who thought he was going to be a major war criminal, and might have been tried later on, on a minor level, jumped off the third railing of the witness wing and was killed. So we had two deaths within a couple of days.

How did Nuremberg compare to other German cities then?

Nuremberg, overall, was in about medium shape. There may be some pictures of [Nuremberg] here. I don't know how these [postcards] got here, but they were given to us, written in English. We got them during the war. So the Germans either knew we were going to win and had the postcards ready for us, or what. [laughs]

The story goes—and I don't know this for a fact—18-year-olds are usually not taken into high-level discussions of what's going on. We hear rumors and put stories together. The story was that our military thought that the SS had a training school in old Nuremberg, and bombed it to pieces. The local story by the Germans who worked with us afterwards, was [that] the only people in old Nuremberg at that time were a battalion of Hitler Youth. These were kids 12 to 14 or 15 years old, or younger even. And they were the ones who were destroyed by the bombing; not the SS, who had gotten out long before that. So believe whatever you wish. But that part of Nuremberg was really demolished, as piles of rubble. That particular part of Nuremberg was saturated. I didn't see places like Dresden or those that got the huge concentration of bombing. So I can't compare it.

Did you get any briefing as to what you were going to be involved in when you went to Nuremberg?

I think it went something like this. "Corporal Carlow, we're going to send you to Nuremberg." And my answer was, "Oh, boy." At that point I didn't know anything about it.

They said, "There's going to be a war crimes trial." This was in maybe October, and the trial started late November. I said, "What am I going to be?" And they said, "You're going to be the Special Services non-com for the Nuremberg prison and court facility—Palace of Justice." I said, "What am I supposed to do?" They said, "Well, if any of the guards need books to read, or they want movies, or writing paper—anything to help the guards, and indirectly the prisoners." I was not supposed to have direct contact with any of the major war criminals for harassment reasons. They wanted them pure. They didn't want any contact with people who might give them a hard time. "And that's what you do?" I said, "How do I do this?" They said, "Well, they have no facility in Nuremberg to accommodate it, but the Air Force has a base in Furth, which is outside Nuremberg, and you have access to their Special Services area. From the Air Force Base, you can go there and get movies or projectors or books. If they don't have it, they'll requisition it from London or wherever. Supplies— pens, pencils, whatever you need. You can go there once a week or call them, and they'll send it if they have a shuttle coming into the courthouse." So I said, "Fine," and I went to Nuremberg, reported in, was given my medallion and my badge. I was given this.

Now, if you look at this patch—this was a photo pass. The guards in the prison had a duplicate of this. So if somebody conked me over the head, like you see in spy movies, and put their picture on there, it would not get them by. But this particular pass I don't think, other than the guards, 150 people in the world had, [it lets you] go in and out of the prison wing. Now, in this prison wing, the overriding fear that I sensed—and again, as an 18-year-old, they didn't give me this as policy—was that somebody was going to try to assassinate any or some of these guys, make martyrs out of them, and get a lot of publicity for it. So the security was super-tight getting in and out of that wing. I had access to it on an ongoing basis. Day, night, whatever.

Why do you think you were chosen?

I think as a favor. I don't think I was specifically chosen. Yes, maybe that is a part of it. The fact that I was young, and it looked [like] I was going to be around for a while. Because there was such confusion [about the end of service]. As I remember, it went like this. Your age plus the number of months

58

Following the suicide of defendant Robert Ley, and because of fear of outside attack as well, one guard was assigned to each cell.

"The overriding fear that I sensed ... was that somebody was going to assassinate any or some of these guys, make martyrs out of them, and get lots of publicity for it. So the security was super-tight getting in and out of that wing." —*Burton Carlow*

you spent in Europe, if it exceeded the number 42, you then were eligible to come directly home to the States. If [the number] was under that, there were certain options. The Pacific war was still going on at that time, and most likely, if you had infantry training, that's where you were going. Or you were going to be kept in the Army of Occupation in Europe, which is what I was technically in, once the war ended. So maybe the fact that I did have some time left to be there was a factor, because everybody else was in a state of flux. They were all trying to fake their birth certificates, and add a year here and there, and a month here [to get out].

There were a lot of young [guards] because there were a lot of young [men] in the military, generally speaking, at that point. Yes, they were relatively young. But again, this particular outfit—I was in the 6850ISDIMT, which is a mouthful to say all the time—was unique, meaning one-of-a-kind. There was only one, and there probably never will be another. The head of the prison was a gentleman named Burton C. Andrus, who, I think, wrote a book called *I Was the Nuremberg Jailer* or something. I read it many, many years ago. What he was responsible for was the overall internal security of the prison. So he brought people in. There was no table of organization, that we have to have one captain, two lieutenants, four sergeants, five privates, whatever. Whatever rank you were to do the job that they needed you for, you became. So we were a totally unbalanced sort of a thing. We had probably 10 times more lieutenants and officers than a unit of this size should have had. We had people doing huge jobs with very minor ranks. For example, the hangman [Master Sergeant John C. Woods] who came in at the end was part of the 6850.

We didn't know who Woods was. We went to shoot baskets one morning in the gym. The gym was closed; we couldn't get into the gym. We saw piles of lumber being dropped off near the gym, and we wondered, "What the heck is going on here?" One of the fellows said, "Hey, you see that new guy that came in for breakfast this morning?" "No, who is he?" "Sergeant Woods." "So what's he doing?" "He's a hangman." "Oh, good." So I ate my eggs, and went about my business. [laughs] But, I mean, that is the kind of outfit 6850th was. It was just individuals who could do a specific job that was needed at that particular point in time. I had probably the easiest job, in that I didn't have a boss because no one knew what I was supposed to be doing. My lieutenant didn't know who I was or what I was there [for]. The only thing he wanted to do was not see me. So I would do what I had to do, and most days, as I said, I had nothing to do, so I'd go to the courtroom. There was a little balcony upstairs, looking down on it, and I'd just go up to the balcony. You've heard about the earphones with the four languages, which was unbelievable. I jokingly would turn it into Russian, and listen to Russian for a while. I didn't understand a word they were saying. [laughs] But what did totally amaze me again as a kid, was how simultaneous the translations were. When I switched to English from where the witness was speaking German, it was coming to me in English, and I could see what they were saying, and how quickly I was getting [it] idiomatically in English. Not just stilted phrases, but very fluent. I knew the Russian guy was getting the same thing, and then the French. The British—I think they had trouble understanding us because I did with them.

The whole thing was absolutely new to me. From my seat, I could look across, where the translators were. They had glassed-in booths opposite me, and I could watch them speaking, and I was fascinated by that. Again, just for the lark. I wasn't honestly that interested in what was being said. Some things really shook me. We saw certain films in the trial that you've never seen.

They've never been published. They were from the German archives [and] were so terrible I got up and walked out. I just couldn't watch them anymore. But that's basically what I did. In the evenings and late afternoons, when the trial was over, I would do what I had to do—get books for the people; just ask around if anybody needed anything. Once in a while I got things for the war criminals themselves. I know [Joachim von] Ribbentrop wanted a certain book that he was not able to get through his attorney. I think he had a German attorney. Yes, it was. So he asked his guard at his window [if he could] help him get this book and his guard came to me and said, "Can you get this book?" I don't remember the book. I said, "I'll try." I gave the name of it to the Air Force people in Furth, and two or three days later they flew it in from London, and I gave it to him. So indirectly I did get a few things for some [defendants].

Did you see any of the defendants?

Yes, of course, I listened to them all. The defense counsel for Admiral Dönitz—whose autograph I have here somewhere—did something that I think you would see on "Matlock" or "Perry Mason," maybe even the O. J. [Simpson] trial. I don't know. But it was very cleverly done. He had his witness, and his witness was a submarine captain on the stand. I think they had him read his orders, like, if you torpedo a ship, and there are survivors in the water, you are not—"not"—under any circumstances, to surface and to assist the survivors in any way, but to continue on your mission. I remember the attorney saying to the gentleman, "Those were your orders?" He said, "Yes." "You're reading it right off your orders of the day?" He said, "Yes." He said, "Whose signature is on your orders?" He said, "Lord Somebody for the British." He was the head of the British Submarine Service. He was bringing out the identical orders that the British submariners had, that the Germans—Dönitz—gave, so it was not a war crime. I mean, everybody did it. That's what you did. You didn't jeopardize your mission to go after survivors. I was totally impressed with that.

How much freedom did you have to move back and forth into the trial room?

Complete [freedom]. There was a control, but it's all in context. My job meant that almost every person who worked in that prison in a guard capacity knew me, and kind of wanted to be nice to me because I was able to get things. If they wanted to see *The Maltese Falcon*, I could get that movie, you know? I was the guy that helped them. I was one of the only people that could bring a dog into the prison. Now you've got to consider that almost every GI that got a dog after the war either got a Doberman or an Alsatian, the biggest, toughest dogs in the world. I had a little German short-haired terrier, a cute little white dog. Nobody was afraid of the cute little white dog, and [it] followed me continually wherever I went, all day. That dog had as much access to the prison as I did. [She] always walked beside me.

Toward the end of the war, the Germans took every able-bodied elderly man and young kid and brought them in. I think they called it the Volksturm. It was a people's army, a last ditch effort to stop whatever was going on. So when the war ended there were hardly any younger people in Nuremberg or in any of the cities. We had an elderly German man. He was, I would guess, in his 80s, hired by the U.S. Army—the boss hired him—to clean our rooms, to make fires, because we were living in bombed-out buildings, essentially, see that our laundry got done. They were paid mostly in food. Money didn't mean anything to them. They got food, and they worked for the army. One day I asked him, "Can I get a *Hund*, a dog?" I spoke a little German I picked up at the time. He said, "Yes. Come with me tonight to *Alte Nürnberg*." That night he took me into Old Nuremberg, which was about a 15- or 20-minute walk from where we were. I was scared to death. There were no lights—no nothing—just piles of rubble as far as I could see. And I said [to myself], "Burt, you did a stupid thing. No one knows where you are. You're walking with a German man you don't know anything about. You're going into an area that who knows what you're going to find there." I was really getting shook. But he took me into the cellar of what was a burned house, and I could hear dogs barking.

I walked in and there was sort of a big room dug out of the rubble [with] maybe a dozen dogs of different kinds, mostly Dobermans and Shepherds or Alsatians. In the corner I saw the white puppy with black ears that reminded me immediately of the RCA Victor dog, which is what he is. I said, "What kind of dog is he?" He said, "A short-haired terrier." I said, "Okay, I want him." They looked at me like I was nuts. American soldiers don't buy those kind of dogs. But I did, and they got their carton of cigarettes. The dog had papers, which I don't have. I don't know what the prefix in German for the word *witch* is. Is it *De Hexia* or *Der Hexia*? Der Hexia Von Nuremberg. The Witch of Nuremberg. That was her name. I took her and raised her, and she became part of me. I took her back to the States when I came back home.

I called her Hexie. She became part of me, and we did everything together. [We] went in and out of the prison together, which [brings] up the classic story. Connecting the prison wing to the Palace of Justice was a winding wooden corridor. Originally there was none, but I think our military built it to protect the goings and comings of the prisoners from the prison wing to the courthouse, to see their attorneys or to appear in court. That's the way I would go back and forth. I was always running into them in this corridor. One day walking down there, Hermann Göring was walking with his guard a step behind him, and my dog, who is the gentlest thing in the world, growled. And Hermann lifted his foot and said, "*Aveck Hund!*" [Away, dog!] and kicked his foot. He didn't hit the dog. He kicked out, at the dog. Stupid me jumped in front of the dog, stuck my finger in his face, and said, "*Nein,* Hermann!" The guard cracked up. From that day on, half the people there would see me during the day and say, "*Nein*, Burton!" So the dog has a little piece of history at that moment because [Göring] did speak to a dog.

As I said, I got to see the prisoners in their cells—I'd walk and peek in. Some I have vivid impressions of; others hardly any at all. Julius Streicher. He was the editor of [*Der*] *Stürmer* [The Attacker], the newspaper, known as a Jew baiter. I'm Jewish. He is what's to me the perfect caricature of what his papers showed old Jewish men to be. He was the living image of what he pictured. Short—at that time nobody looked grandiose. Nobody had fancy uniforms. The military had military tunics, but no medals—no nothing. And he looked like just a little old man. Baldur von Schirach. I think he was at one time the head of the Hitler Youth. Very nice-looking guy, as I remember. Very young. I think he had to be 30. I just remember him as being relatively young-looking and nice-looking, and I always kind of thought when I saw him, "Too bad a young kid like that has got to go through this."

I want to mention Ernst Kaltenbrunner. Was he a war criminal? Because people tell me, "No, he wasn't," and I know he was. He had a scar, too. And he was basically, I think, replacing Himmler. Himmler should have been in his spot in this trial. But because he wasn't, they needed someone from the SD, or one of the security services, which is probably why he got the prominence of being in the trial. He was a vicious-looking man, as I remember. That's why I remembered that man. Because he looked as bad as he sounded. He just had that kind of a look. The military I was totally impressed with. They looked military. Keitel and Jodl. Typical. Without medals, they looked like a field marshal and a colonel general. Jodl—he was the head of the *Obercommando*, High Command. And Keitel was the field marshal in charge of the *Wehrmacht*, I think, if I remember. They looked the part. Keitel was very old and looked it. Jodl wasn't, but he looked military. Of all the military, the most impressive, I thought, was Dönitz. Keitel, again, was an older person. The two governor generals, Frank and [Arthur] Seyss-Inquart—people talked about the most. When I say people, I mean the GIs—the older people who knew because of the atrocities. Particularly [that] Frank in Poland was particularly responsible, and Seyss-Inquart, as well. The politician, von Ribbentrop. Schacht was the financier. I think von Papen was a diplomat, too.

Certain people I don't remember. [Konstantin] Von Neurath and Sauckel and [Hans] Fritzsche and [Wilhelm] Frick. I don't know what they really did. I don't remember. I didn't know then—I still don't know. Someday I'll read about them, and find out what they really did. Who else? Well, Göring was Göring. He lost a lot of weight at that point. He apparently was weaned off drugs. If you read Andrus's book, he was an addict when he came in, and got off it and lost a lot of weight in the process. Hess was vacant. In other words, I never saw any emotion, whether he was in the courtroom, in his cell, walking in the exercise yard, or passing [by] in the hallway. He had the same look on his face, like he was out of it. I don't know whether this was an act all the way, or whether at that point, he was sort of out of it. But those were the ones that I remember.

Did you ever go into the cells, or was everything through the door?

Through the door. No one was permitted in the cell except the cleaning people. Again, these were German citizens who worked in the prisons, so they did have fairly close access. I mean, these fellows had haircuts and shaves, and I'm sure none of our people did that. I wouldn't think they did. I did look into the cells, as I say. Now, there is a story. There were all kinds of stories floating around there, and this is one that I heard. I'm not sure it's true. It sounds way out, but it could very well be because a lot of weird things happened. Streicher was at one time being guarded, and all these guards were from our First Big Red 1—the First Division, from Brooklyn, New York. Each prisoner, we were told, was allowed one uncensored letter a week to Colonel Andrus to complain or to commend, something that didn't go through the chain of command. It went right up to the top. And he complained to Colonel Andrus that this guard was putting him on the verge of a nervous breakdown because [of] what this guard would do. The cells were never dark. Twenty-four hours a day, there was light. [The guard] would make a noose on a piece of string and wave this in front of his light, making a noose shadow on the window. And it was driving [Streicher] completely crazy. The story we got back—and this whole thing may have been fabricated just to stop that from happening, but it was disseminated throughout—[was that] this man was taken off the job, was court-martialed, sentenced to 10 years at [Fort] Leavenworth, and sent back to the States. The true story is—and I don't know if it's true, but apparently for most people, none of it ever happened—he didn't do it. He wasn't court-martialed. There was no such person. But it had a deterrent effect—nobody stepped out of line because they didn't want, like the O. J. trial, an appeal that the prisoners were being so harassed they couldn't get a fair trial. They wanted everything straight and above board. They knew they were going to [convict] most of them anyway. [Otherwise], they wouldn't have built the gallows so far in advance.

Was this Andrus who did this, do you think?

I can't see him not being aware of it. I have a letter here signed by him. This is a commendation. We showed some movies to guys who wanted certain movies that were very hard to get, and we went all over Europe to get them certain films. He was so proud. His men were so happy.

I saw him occasionally. He would come through the prison on occasion, very military and very responsible. He had a tough job there. If anything went wrong in that prison—it was his prison, basically. If anything went wrong outside, that wasn't so much his responsibility. But within the stone walls of that prison, if anything went wrong—like the people who got killed in there—I think there was this fear during the whole thing, that something was going to happen that was going to look poorly for us. So I think he was under quite a bit of strain.

This is a letter that's dated January 28, 1946, to Commanding Officer Third Special Service Company, and it says, "I desire to commend Technician Fourth Grade Radford W. Yates 33895966 and Private First Class Burton Carlow 11138393 of your organization for the fine work they have done for this detachment as a Motion Picture Projection Team. These men have displayed unusual cheerfulness and cooperation in making successful a program of motion picture entertainment for the guards of the Nuremberg Prison and the enlisted personnel and officers of the 6850th Internal Security Attachment. These men have had to put on numerous showings each week to make certain that the motion pictures reach the maximum number of personnel. To this end, they have been more than willing to extend their schedules when necessary, and the resultant irregular hours have brought forth no complaint from them. Their sincere desire to see that the shows conform as nearly as possible to the dates of the audience is commendable." [signed] B. C. Andrus

There you go. [laughs] I think he expected everybody to do what they were supposed to do there. But there was one thing. This was kind of interesting too, in a way. You probably heard this from other people you talked with. The fraternization rules that were in effect in Germany at that time. We could, under no circumstances, converse with Germans, have anything to do with them on a social basis, [we could] speak with them only strictly in a business category. If you found a family that was willing to do your laundry for you, and you were caught bringing your laundry to them, you were subject to court-martial. I mean, it was that stringent a restriction. So for you to be with a German, you had to have one darn good reason to have that person with you without breaking the rules. So whenever you had to take people—like in the Jeep with me, I'd take someone out to pick up something or do any work—I had to have an authorization, with that person's name listed, giving me authority to be with that person without it being considered fraternization. So any time you had a German civilian that did anything for you, you made darn sure you got their name on an authorization saying it's okay to do it. But they were very, very strict about that.

How did you get those autographs from the prisoners?

Very difficult. I put the paper through the guard and I said, "Can you have them sign that for me?" And he'd sign it and hand it back to me. [laughs] I mean, I didn't know what else to do. But you notice, some of those autographs are not the war criminals. I didn't know that either, but I do know that one of them was an SS general, who was being kept as a witness. Another one was a *Corvettan Kapitan*—a naval captain. He might have been involved in that incident with the not picking up survivors. There was another wing of the prison adjacent to and above where the major war criminals were, where witnesses or potential witnesses were sequestered, most of whom were going to be tried themselves, later, at a lower level. Because there were loads of trials after, [such as] the judges. You know, *Judgment at Nuremberg*. The legal profession. So there were war crimes trials going on for quite a period of time after this. This was a show piece. This was *the* one that the world was involved in.

How were the witnesses treated as compared to the people who were on trial?

Good. I think the way it was originally, downstairs, was one guard for four prisoners, walking back and forth, looking in the cells. Then after the incident with Ley, they changed it to one-on-one, 24 hours a day. But no, basically anybody in the prison, whether as a witness or as a defendant, was treated pretty well because the prison was a show place. I mean, people from all over were constantly in and out. Our people from our Congress would visit and sit in the gallery to watch the trial, and the world leaders [would visit]. It was a thing that people wanted to be involved in, in one way or the other.

Getting the autographs—wasn't that against the rules?

It might have been. I never saw it in writing, anything saying, "Don't get an autograph." It was done constantly. I mean, the officers and the people in the court itself that never got to the prison wing, wanted them. So they'd pass sheets of papers back and say, "Please get me this, this, and this," and they'd bring it out to them. In fact, some of the guards were selling them. They're getting them and selling them to other GIs in their outfit that didn't have access to them because they realized the historic value of these things. I didn't maybe as much as others did, but some of them made a business out of supplying autographs.

Was there a feeling that this gave sort of respect to the war criminals?

I don't think anybody respected them. I do feel that most people didn't hate them. In a general way, most people I spoke with—the guards, the others— treated them as criminals, but not hateful criminals. I mean, we knew what they were responsible for. But for some reason, I just didn't get that feeling that people were snarling at them through the cages, you know, like animals. They weren't. And they were under orders [not to]. You know, it would have reflected badly on them had they done something, and it [would have shown] up in a letter saying they were harassing one of the prisoners. They didn't want that on their record. So they did their job, and marched them into the court-room in the morning, and marched them back to their cells in the afternoon. During the time I was there, I had never heard of an incident of any sort, on a serious note.

You were 18. Your background is Jewish. Did you have a sense of what had happened in Germany?

Not until almost the time I went to Germany. I mean, I read what every-body else here read in the papers in those days, and there was a lot of finger-pointing and a lot of discussion. No proof. You know, everybody heard these things about concentration camps, and so forth. But the extent of it, I don't think was public here, other than what people heard and repeated. We didn't have the films then that we have now. We had word-of-mouth discussions that were mostly not believed, even at the highest levels of our government, if you believe what you read today. Most recently I read about the Polish head of something that went to the president, and nobody believed him. So again, yes, I've heard about these things, from what the average American citizen knew at those times. The young ones might have heard it and not even cared about it. It didn't register. I had more important things on my mind than what was going on in Germany when I was 17 or 18 years old, like getting good marks in school. A car was no problem; I didn't have one anyway. [I had] just a whole different sort of interest. But during the course of the trials, when you saw the lampshades that were presented—there were lampshades made from the tattoos on people. You know, you saw things like that and you began to realize this was for real. Last summer, a year ago now, I was in Auschwitz. On a tour my wife and I went through Auschwitz.

As a soldier, were you given an opportunity to visit the concentration camps?

No. I think basically at that point, the military that were involved in those areas did get to see them. But they did not have a travel agency set-up to bring GIs in from other parts. Some of the higher officers, they would come in their car and drive and get in, but [not] the average GI.

What were the Germans' attitudes toward the trial, towards you?

The Germans that I spoke with—legally or otherwise, and I did both, as everybody did—loved us. Not one of them was ever a Nazi. No one ever knew an SS man. We used to search houses. We called them Hans Zoochen assign-ments. Like you see in the movies today, like *Schindler's List*. They block off a street, the German soldiers go through the apartments. They were bringing the people out. We did exactly the same thing, but not for the people. We went looking for uniforms, for soldiers who might be hidden; anything, any artifacts, anything that related to it. This was common. We did that all the time. But no one, no place, ever had any connection with the Nazi party [or] with the SS, with Germany and Hitler. [imitates a German spitting in disgust] That was the general theme you got from everyone. Again, I think you might expect something along those lines. So yes, they loved us, in appearance.

You never got any sense of hostility?

Never, no. They dared not, at our level. I mean, don't forget, they [were] dealing with armed soldiers. That's a little different than civilian [to] civilian. You're talking about someone who [has] got a .45 on his hip or a Thompson machine gun in his hand, and don't forget again, it's important—there were no young men here. You were talking to very old men. *Very* old. I mean, 80s and above. Women of all ages, from two to 92, and little, little boys—up to age five or six years old. In between, there was a great void. There were none. Everyone that you talked to was waiting for someone to come home—from the eastern front, from the western front, from a Russian concentration camp. Everyone [was] waiting. They didn't know, like we know, in hours, if someone gets hurt in the military operation of our country today. There, they had no communication. Nobody could tell them. They knew their husbands or sons or grandfathers left, period. That's it. Whether they'd ever see them again, they had no idea. Most didn't come back.

Did you have empathy for their suffering, for what they went through during the war?

In some individual cases, yes, I did. Yes. Most not, but I met some people who were families. You know, a mother and her two little daughters, whose husband had left three years ago for the Russian front. They didn't know if he was alive or dead. They had no food. They had no nothing. This was a general thing. This wasn't isolated. Yes, some of them I did feel sorry for. My mother used to send me gift packages. She always thought I was starving to death. To this day she does, or did. She would always send me food. I would share a lot of that food. I had all I could eat over there. They fed us very well at Nuremberg. They even had a hamburger stand set up for the Americans so they wouldn't feel homesick. The old man who cleaned my room—I quite often gave him things. Canned pineapple or canned chicken. Things that my mother had sent, that I knew I didn't need, and wasn't going to eat anyway. So, yes, there were cases [where] I did feel sorry.

Did you know German before you went [abroad]?

No. My grandfather spoke Yiddish when I was a little boy, so I picked up a little bit. I was not [fluent] in it at all. But like anything else—I was there for

16 months or whatever—just by listening and trying, I had toward the end, very little problem understanding or being understood. You know, I do it in the most rudimentary terms. I wouldn't be very flowery about it. But almost all the time they knew what I was asking for, or requesting, or whatever, and I could understand what they were saying. And if I didn't get it one way, they'd rephrase it until I did. Or I would do the same thing. So I had really no great problem at all.

What was your impression of the [American] lawyers and the judges?

I think I was impressed with all of them, but not to the point that I oohed and aahed. I knew they had a job to do, and I didn't know what their job was. I do today. But then I didn't. I would listen to what they'd say, and sometimes if they'd come up with something I felt was rather astute, I would nod my head and say, "Good boy," or some such thing. But other than that, no. I figured they were all competent people, or they wouldn't have been there in the first place. At one time or another, I did hear them all. I don't remember much about what they said because there was a lot of jockeying amongst the prosecutors interrogating the witnesses. But I did see everybody and hear everybody, because I was there almost every day, from the end of November until about the middle of May, when I started getting ready to come back home.

I was there [at the trial] almost on a daily basis because I had nothing else to do. I got home [and] was discharged on June 6, 1946, [but the hangman] was part of our detachment before I left. He was there. Woods was there.

There was lumber. Our gym was closed—the building we used for a gym—and lumber was being delivered to that site. We saw it outside. And that's when everybody put two and two together and said, "We got a hangman. We got lumber. We're going to have a hanging." As I said earlier, they knew early on that there were going to be some [hangings], as they knew early on that there was going to be a trial long before anything happened. So it was sort of predestined that it was going to work out this way.

What about Tom Dodd? He was one of the attorneys.

My relationship with Tom Dodd—I mentioned to you this hamburger joint. You know, it was a little section of the Palace of Justice, where the Americans brought in a couple of their cooks and put up a hamburger grill with coffee and Coke, and whatever. Any of the American personnel off-duty could go there, and for a nickel apiece, or some ridiculous [price]—I have some German money that wasn't worth much anyway. Fifty marks. But this was Allied money, which wasn't worth much. You couldn't buy dogs with that. But anyway, you could buy a hamburger for a nickel or dime or whatever it was. And one day I was in there having coffee in the morning [when] there was a break in the trial. Whether it was just a normal break or lunch, I don't know what it was. And I didn't know Tom Dodd at all. I had no idea. This gentleman came over—two of them—and one of them said, "I understand you're from the state of Connecticut," and I said, "Yes, I am." They said, "Where?" I said, "New Haven." One of them turned to the other and said, "This is Tom Dodd. He's from your state." [He was from Norwich.] We shook hands. Of course, he was older, and he said, "How are you doing? What are you doing here? How did you get here?" You know, I gave him a story about being assigned here. He said, "What do you do all day and night?" I said, "I sit upstairs and listen to you." So that was about the extent of that first conversation. He said, "Are things pretty good back home?" He said, "We don't live that far apart, and I understand that the weather is great back home right now." I said, "Yes, my last letter told me." We kind of talked, very small talk. And then periodically—maybe once a week, once every two weeks—the same thing would occur. He would happen to be there when I was there, and we'd shake hands and talk, and I would make a comment, "Hey, you did good with Göring." Well, I didn't know if he did good or bad. But it seemed to be the thing to say. So that was the extent of my relationship with Tom Dodd. But I did see him, and finally found out what he was doing there. At first I had no idea what he was. I didn't know what a prosecutor was. That makes it even more difficult. But that [was] my relationship with him.

What impact did Nuremberg have on your own life?

Then, none. Now, a lot. I am much more interested in what happened there and why it happened. I'm going to get some books—you may recommend a couple for me—of the trial itself, and read about what I saw. Because a lot of it, I had no idea when I was watching it, what was really going on in front of me. To me it was like a show. I was sitting in an audience watching a show. No. It had no impact at all then. I came home and I completely forgot about it.

Was the film Justice at Nuremberg *realistic to you?*

I thought it was. You know, I had no sense of comparison. Even the O. J. trial doesn't seem realistic to me. It seems like a show. And this, in a way, did, [too], because although they didn't have TV cameras on it, between the news-reel broadcast and the print media, they covered this thing pretty well. And the world was hearing what was going on there.

GEORGE KREVIT

Court Page

George Krevit enlisted in the U.S. Army in 1945. In his first assignment in Germany, "we were the mayor, and the police chief, and the tax collector for the town." Krevit was sent to Nuremberg in early 1947. As a page, he was assigned to a different courtroom every day. Krevit is proud of his involvement in the subsequent trials. "The trial of the top Nazi criminals was show and tell for the world. The trials that went on afterwards were the trials of the people who actually committed the horrible war crimes." Krevit went into the family chemical business and is now president of H. Krevit and Company.

I was born December 23, 1927 in New Haven, Connecticut. My father, Allen, came to this country when he was a year old, in 1901, and my family—my grandfather and my father—settled on a farm in Storrs, Connecticut. . . . They eventually sold the farm and moved to New Haven, Connecticut. . . . In 1919 my family went into the chemical business in New Haven, Connecticut. Our family was the first producer of liquid bleach in the United States of America. Some people came down from Syracuse, New York—the old Solvay Chemical Company—and showed my father, who was then 18 years of age, how to make this product.

It was called Solvay process. They were a division of a company from Belgium. So our family went into the chemical business and started to produce laundry bleach for all the small wash and dry laundries around New Haven. And over the years business expanded. I went to Syracuse University. My wife came to the University of Connecticut. During World War II, I became of draft age, and rather than wait for the draft, I enlisted in the regular United States Army.

I turned 18 December 23, 1945, and I became eligible for the draft. Well, rather than wait for the draft, not knowing where they went or where they would send me, I went down and enlisted in the regular army. They gave me a six-month extension to finish the semester that I was in, and then I reported for duty in June of 1946. I took basic training at the Aberdeen [Maryland] Ordinance Grounds, and eventually was shipped to Germany in the early part of 1947. The [Nuremberg war crimes] trials were ongoing at the time. The major war criminals, the top echelon of the Nazi government, had had their trial and had all received their sentences. There were 10 enlisted men on my troop transport. When we got to a troop processing center in Germany, a call went out from the United States military government from Frankfurt. The last 10 enlisted men assigned to the European theater with IQs of 125 or above were requested to report for duty at the Nuremberg war crimes trials.

On March 28, 1947 I received my orders to report to the 7740 military detachment, Nuremberg, Germany. It was called the Office of War Crimes. Our particular unit in Nuremberg handled all of the paperwork. We worked directly under General Telford Taylor. Telford Taylor became the chief prosecutor after Senator Dodd left. In other words, he eventually was in charge of the prosecution of all of the trials. And in 1993, my grandson and I went up to visit him in his weekend home in Kent, Connecticut. He had written a book, *The Anatomy of the Nuremberg Trials,* and I got a very nice endorsement: "To George Krevit. You were there. Telford Taylor. January, 1993." Being on the verge of turning 19, it really did not have an impact on me until later years. In my own personal opinion, the trial of the top Nazi criminals was show and tell for the world.

The trials that went on afterwards were the trials of the people who actually committed the horrible war crimes. Starting down from Adolf Hitler, to Göring, to Himmler, to Hess, we would put these ranking in the top echelon of any government, whether they were good or bad. But the people who were involved in these trials—the SS, the judges, the industrialists—these were the people who did the dirty work, who were out there, as we say, in the trenches, committing the Holocaust, using the slave labor to make munitions, going into Russia, killing everybody in back of the troops. There was a group of SS called the *Einsatzcommando*, whose job was to just kill anybody who got in the way of the German army. Any collaborator, any traitor, any spy—anybody. They just decimated the country. They would go in back of the *Wehrmacht*.

We sat there—my fellow soldiers and myself—and I think it really started to hit us when they brought in the trial of the doctors who did the experiments in the concentration camps. Witnesses started to come forward, and it was probably the most horrible time in my life. Men and women came into court, showed the results of operations, torture. I don't even want to mention some of the things on tape—they were just too horrible. These were the people that should have been tried first, in my mind, and the rest tried second. I mean, opening up a man's leg and putting seaweed into his veins to see how he reacted to foreign bodies. Castrating people of low moral character, or just to get them off the face of the earth. Experimenting on twins who had the same color eyes. And these people just sat in the dark and showed no emotion whatsoever. And, of course, the old defense, "We were just obeying orders."

What were you doing at that trial?

We prepared all the documents for the judges. Every night we would work until ten or eleven o'clock at night. We would prepare the indictments, the paperwork, get everything ready for the prosecution. If there were requests

Eighteen-year-old Corporal George Krevit (left) presents Alfried Krupp with papers for his indictment on August 18, 1947. Also seated in the dock are Ewald Loeser (center) and Eduard Houdremont. Krevit was chosen for this honor because he was Jewish.

"This photograph depicts probably, I guess, the crowning glory of my life.... [It] was on the front page of the New York Times.*" —George Krevit*

from the defense witnesses, we would prepare documents for them. [We] collated, mimeographed and prepared all the documentation that was used in the trial. If one of the judges said, "Go get this," [we got it]. We were called pages. In today's court, [we] would be a bailiff or a court clerk. We were ready at their beck and call—our particular department—to have everything ready for General Taylor. This photograph depicts probably, I guess, the crowning glory of my life.

I happen to be Jewish. My colonel—Colonel Mays—called me into his office one day and he said, "Corporal, Alfried Krupp von Bohlen und Halbach is getting ready to be indicted." He was the big munitions man, whose family owned all the factories in Germany. He said, "I want you to go into court, get a haircut, get your pants pressed, and present him with documents for him to arrange for an attorney." I said, "Colonel, why me?" He said, "Open up your shirt, take out your dog tag." Your religion is imprinted on your dog tag. He said, "There's an 'H' on there, isn't there?" I said, "Yes, sir." He said, "Go in and give them hell." This picture was on the front page of *The New York Times*.

This is August 18, 1947. This is Colonel Mays here. This is the other trial, as I said, with some other people. It was an amazing time in my life because here I am sitting and watching what had happened during this horrible time. This is Alfried Krupp von Bohlen und Halbach. This was the son. In other words, they used slave labor to run all their factories. So this was a war crime. It was a very proud day for me. When we walked into court that day, he had to apply for an attorney. So these applications on these papers were for whatever attorney he requested, which would then have to be approved by the military government to see if these lawyers were presentable and people that could be used in his defense. This particular gentleman and General Taylor and I had many conversations. He was sentenced to, I think, a term of maybe 7 to 15 years.

[Sitting next to Krupp was] Ewald Loeser and Eduard Houdremont. These were all officials of the Krupp. He was released from prison after serving, I think, approximately three years. I called General Taylor in New York and I said, "General, all the work and all the time and all the hours that we put in getting this case ready—why?" He said, "George, politics." He said, "They need him now to get the country back on [its] feet." So a lot of these lower-echelon Nazis were released from prison to get the country back on its feet. I know there's been a lot of comment and a lot of articles on why did we have the Nuremberg Trials when so many of these people, other than the top Nazis, who were either executed, committed suicide, or served long prison terms, were released? Well, West Germany then was an ally against the Soviet Union, so they needed them back.

[The Medical Trial] made the biggest impact on me because they brought many witnesses into court whose bodies had been decimated by surgery and horrible experiments. [The defendants] all belonged to the SS. They were all high-ranking medical officers with military ranks, who thought nothing of doing these kind of things. And the famous one who escaped to South America, who some people still think is alive, [Josef] Mengele. Of course, he wasn't there for the trial because he had escaped through the route of the SS.

Who made the biggest impression on you?

Well, of course, the man who I considered a hero was one of the judges, Michael Musmanno, who was a captain in the navy [from] Pittsburgh, Pennsylvania. His case was of the high ranking SS officers who ran the *Einsatzcommando*. He made more of an impression on me than any other official, other than General Taylor. He was a no-nonsense judge who just would not take any nonsense from these people. When they got up and said, "We were just obeying orders," he would say to them, "Do you think there's a military person who is a legal order?" Well, of course, they wouldn't answer because under military law, even though you can be shot, you have the right to refuse an order that you don't feel is right. The consequences, of course, you may have to accept. But there are laws from the Geneva Convention that say certain military orders are not legal. But this is what the background of the trials were. They were obeying orders. Now, this was a defense for many of these people, starting right from the top, down. All throughout the trial they would get up and say, "We were obeying orders."

Were some of the other judges softer in their approach to the defendants?

I don't think they were really soft because the judges were English. Then, as the years went on, judges were brought over from the United States to run the secondary trials. They were very strict. Strict and stern. They took no nonsense from the defense attorneys. They went by the letter of the law. You know, a movie is a movie. When they made the movie *Judgment at Nuremberg*—I probably have seen it a half a dozen times—the part that Spencer Tracy played reminded me of Judge Musmanno. Even though you thought he was going to do the opposite, he gave them all harsh sentences, death sentences. Because during the movie I said this guy is going to bend. You know, he's being soft-soaped especially by the general's wife who was played by Marlene Dietrich. He was strict. He was like Judge Musmanno. He took no nonsense. He sat there. The other judges in the movie tried to convince him that there would be political ramifications but he didn't want to hear it.

You mentioned that you were chosen to do this, to present the documentation because you were Jewish. Was there anyone else who was Jewish?

I don't remember one other person in my company being of my religion. I was the only one. It's in your records. It's in your military files. Colonel Mays, I found out much later, was from Old Lyme, Connecticut. I didn't realize that then. He was a career artillery army officer who had been in the army for 30 years. A lot of the officers originally were picked for spit and polish. Our executive officer, who was a West Point graduate—at that time he was lieutenant colonel—his name was Autry Maroon. [He] retired as a major general. I've had conversations with him. It's a very strange thing. We have a country that everybody thinks is very democratic. I tried to find out where all of my military counterparts lived so we could have a reunion. And the government tells you that's private information. You have to get to them to get permission. I spoke to the Library of Congress. They told me to contact the Records Center in St. Louis, Missouri. I still could not get any information. I think two years ago I put an ad in *USA Today,* and I got one reply from a friend of mine, and we still talk—Henry Pusey, who lives in Virginia. In fact, we were on the phone a couple of weeks ago. The government will not let you find anybody who you served with because they say it's private. I was never able to have this come to being, which I would have loved to because we had a very unique group.

Have you gone back to any of the Nuremberg reunions that they've held?

No. I went to Nuremberg myself. I did business with a French chemical company in Paris, and five years ago during the time that I was in Paris, I took a commercial flight to Nuremberg and went back to the courthouse and walked up the steps to this particular courtroom. I opened the door and there was some kind of conference going on, and somebody said to me in German, "What are you doing here? This is private. Close the door." But it was awesome to walk back and look at it.

The building was absolutely the same. In fact, there was a plaque on the wall, telling about the IMT. I went back to our barracks, which at that time was a schoolhouse. They had taken over a schoolhouse, and we lived right next door. One of my marvelous experiences while I was there: Our commanding officer one day said, "Go to the armory, pick up a sidearm and go out to the airport and pick up a VIP, and you will escort that individual for the day around the courts." Well, I go out to the Nuremberg airport, a C-47 lands, and the hatch opens up and out walks Rita Hayworth. And here I am 19 years old. She was my idol in the movies. I used to have a picture when I was a kid— her famous World War II picture, kneeling on a bed in a slip. She got out of the plane. I think she had a mink coat that went all the way back to New York. I took her in the Jeep, brought her into the courts, showed her the whole building, and then brought her back to the airport late in the day. So that was an interesting time.

I guess [it was] publicity for her. She took a lot of pictures with a lot of the officers, a lot of the enlisted men. One of the other trials that I found a little bit above me was the trial of the bankers. They were the backbone of the financing for the Nazi government, and of course, they were all brought to trial. But their sentences were not harsh. Most of them were released after a few years, probably in high positions back in the German hierarchy. The first case—the one I was telling you about—was against the doctors. This was the first case brought to trial after the IMT was finished. Here are the names of them. These are the ones that did all of the horrible experiments. Case #2 was against Erhard Milch, who was a member of the Central Planning Board, which planned all of the production of anything that was made in Germany during the war. Case #3 was the case against the judges, and all of their cohorts who ran the court system in Germany during the war.

We would go from courtroom to courtroom. Every day we would get a different assignment. You know, what court to report to be the page in that courtroom. Case #4 was a horrible one. This was against the SS. The *Einsatzcommandos*—all of these men were either ranks of colonel or above; some majors, but mostly generals—committed the horrible atrocities in Russia. You know, just hanging people right and left.

We really didn't have too much contact with the defendants unless we brought something over to them. At the opening day of a trial, we would bring a microphone over to them when they pled "not guilty" or "guilty." So we really never came into contact. The only people who came into contact with the prisoners were their guards and their defense lawyers. The guards were all veterans of the First Division—the Big Red One. So they had guard duty from day one, right until the end of the trials. Case #5 was the one against [German industrialist] Friedrich Flick and his associates, who ran most of the industrial complexes in Germany. I'm sure you heard about them. They were all convicted. And the last case that I was a witness to was a group of generals who were accused of using prisoners of war for slave labor. These were all high-ranking generals, representing all the military services in the German army, navy, air force.

Then came November 1947. I got ready to come home. Very strange trip home. I went to Bremerhaven, which was the port of embarkation. When I got there, there were about 20,000 soldiers—officers—ready to come home. We were housed in these huge barracks. I sat there. I was one of the last 10 enlisted men in this building. The port commander called us in, and there was one second lieutenant by the name of Anthony Marcucci from West Haven, Connecticut. He said, "I've got some good news and I've got some bad news." He said, "You're going home on a Liberty Ship." Well, if you ever take a cruise, don't go on a Liberty Ship because it's like taking a ping pong ball and putting it in the Atlantic Ocean. He said, "You're going to do some escort duty home." One of the soldiers said, "What do you mean by escort duty?" He said, "You're going to be escorting 54 animals home. Officers' pets. All dogs."

We got aboard ship, and our bunks were in the rear of the ship. The ship had an odor like you can't believe because all the animals were down below deck. When we left Germany, as we were going through the English Channel, they piped on board [that] this was the day, late in November 1947, that then the princess—now Queen Elizabeth II—was married. When we got out in the Atlantic Ocean on that Liberty Ship, it took 15 days to get to New York in the height of the winter. I mean, all of us—we just wanted to jump overboard and say, "It's been nice knowing everybody." We all got horribly seasick. My buddies had to go down into the hole, clean the cages, bring the dogs up and walk them. As a ranking noncommissioned officer, even with the rank of corporal—all the rest of them were privates—I got what they called a so-called privilege. I waited on tables. I served the mess. So I didn't have to go below deck. And about two days out, I went to one of these deck hands. I said, "Look, I can't sleep in that bunk anymore." I said, "Can you rig something for me? I don't care if I sleep outdoors the rest of the trip. I've got enough clothes." So he got a bunk for me and bolted it to the deck. So I slept out in the open air the rest of the way home, with my overcoat over my army clothes.

When we got into New York Harbor, some of the animals had delivered puppies, and we had to sack them, weight them down, and dump them overboard because they weren't inoculated and nothing could come into the country. But each time I see something about the trials—when I see a movie, or when I saw this magnificent edifice going up—that brought back all the memories. It was probably the time of my life that I would remember more than anything else. As I said, [it was] being close to history. But I say again, "Was it a waste? Did we spend hundreds and millions of dollars for a show?" A lot of people think so. Even though the eight or nine were hung. Göring cheated the rope. Allegedly this first lieutenant from Texas was able to get him some suicide pills. It was quite a time—quite a time in my life.

When you first came to Nuremberg, what was it like?

Part of the town was still decimated, still in ruins. The courthouse didn't have a scratch on it. Not a scratch. People were still living in squalor. A pack of cigarettes could still get you anything you wanted. In fact, I was a nonsmoker, so I used to sell the cigarettes and send the money home to my folks, which in turn, bought my wife her engagement ring when we got married. We in the military, of course, didn't suffer for anything. But the German people did suffer. A lot of them resented these trials because as the years went on, I guess there's an expression, "The victor gets the spoils." A lot of this was a waste. Pure, absolute waste of time and money because now we're hand-in-glove with West Germany, and East Germany has become part of West Germany. I would [ask if] the top echelon in any government—and we could look at what's going on now in Europe—are they actually responsible for these things? If we took our own president—President Clinton—and let us say he was president during [the] Vietnam [War]. Do they actually know what the troops in the field are doing? Or are they committing atrocities? This happened to be a different time in our lives because we did have the Holocaust.

I think a lot of this and a lot of these trials came forth because of this horrible time in our life when 50 million people died during World War II, plus the murder of all these other people. Will it end war? I don't think so. It's going to happen again. Someday. We hope never. But when you look back on everything we did there, and of all the conversations—because General Taylor and I speak together at least once or twice a year—I don't know if you read his book—the politics that went on. Especially France and England and the United States. If you read the book and you read it again, you wonder, "My God, the nonsense behind the actual courtroom scenes." "I'm not going to do this," or "I'm not going to do that." Everybody wanted their piece of the action.

Did you work very closely with Telford Taylor?

Absolutely. General Taylor was a very soft-spoken individual. There were many nights that everything was a rush job, getting the documents ready. Because we had people out in the field, getting information from the concentration camps. The one good thing—and it sounds crazy—that made these trials possible is that the German government is fastidious about keeping records. If a lot of these records had been destroyed in the normal course of events, say in the last six months of the war, when I assume most of them knew they were losing, it would have been very difficult to bring some of these lesser people to trial. But everything was there. [We would] just go out and find it, and bring it into the research rooms and collate it and mimeograph it, so that when he stepped up to the podium to make a presentation, they had all the evidence. Nothing was hidden. It was all on file. I'm sure there are a lot of Germans that felt, "What did we do? We made it easy for them." But they were there. General Taylor was very soft-spoken. His wife was there. The funny thing here—this is a strange incident. During that time we all wore what we called Eisenhower jackets, which was the short military jacket. He had been awarded a distinguished service medal by President Truman, and his wife called me up one day and said, "The general is going to be presenting opening evidence, and I want to get his jacket with all his decorations in order." So what had happened—under military regulation, your highest-ranking medal sits on the top or as first. She had sewn all his ribbons on backwards. I had to rush and take the jacket over to the tailor to get everything reversed so that nobody could say, "My God, he's a general in name only." We rushed to have that done. But he was marvelous to work with. The tough one was his executive officer, this Colonel Maroon. He was all spit and polish. He had every medal on his chest except the Medal of Honor. West Point graduate. Combat officer. Most of the officers who came to Nuremberg who were not related to the legal part of the trial were all decorated officers. All wartime decorations, under fire, Purple Hearts, the whole works. Again, show and tell.

The soldiers from the First Division [were] spit and polish. I mean, you could cut a slice of bread on the creases in their pants. So it was a time when our government made a huge effort to make sure that the world realized what happened behind all those closed fences. And they brought it all out. The evidence in the concentration camps was unbelievable, and these doctors who did these horrible experiments.

As an 18- or 19-year-old, how much did you know about this before you were at these trials?

I grew up during the war. We read the newspapers, we saw the newsreels. The Holocaust, I don't really think, came into our minds until probably a year or two after the war was over. As it came on later, our government knew what was going on, but it was a matter of priorities. I think one of the Jewish agencies sent an emissary to President Roosevelt [to ask him to] bomb the tracks, destroy the entrance to these concentration camps, make it difficult for the Germans to bring these poor people to their death. And they said, "No, we have other more valuable targets." The one thing that I don't think I'll ever [forget]—and I will make this statement from my heart—I would say that if it was not for the Holocaust, the Germans would have had a very good chance of winning the war, [or] creating a stalemate. Because if you look at the effort, the troops, the rail system, the guards, and the resources that they used to kill six million people—if they had taken that and turned it around to kill the advancing armies, who knows [what would have happened?] Because evidence was brought forth to us that if a train was coming through a combat area, and some SS officer said, "We want that train for Jews," soldiers got off the train. Off. They would take the train and just reverse it and send it back to the camps in Poland with the people who were going to be exterminated. You know, when you think about it, it's mind-boggling. The war could have gone on for years and years and years if this effort to exterminate people was used on the other side of the coin.

Did you have a sense of the Holocaust before you saw these witnesses in the medical trial?

Not a bit. Just a few instances in the paper that you read about, but it didn't affect you. You know, you were young, you were growing up, you were in your teens in 1941. I was 14 years old when our war started with [the bombing of] Pearl Harbor. I was eleven years old on September 1, 1939 [the day Germany invaded Poland]. So you were growing up, you had your life. I've been back. I went to Israel in 1987, and it's still in its original state. [I] went over on a UJA [United Jewish Appeal] mission. We went to Mauthausen [Austria]. The walk from the town up to the camp is about a three- or four-mile walk, up an incline. This is one particular camp where the trains did not run to the camp. The people got out in the town and walked up the hill. And, of course, they never came back. And when soldiers from the United States Army broke into the camps and then they started to interrogate people around, they said, "Didn't you know what was going on?" [They said], "Well, we heard some noise but that was about it." "But how about all these thousands of people that walked up the hill?" Nobody ever walked back. [They said], "We didn't know what was going on." They knew, but they didn't want to know probably because the smoke was going up the stacks, and bodies were being burned.

Did you have much to do with the German people as a soldier?

You would take a German girl out. You would become associated. I had a girlfriend. One part of the story that I neglected to tell you, when I got to Germany I did not go right to Nuremberg. We were assigned to what were called these military government detachments, where two officers and two enlisted men would run a town. My first posting after I got off the boat after a couple of days—I went to a town called Buchen, and was there for about a month before these orders came down to report to Nuremberg. We were the mayor, and the police chief, and the tax collector for the town. So we had everyday functions with the German people. You know, we were there to run their towns under the United States military government. They had no people, no politicians running their towns for quite some time, until things got a little looser. So it was from this small town in Germany, north of Stuttgart that I then went to Nuremberg. But we had a lot to do with the German people. And our only life in Nuremberg was social life with the opposite sex.

Being an American, being a Jew, what was it like in dealing with the ordinary person? How did they react to the trial?

That never came up in my everyday life. I never had one problem in the army because of my religion. Not from day one. Everything went fine. We all got along. Our unit in Nuremberg was very close-knit. We had our own club house. We had our own meals. We did what we wanted. We played softball or baseball every night, or we played football, or, if we found a German girlfriend we would bring her to our club or go to some local club that opened up. The young lady that I met in Buchen—I would get on the train on the weekend to go 150 miles and spend the weekend with her and her family. You know, bringing goodies for them—coffee, cigarettes, whatever. They were happy. Here was somebody that was going to give them some of the things that they couldn't get. Most of the German people, I would say, reacted in a favorable manner to the army. What they did in their own homes, who knows?

When I went back in later years, the cab driver who took me from the Nuremberg Airport into town remembered everything. I think what the German people resent was being forced into war, and the air raids. I just got through reading a book about the RAF Bombing Command. The book more or less intimates that the philosophy of the commanding general, Air Commodore [Arthur Travers] Harris, that besides inflicting damage on the German industrial centers, he just wanted to bomb the living daylights out of the population. He felt if you could bring the population to their knees, you could bring the country to their knees. You know, he would have argument over argument with officers of his own rank that the main theme in bombing during World War II, as far as the British were concerned, was rails, munitions, and oil. Oil, of course, being number one. Well, he went along with that, but then they had some of these horrible raids on Cologne, Dresden, where cities that had magnificent culture, going back hundreds and hundreds of years, were wiped out. I think this was the major resentment of the average German person who was not a member of the Nazi party. We have to realize in this country that not one bomb ever landed on the United States during World War II, so we never suffered the horrors of aerial bombing.

But they brought it on themselves. Not the German people, but the Nazis. They would get up, and in their mind they did nothing wrong. They did nothing wrong. Somebody told them to do this. A general in the SS told a colonel in the SS, "Go out and kill these Russian prisoners of war." There was no "I can't do it. It's against the rules." They would go out, string them up, hang them by telephone poles. There was no talk back. You either took an order or they would execute you on the spot, as they were doing toward the end of the war. But the German people themselves that we had contact with were good. It's like being with your own neighbors. They were friendly. They would bring you into their house. They would talk to you in broken English or you'd have an interpreter. Life there as a soldier—you know, after the hostilities—was not unpleasant. It was not a difficult thing.

Did your job take you out of the courtroom to get information?

No. We collated all the information. There was a part of our unit that went out into the field with lawyers, who brought information in. Our job was strictly to maintain the presence of the courtroom, have documents ready, if the judges needed something. Strictly in the courtroom. That was our job. We never went out in the field at all.

When you came home, was there much interest in the Nuremberg Trials—that you had been there?

Yes. All of my friends—we used to get together and talk and talk for hours.

Did you ever think about a legal career? Did the trials affect you in that way?

Not at that stage of my life. You see, my family had been in business since 1919. In fact, when I got home from the army, I got involved with a lady. I went back to college for six months and I said, "You know, I'm going to go to work in the family business." So in July of 1948 I came home, went to work for my dad. I'm still there. My father's passed away but our family is still in business. I got married in 1949. But this is always the fondest part of my life, always the thing that brings back the most memories and the most excitement—to say I had my picture in the newspapers [*The New York Times*] at a very spectacular time. My father called me 10 days after this and he said, "What's going on over there? Your picture is in the newspapers." You see, when I was presenting [the indictments], there were cameras all over and I wasn't paying any attention when they were snapping all kinds of photographs. This was one of the photographs that they sent back to the U.S., and I had no indication—nobody told me—that they were going to publicize this until it happened. So it was pretty exciting. So I was in the forefront of many of the trials. In fact, I went down to the Holocaust Museum in Washington and they have a moving picture of these—of the secondary trials—and there I was, doing these kinds of things every day. We had a pretty good life. We had decent barracks, we had a lot of athletics. If you remember the famous wartime scene at one of the massive stadiums in Nuremberg where they blew up the swastika. Do you remember that scene? [That was] where we played ball every night. There was enough ground to have six baseball fields. And we would go every night to play ball. Because of the shortage of power, they [changed the time so] that it really never got dark in Germany until four o'clock in the morning. We would be in the courtroom at noon and it was still pitch black. It would start to lighten up in the afternoon. So there would be more light available later on. But we played ball every night and we took our furloughs. I spent a week in England. I flew over on General Taylor's plane and had a good time in London for a week. I burned a hole in my pants, [which] left me with one pair. I had to go to the embassy to get some clothes. [laughs] But it was interesting. I would do it again anytime.

You kept the relationship up with Taylor.

Absolutely. I call him every year to see how he is. We talk. He was going to write a book about these trials, which he's in the middle of doing now. I don't know whether he's going to have the physical stamina to do it. When I spoke to him over the weekend, he sounded old. He's got to be in his 80s now. [Telford Taylor died in May 1998 at age 90.]

How often do you think about Nuremberg?

Oh, every time a movie comes up or I look at [these photos]. These were hanging on my wall in my office. Every time I walk in, it brings back memories. It does. I would think the trial of the SS doctors who experimented on all these hostages in the concentration camps is probably something I'll never forget, and the trial of those SS officers who ran these killing squads. That's probably a lasting effect on my life. The bankers, the judges, the munitions people—probably if we were to reverse circumstance, would we bring these kind of people to trial? Well, I guess they had to do it for the world because they were using slave labor.

Has it had any effect on your own thinking or politics?

Well, I don't know where this country stands today. Can we ever trust the German people? They are now, of course, trying to make every effort to be peaceful citizens. But there are still people there who still celebrate Adolf Hitler's birthday. There are still people in South America allegedly who took off with vast sums of money. I'm sure that there's tons of money sitting in Switzerland that nobody can get their hands on because they couldn't get there. But I would hope that this would never happen again.

Don't forget that in this country, there is no legal limit to prosecute somebody for murder. It should be no different than somebody who killed innocent people. They should be hunted until their days' end. Absolutely. Have you contacted the Simon Wiesenthal Center in [Los Angeles] California at all? I have talked to them, and we've written back and forth. I got a little upset with them one time because I think they were more interested possibly in raising money for all of their ventures. But they have done good work, and they keep the people on top of the events in the world when it comes to anti-Semitism or these Nazis that are still hanging loose somewhere in the world, even though they're all in their 80s. If you're going to bring them to trial, they're going to be dead in a year or two, or whatever. But it was an impressive time in my life. I don't think anything could ever replace it. Ever. Ever.

INTERROGATORS AND
TRANSLATORS

HARRY FISS

Translator/ Documentation

As a Jew, terror fills Harry Fiss's memories of his Austrian childhood. Fiss's family came to America in August 1939, when an American philanthropist, Abraham Felt, sponsored them. "We were just numbers to him; he wanted to save Jews." Happily drafted into the military in 1944, Fiss arrived in Europe with a great anger toward Nazis. Fiss listened to parts of the IMT Trial. "I was there when they all pleaded 'innocent,' or 'not guilty.' I couldn't believe my ears." After a career as a journalist, Fiss became a clinical psychologist.

I was born April 15, 1926 in Vienna, Austria, of parents who were both born in Vienna. I had a rather traumatic childhood because my father died when I was three years old, so I never really knew my father. When I was five years old, my mother married Mr. Fiss, whose name actually was Fishman, but they changed the name when they came over here. He was my stepfather, but I don't remember any other father.

Austria has always been a very anti-Semitic country and had plenty of trouble before the *Anschluss* [annexation of Austria, March 1938] came. There was always discrimination and quite a few beatings; mostly [I was] getting beaten up or insulted by fellow students and kids on the street or in the park whom I didn't even know. In all fairness, though, I must say, there were some students who were definitely anti-Nazi. They were not anti-Semitic. There were some teachers who were exceptionally nice to me. I'm not saying that everybody was that way, but the large majority was. I had completed elementary school. In Austria you had four years of elementary school. It's called *Volkschule*, followed by eight years of *Gymnasium*. Then you took the "*matura*," oral exams, the completion of which was more or less the equivalent of a college degree. If you are a graduate of *Gymnasium,* you get an automatic commission in the army. Anyway, I got as far as my second year of *Gymnasium* when the Nazis occupied Austria. That was March 11, 1938.

I'm currently writing a book, which has nothing to do with the Holocaust. It has to do with dreaming. That's my specialty. I do dream research. The book has to do with the importance of dreaming and how important dreams are in helping us live better lives. I start out with a chapter called, "The Dream That May Have Saved My Life." The reason I'm going to read this to you is because it has to do exactly with what I'm talking about.

It was the day after the *Anschluss*—German for annexation. Hitler and the German army had just marched into Vienna, Austria, where I was born and grew up, and had been given a jubilant reception by the great majority of the non-Jewish population, and I, an 11-year-old Jewish Gymnasiast, high school student, about to celebrate his 12th birthday, was on my way to school full of fearful anticipations. When I arrived, I found that the Jewish students had just been segregated from the non-Jewish students and were now confined to the last two rows in the classroom. This happened overnight. I heard a few snide remarks from some of my fellow students that the seats formerly occupied by the Jewish students would now have to be cleansed with Sidol, which is something like Ajax.

There was tension in the air. The first class was in German composition. Our teacher, who had always been kind to me, gave a desultory Heil Hitler salute. [He] was not a Nazi. You could tell by the sloppy way he said "Heil Hitler." He sat down at his desk and announced the day's class exercise. Almost all exercises and examinations were oral in those days and carried out in front of the class. The assignment was to write an essay about "Why I love my Führer, Adolf Hitler." The Jewish students could deliver a talk on a subject of their own choosing.

When my turn came, I decided to describe a funny dream I had the night before. I have no memory whatsoever of the content of this dream, but I vividly remember the impact it had on the class. It made everybody roar with laughter. For one split second in the history of the Holocaust the gulf between tormentor and victim had been breached. Both segments of the population were, for a fraction of a moment, members of the same human race, not supermen and subhumans, but united in a pleasurable experience they both shared.

88

But the precious moment didn't last long. No sooner had I completed my dream talk than the uniformed head of the local Hitler Youth, an upper-classman, burst into the room, gave a snappy Hitler salute, pulled out a decree which had just been issued by the local Nazi headquarters, and announced in terse terms that as of this moment all Jewish students were to be immediately expelled from all public schools. What followed was one of those mini-*pogroms* that heralded similar demonstrations on a much larger and lethal scale. Not a single Jewish student emerged from the school building that day uninjured—not one, except me. Some had even sustained serious injuries. Did my telling my dream keep me out of harm's way? I'll never know, but the incident has remained ingrained in my memory. The dream also encapsulates what this book is all about. It is an ode to the dream.

I remember religion was a compulsory subject. This was before the *Anschluss*. We all stayed in the same room, even though this was high school. When it came to religion, the Catholics went to one room, the Lutherans remained in the room, and the Jews also went into another room. There were always comments about the Jews.

Also, we had religious instruction on Saturday. We had Hebrew or whatever it was. I remember one particular Saturday morning the local hoodlums, they roved around in bands looking for victims. Two kids came closing in on me with sticks, rocks, and whips. I was terror-stricken, since I couldn't run this way and I couldn't run that way, and I couldn't run back—I could only run forward. I was, literally speaking, struck blind with terror because I basically ran against a building and knocked myself unconscious. When I came to, there were some civilians expressing concern about what had gone on. They told me to go to the police, but I knew that if I went to the police, I would only get my parents in trouble. The police were no help.

There was all this unpleasant business for years, this anti-Semitism every-where, but it became even more horrendous after the *Anschluss*. The Germans accomplished in six months what it took the Austrians five years. I got kicked out of school. My father's business was "Aryanized" by his foreman. He was kicked downstairs and had to scrub sidewalks. In fact, at the Holocaust Museum in Washington, there's a blown up photograph of Viennese Jews scrubbing sidewalks and I was looking for my father there, but his photo just happened not to have been taken that day.

I was also looking for myself on line waiting for the passport, which might be interesting to you. I have a copy of my passport. [shows passport] This is what I came to the United States with. Look at the letter "J."

I started [a] diary two weeks before *Kristallnacht* ["night of broken glass"; November 9–10, 1938; 815 Jewish shops and 76 synagogues were destroyed and at least 20,000 Jews were arrested]. My mother must have had a premonition. My mother said, "You should start keeping a diary." We had had an earthquake two days before the *pogrom*. All this is written up.

Aside from watching synagogues burn, which everybody did, the night before I was at my grandparents' for dinner and there was an announcement on the radio saying that a Jew by the name of [Herschel] Grynszpan had assassinated a minor German foreign office person by the name of [Ernst] vom Rath in Paris and because of this dastardly deed, the Jews are being fined two billion marks. I heard that on the radio and that's when the trouble started.

Personally, the first thing I experienced was 6 A.M. that morning—it was November 10—there was a loud ringing of the bell. My father was not there. My father was already in the factory, which he soon lost, but he was at work. Two SS men came. These were the guys with black uniforms and they said, "We're looking for weapons. We have to search the house. We're looking for weapons." The German word for weapon is *waffen* and I misunderstood *wappen*, which means emblems. I had a collection of war medals that my biological father in World War I was awarded. Interestingly enough, my biological father, who died when I was very young, was an officer in the Austrian army in World War I, and had earned all these decorations. He was wounded in the Battle of the Somme. So I brought out all these emblems and they said, "No, we're not interested in that." I tried to assuage them. They went through the whole place and turned everything upside down. The place was a total mess, but they didn't hurt anybody.

So then they wanted to arrest my father and he wasn't at home. So my mother called the office and asked if they would call him. So she called and said, "Is Mr. Fiss there?" and he said on the other side, "Yes, I am here." She says, "Well, where is he?" "I'm here." He wasn't too bright. I think he finally caught on that there were people looking for him, and they got impatient and they left. They put a seal on the door, which meant that we had been searched and there's no point in being searched anymore. The real scum came afterwards. That was the Brown Shirts [the SA, the storm troopers] and they really caused trouble. Fortunately, they passed us by because we had already been inspected by the SS.

That was the day that my stepfather was knocked down the stairway and had to wash sidewalks. My cousin and her parents were thrown out of their apartment, which was confiscated. They had to move in with my grandparents. My uncle was in prison. Another uncle ended up in jail and my cousin and I were standing guard duty, on the lookout, in case he came out. He never came out and we got a card from Dachau that he was [there] and they were picking up people on the streets in these green cars. They called them "Green Henrys" [*Grine Heinrich*]. They just disappeared and were never heard from again or they were beaten up in jails or ended up in a KZ [concentration camp].

Oh, and I remember my father was arrested by a 14-year-old hoodlum with a pistol. I don't know what happened after that. My mother was stopped by two SS men who wanted to drag her off, they said, to clean the windows at the Gestapo headquarters. They needed window washers, and ordered her, "Come with us." My mother was the most amazing woman. She was very good in a crisis. She said, "Well, I'd be very happy to do this, but I have a bad heart and I'll just drop dead on you." It was like quarter to five and one SS man said to the other, "Oh, let that fucking Jew bitch go home" [in German]. I was there waiting for her at home and I thought I may never see my mother again.

A lot of close calls and it was just terribly frightening. The thing that remained was not the incidents so much, but I gave you a sample. It's the fear, this constant dread. I think at some level we knew that if we didn't get out of there we'd get killed.

Look at the last page [of my passport] for the precious American visa that saved my life. Notice it says "Vienna, Germany" on the bottom.

Was there a Jewish school that you attended?

That was a big joke because the Jewish students somehow didn't have any discipline. I guess when you suppress a people and suddenly you give them freedom, there was so much disorder and such lack of discipline in that school, I decided it was a waste of time. Also, going to school and coming back was always extremely hazardous. Even if I was accompanied by an adult, I would get rocks thrown at me and beaten up.

When I arrived in the United States in August 1939, I was so afraid. I had real post-traumatic stress disorder. I remember we lived on Sherman Avenue in Washington Heights and I didn't understand a word of English. Whenever I saw some kids, I immediately went to the other side of the street. I still had this built-in fear and as soon as I saw some kids, I started running the other direction.

My wife went to England. My wife is from Darmstadt [Germany] and she went to England on a children's transport, about the same time.

How did you get out of the country?

As you realize and I'll tell you, the whole world bears a responsibility for the Holocaust because, except for Shanghai, there was no place to go. It was extremely difficult to come to the United States. You had to have a sponsor with money in the bank. I think it was $4,000, which was an awful lot of money in those days. We had no relatives there and the reason we came to the United States was simply because of the fact that my father happened to be a joiner. Among other things, he was a Freemason and the American Jewish Masonic Lodge had a philanthropic person on its board by the name of Abraham Felt, who was the father of James Felt, who was Housing Commissioner for New York City about 30 years ago. Anyway, he was a Jewish philanthropist and he had a list of people that he wanted to save. It was a Jewish Schindler's List, you might say, and somehow we got on that list and when we arrived in New York, he signed all necessary papers and sent us on our way. We were just numbers to him. He just wanted to save Jews. He wasn't interested in having a relationship with any of them.

I still don't know him. I saw him briefly when he put us in a taxi and that was all. I was asking for a summer job once and he refused. [laughs] This was not his line of work.

How difficult was it to get a visa to the United States?

You had to have a sponsor and also you had to register at the American consulate in time. If you registered late, you might not have gotten out. Also, they had different quotas for each country. Polish Jews were far more restricted to come to the United States than Austrian Jews.

My grandmother was born in Vienna but my grandfather was Polish. They managed to get out of Vienna in 1941! Can you believe this? It took him two years longer because he was Polish. So the country of origin made a difference. You had to have the right connections. It was even harder to get to Australia. It was even harder to get to Canada. All these countries had space, you know. In fact, it was the South American countries like Bolivia and Paraguay who were most generous. At least you could buy a visa, but we didn't have enough money for that.

The Dutch Reformed Church tried to help us. The best they could come up with was getting my father out. So what's the point of that? I have a French uncle who was very well-to-do. He tried to get me a visa to come to France. That's why I spoke French before I spoke English. I even passed the entrance exam in Paris and the French government never granted me a visa. Of course, the French were just as anti-Semitic as anybody else, and that's very fortunate because I don't think I would have been alive if I had gone to France. A year later my rich uncle was a refugee himself. We were his guests on the way to America. It's a crazy story.

So that's why it was difficult. No country wanted us. You know the story about the *St. Louis*, the ship that was sent back. There was a ship that was actually turned back and Eleanor Roosevelt tried to intercede. But anyway, the Holocaust Museum makes a very good point. It doesn't mince any words about the responsibility of the entire "civilized" Western world for the "Final Solution."

Was it all Jews [on the ship]?

No, but there were a lot of Jewish passengers. About three months ago I went to a meeting at Adelphi University in the Unified Germany, and one of the people in the audience I started talking to turned out to have been on the same ship. Can you imagine?

It was the *S. S. Manhattan*, United States Lines Manhattan. We left from Le Havre and it took us three weeks. It was a long trip. There were no transatlantic planes.

I remember playing with an English boy called Hugh, whom I didn't understand but we played together anyway. It wasn't a refugee boat. There just happened to be a lot of refugees on that boat, among other passengers.

What was life like when you came to the United States?

[It was] difficult. Of course, we were very much aware that we had barely escaped with our lives. It sounds like a cliché, but to breathe clean air, this is something that you don't appreciate until you are deprived of it. You don't walk around saying, "Gee, it's wonderful to be in good health," unless you're sick. The first free place, I think, was Zurich and I cannot tell you the feeling of liberation, as if a tremendous load had been lifted off me. It was just unbelievable, after living in terror and fear for so long.

I still had flashbacks, like I explained to you, but they didn't last very long. I must say that on the upside was the feeling that we were saved, we were safe. On the downside I can say a lot. First of all, two weeks after I came here, I had to go to school.

Did you speak any English?

Not a word because I had spent all my time learning French. There were no special classes for refugee students, though the majority of students, at least 60 percent in that school were refugees.

It was Washington Heights. It was George Washington High School. You know, like today you hear about Spanish-speaking people, but all I can say is there were no efforts made to help us in any way with the English language. We had to sink or swim.

My parents had to go to work the very next day after we arrived. That's another thing I really experienced for the first and only time in my life. We were really destitute. We actually were completely penniless. We had 16 pieces of luggage and not a cent in our pockets. We were completely stripped of everything at the border, all we had left, by the Nazis. My parents had to find a job the next day and they both worked in factories. They each made $12 a week.

Luckily, I had an aunt and an uncle who lived in Washington Heights who had arrived here a few months before us, and she helped me with my homework. She translated to me in German. It was a terrible struggle, but I have a flair for languages, so I picked up English in about a month, enough at least to understand what was being said to me and to do my homework. I got a 65 in everything and the next term I got a 78 average. It wasn't until I was a senior in high school that any American student would speak to me, though. The American students had absolutely nothing to do with us. All I heard most of the time was, "Dirty refugee, why don't you go back where you came from?" It was an Irish neighborhood.

Were there other students like you who were refugee children?

Oh, 60 percent at least. All my friends were fellow refugees. I would say one thing. The Society for Ethical Culture did a lot to help me. First of all, they formed a club of refugees like myself, under the leadership of an American youth leader, who later became a social worker. He taught us how to speak English properly, how to whistle at girls properly, how to use profane language properly, etc. It basically was an Americanization group that was funded by the society. The society also sent me to summer camp for two or three summers.

They also arranged for my bar mitzvah. It was interesting. I was 13 when I came here and the last thing my parents had on their mind was my bar mitzvah. They couldn't care less. We were never very religious anyway. But I had to have a bar mitzvah, so the society paid for the rabbi, paid for everything.

I could have graduated at 16, if I had had the proper guidance. In spite of the poor advice, I graduated at 17, went to college [for] one year, and was drafted into the United States Army at age 18, and was quite happy about it.

I was thinking of volunteering, but why volunteer if I'm going to be drafted anyway? In fact, I was in the middle of a summer course I was taking at Queens College. I knew I was going to be drafted. The day I got the notice I had to report immediately to the draft board.

Did you have any contact with anyone back in Austria?

My grandparents were still there. These are my mother's parents. We wrote to each other and my parents desperately tried to put together money for a visa and eventually succeeded. That was a very close call. They must have been the last Jews to leave Vienna.

They came in the fall [of 1941], just shortly before [the attack on] Pearl Harbor. Until the United States entered the war, you could still get out, technically. But my father's parents were of course wiped out and all my Jewish friends, the ones that I knew from high school and elementary school, they all died in the Holocaust. I know that. I'm the only one that survived of all the Jews in that class. One went to Czechoslovakia and disappeared. One went to Paris and disappeared. One came to the United States and was drafted into the army the same time I was and he was killed in combat.

At that time I was trilingual. I was fluent in German, French, and English. I also knew Spanish. I had to take one foreign language in high school, so I chose Spanish. Actually, I was quadrilingual and I scored very low on the mechanical aptitudes. Wouldn't you know it, they sent me to airplane mechanic school. [laughs] In a way, I suppose that's why I didn't see any combat because it delayed my training just enough. I kept saying, "I should be in the intelligence service, for Christ's sake." They were training airplane mechanics to become linguists and they thought they would teach them German in the Army Specialized Training Programs. What they did, instead of taking cooks and sending them overseas as cooks, they took cooks and turned them into linguists. It was stupid, like [they were trying] to make me into an airplane mechanic. I barely graduated, but I never used it much. I kept bothering and badgering them: "This is ridiculous. I really want to go to Europe."

I was drafted into the army air force. The air force was not a separate service then. It was just a fluke. There just happened to be a slot open in the air force and so I ended up being sent to Europe in April on my birthday. On April 15, 1945, my troop convoy left New York and I was in the Ninth Air Force Intelligence. Believe it or not, my boat landed in Europe on V-E Day [May 8, 1945]. It's really amazing. We heard Churchill's speech on the deck of our boat. At that time, all the combat veterans were being sent home and we were the vanguard of the occupation forces. So that's how I eventually ended up in Nuremberg, but I did so only on my own initiative. If I had left it to the army, I would have done nothing.

Why did you want to go to Europe?

There is a mixture of reasons. See, all my basic training was in the South: in Texas, in Mississippi, Louisiana, and I absolutely hated the South because of the discrimination against blacks. I remember going to a USO thing. I was stationed in Biloxi [Mississippi]. I became a citizen in Biloxi. I remember once waiting for a bus to go to a USO dance in New Orleans and I noticed the bench at the bus stop said, "whites only," and I remember five years before that I'd seen a similar bench in a park in Vienna that said, "Aryans only." I said to myself, "What kind of a country did I come to?" It was terrible. I saw blacks had to sit in the back. In other words, the blacks were being treated the way Jews were treated in Germany and Austria, and I was absolutely outraged. I got in trouble a couple of times. I almost started a riot on the bus because I offered a black woman a seat.

So I didn't have very terrific experiences. I felt very bitter because I came here and I expected democracy and then I heard about blacks being lynched. It made me sick. And then the blacks were segregated from the whites in the army itself!

How did you get to the Nuremberg Trials?

I was one of the first Americans to occupy Germany and I was given a Jeep and a driver and told to find an intelligence outfit. Nobody knew where the outfit was that I was supposed to join. So after a week of cruising around just about all of Germany from the back of a truck, I finally found my outfit in what later was to become East Germany in Thüringen, in a place called Eisenach. It's a small city and the capital of Thüringen. Very beautiful. It's opposite the Wartburg, where Martin Luther had once been imprisoned.

Anyway, we were lodged in one of those hills. We weren't at war. It was the demolished BMW plant. BMW made the V-1 and V-2 rockets, which rained on my poor wife when she was in London during the blitz. I was stationed in the ruins of this bombed-out factory, and I was given this Jeep and a driver and told to find the blueprints of the V-2 rockets because the Russians were coming very soon and we wanted to get our hands on them before the Russians did.

I had very little trouble locating the blueprints because the Germans are such authoritarian people that they always cooperate with whoever's in power. So I had very little difficulty getting information from mayors and other informers. I was only 19 and very angry, but after a couple of bum steers I found the blueprints at the bottom of this abandoned salt mine in East Germany. There were also other things. There was valuable art crated away and silver jewelry. We confiscated all of that and I went over the documents with a German engineer who had worked there. I had to hunt him out because I couldn't ship all that stuff. Not all of it was worth shipping.

Anyway, we sent a whole crate of documents to Washington. In a sense, you could say I started our space program, as this happened before [German rocket scientist] Wernher von Braun was put on the U.S. payroll. It was a matter of days before the Russian army moved in and we moved out. So it was in the nick of time. I'm not saying this proudly or anything, but you asked me why I wanted to go to Germany. One was to get revenge. That's why I went there. I think that was my primary motive. Secondly, I felt that with my knowledge of German I could be of some use, which I was.

How did you feel when you arrived in Germany and saw what had happened to it?

Good. I loved to see all those ruins. [I arrived first] in Oberursel, which is a suburb of Frankfurt. It was totally demolished. Except for Heidelburg and Wiesbaden, I didn't see anything but rubble. This March I was invited to be a keynote speaker at the Sigmund Freud Institute in Frankfurt at an international conference. I know these people extremely well and two weeks before that, I was still saying, "You know, I don't really want to go back to Germany. I'd like to remember it the way I last saw it, even though it was in rubble." But it didn't turn out that way and I had a very good time. I was treated incredibly well. I can't say enough in praise of my hosts. That's a different generation.

So after this incident with the blueprints, the army had nothing to do for me and that's the worst trouble you can get into: nothing to do. What do you do? Stand guard. Work in kitchen duty and stuff like that. So I was looking for something to do and I read in *Stars and Stripes* that they were starting a war crimes trial. I wasn't too far from there and being in the air force I had little trouble getting around. I could get a pass and I hitchhiked on a plane.

I went right to the Nuremberg courthouse. They were so anxious to have linguists. I started out as a translator, but I rose very quickly because of my German and English. Soon I was in charge of an entire translating section and before I left I was in charge of all the documentation for the American prosecution, which actually was a job that I didn't realize would carry the rank of a full colonel. When I was ready to be discharged after I had done my tour of duty, I was urged to take my discharge at Nuremberg and remain on as a civilian, and they offered me a colonel's pay. While in the service, all I got was a promotion to corporal from private. After the blueprints I was given one stripe and then in Nuremberg I was given another stripe, so I came out as a corporal.

There was a guy called Sonnenfeld, who was in charge of all personnel. He was probably the single most important person at the Nuremberg Trial. He was so powerful he could take anybody that the State Department had sent there and send them back to Washington as unqualified. He was in charge of personnel at the Nuremberg Trials and his name was constantly on the intercom.

The point I'm making is the army is hardly what you'd call a meritocracy. At the IMT, I was completely responsible for the processing and safekeeping of all documents for the American prosecution. By that I mean I would get a call by an attorney who needed Document So and So for cross-interrogating Göring. I would have to come up with it translated, analyzed. All that work would be done by the whole translation division under me. So the documents had to be analyzed, translated, and copied. I had full responsibility for that.

All of that stuff was top secret, otherwise I would have loved to take some of it with me. I was 19. I was aware that I was witnessing history, though I didn't think of writing a book, as I should have, since all documents went through my hands. When I went to Israel to the Beth Hatefutsoth Museum in Tel Aviv, I saw documents that I translated myself on exhibit there. There's a scene in William Shirer's book [*The Rise and Fall of the Third Reich: A History of Nazi Germany*] that I personally witnessed, which I'm going to tell you about. So I was very much involved.

Also, I had a buddy who was in the press corps and that was something interesting. See, this went on and on and on. There were a lot of dull periods in the trial, but whenever something exciting was happening, like say Göring would be cross-interrogated, then he would give me a call and I would leave my desk and go in and listen for a while. So I also got to listen to parts of the trial.

Another thing I did was I interrogated witnesses for the prosecution and one of them was SS General [Otto] Ohlendorff, the head of the mobile extermination units [*Einsatzgruppen*; in 1941–1942]. How I was able to do this, I'm wondering. It's amazing that I was able to not manage to feel anything at all. I just did my work. I wrote a paper once which I presented to the American Psychological Association, in which I talked about the numbing of feelings. The point I made in this paper is that the same numbing of feelings that helped the SS execute people also helped the survivors. My wife's father, for example, who was in Buchenwald for six months, was able to eat his soup next to a corpse. I was able to talk to this SS man who had killed I don't know how many hundreds of thousands of people, smoking a cigarette and telling me with great pride how he made this killing machine more and more efficient. That was Ohlendorff. I also translated [Alfred] Rosenberg's diary, which was one of the main exhibits that sent him to the gallows, and I'm very proud of that.

The highest-ranking war criminal that I interrogated was the commander of Auschwitz, SS *Obersturmbaunführer* Rudolf Höss. I actually wrote a book about it that was never published. It was kind of a novel. I'm thinking of rewriting and maybe publishing it, but right now I'm working on something more professional. I've put this thing behind me now. I may or not get to it, but this was the excerpt from my novel describing my interrogation of Höss.

> Room 167 was cheerless and whitewashed, just as you would expect, with hard wooden benches and a hard and cold stone floor. It had two large windows facing the prison courtyard, where for an instant I caught sight of a white-helmeted guard pacing by on his eternal rounds.
>
> Suddenly there was a draft in the room. I saw Mr. Booth open a voluminous manila folder with a jerky motion and glance expectantly at the door. Only now did I notice it was open. Something stiff and gray entered noiselessly. "Please sit down." Mr. Booth pointed to SS *Obersturmbaunführer* Rudolf Höss.

Do you know what *Obersturmbaunführer* is? That's an SS general. By the way, he appears in that movie *Sophie's Choice,* but much too young and handsome. This was an old, old man. You would never look at him twice, a very unspectacular looking man.

> He bowed and an arm's length away from me stopped and bowed a second time, this time more noticeably, and clicked his heels together. He wore black boots, gray knickerbockers and a heavy gray woolen sweater. Höss sat

down without waiting for another invitation, crossed his legs and folded his hands on his lap. I looked at the cord-like veins showing through the epidermis. What was he doing, praying?

Mr. Booth was saying, "What's your name?" and I was acting as the interpreter. Höss answered in a controlled voice. "Your rank and arm of service." Mechanically the questions and answers came in one language and were converted into another.

"You were at one time Commander-in-Chief of the Auschwitz Concentration Camp, is that correct?"

"*Ja*," Höss nodded emphatically. There was no expression in his eyes. They were two colorless, bottomless pits, embedded in ash gray flesh. With a motion of his hand, Mr. Booth beckoned to me to offer Höss a cigarette. I was about to comply, then suddenly shook my head. Mr. Booth muttered something about insubordination, grabbed the pack and reached across the table. Höss took a cigarette and nodded a silent thank you. There was a brief flicker of flame, followed by a little puff of smoke, like smoke coming out of a chimney, I thought, a chimney on top of a brick building and inside the brick building there were ovens containing bones, human bones.

While Höss smoked, Mr. Booth opened another folder and took out the top paper. He scanned it briefly.

This is the paper that was signed. I did manage to spirit a copy of it out. Here you have it. That is the confession he signed. This is the most unbelievable thing that I have experienced in my entire life.

I said to him, "You told us once that you'd be willing to sign this confession," and Höss stared at the document and said, "Yes, but there is something wrong," and then he pointed to the second line. "What's wrong?" Höss said to me, "Right here." He moved his finger across the page. "It says here that I personally arranged the gassing of three million persons between June 1941 and the end of 1943." "Well, isn't that what you said?" "I'm afraid not. I said that only two million were gassed. You have to get the record straight. The rest died of other causes." "Other causes?" "You know, the usual thing, malnutrition, dysentery, typhoid. We had an awful lot of typhoid cases." "I see." Mr. Booth leaned back and sighed, "Okay, change it then." He pushed the fountain pen across the table. Höss picked up the pen, unscrewed the top *and without further ado crossed out the three million and put in two million over it.* Then he signed his name and then he blew on the paper until the ink was dry. I never could remember what happened afterwards. It seemed as if the very next moment Höss was gone and the whole thing had just been an apparition, but there was the signed confession, the cigarette still smoldering in the ashtray and there we were, sitting in the captor's chair.

That part of this book I wrote when I was 24, which I never published because in those days nobody wanted to hear anything about the Holocaust.

Booth was your superior?

Yes. Well, actually there were two of them: Mr. Booth and Captain [Drexel] Sprecher. I pissed him off once because I wanted to go to Vienna in the worst way and he said he couldn't spare me, but I went anyhow. But he was a good guy. It was actually on official duty. What happened is I overheard two colonels going there and they wanted someone to check the prison rosters, in case they needed witnesses, and I offered my services to them. I think he's forgiven me for it.

What was it like going back there?

Well, I was angry. I just wanted to create a lot of trouble, that's all. I don't know. I just wanted to go back there and create trouble. [I did] stupid things, like breaking into my apartment because the woman there was hysterical when she saw an armed soldier on the floor. I wanted to see the apartment, and I had to break in because she wouldn't let me in. The neighbors recognized me and they tried to calm her down. They said, "He only wants to see the apartment." She must have thought I was going to rape her, so she called the police and the police couldn't arrest me because I could arrest the police. [laughs] Crazy things like that.

I was looking for one of the Hitler Youth that had been my chief tormentor and couldn't find him, but I thought I found him because the name was rather uncommon. His name appeared on one of those POW lists and I swear that I would have killed him. That was my plan. If he came out of that formation, I was going to shoot his head off. That was what I was planning to do. I'm very glad it wasn't him. He was a Czech National.

I also went to the person who had Aryanized my parents' business. I told her that I'm taking legal action against her and I did. I started the whole legal proceedings, but my parents didn't bother following up.

How long were you in Austria?

Just two weeks. I didn't enjoy it at all. I was ready to go back. I mean I hated it, but then I was back in 1990 and I loved it. I think that a lot of people kept silent and tried to repress it and not think about it and not talk about it. They repressed everything, including anger. I always talked about it and acted it out. I still get angry, even to this day. I'm not angry to the point where I'm blind. I can see this is a new generation and I have very close friends in Austria and Germany that are not Jewish. I felt very much at home in Germany in March.

100

I couldn't believe it. I felt very comfortable there, although before I went I had a lot of anxiety. Children, grandchildren of people that committed those atrocities are not responsible. They were very nice to me.

How did you feel about the ordinary German on the street?

Oh, I wouldn't have anything to do with them. I had a problem because I was at that age where I wanted girlfriends and I couldn't get myself to make love to a German girl. So there was this conflict of being attracted to women and not allowing myself to do anything. That was a big problem. I didn't have any relationships. Unfortunately, not in Nuremberg but before in East Germany, I was the only Jew in a German-speaking outfit. The others were all German Americans, and they were rather sympathetic to the Germans. They were slightly anti-Semitic and they made remarks like : "It's a good deal, Fiss," or, "You can't hold a grudge forever. You've got to forgive and forget." They were fraternizing right away and I had problems with those guys.

I did have one positive contact with a German family that had actually helped a Jewish family and this Jewish family was sending care packages and I delivered them. Then the only other contact I had was in the black market because I always sold my cigarettes. I was a nonsmoker and I got a carton of cigarettes that was worth $50 and I would sell them. I didn't think twice about that. Everybody did it.

But really, other than that [I had] no contact with the German people. All our German secretaries, people like that, I had normal relations with those. I wasn't particularly nasty to them.

You said that you didn't have too much direct contact with Telford Taylor.

Very little. I think I was at his house once for a dance and I was introduced to him by Sprecher. It was a very distant relationship. All my contacts were with Sprecher and Booth.

I want to mention, I had one other assignment. I was also charged with preparing the case against the German industrialists.... I remember getting hold of bills of sales from IG Farben [for] Zyklon B [the gas used to exterminate concentration camp inmates].... I proved that these people knew exactly what it was used for....

Do you know something? I never heard once the name of [Adolf Eichmann] that guy who was tried in Israel. Do you know that I can't recall seeing that name once, and I thought I had read every letter that Hitler and Göring and Goebbels and all these people wrote in Germany, every memo. I don't remember. I must have seen it, but I don't remember seeing it.

You said you were called in sometimes when there was special interrogation?

Like Ohlendorff and Höss, I witnessed those. I also interrogated former Reichsminister [Hans Heinrich] Lammers. I don't know whether he was tried or not. He was one of the witnesses. As I said, I didn't work inside the courtroom. I could only translate; I couldn't do simultaneous interpretation.

You weren't an interpreter in the trial.

I failed the exam! I couldn't do it! Not because my German wasn't good enough. I just couldn't do it. You have to have a special talent for that. It takes a lot out of you. These guys need a rest every two hours. It's a very, very strenuous job.

I think my work was far more interesting. I have a couple [of] documents here that are absolutely hair-raising. I really knew a lot about every single camp, and then also another important experience in Nuremberg was my charity work for DPs.

You asked me about contact with the Germans. The only contact I had and that was very frequent and very intense, was with the DPs, the displaced persons. There was a DP camp right near Nuremberg and I spent practically all my free time [there], practically lived with these people.

These were Jews mostly?

Yes, all survivors. I guess I have a lot of survivor guilt myself and I couldn't do enough for these people. I would collect food and clothing and practically lived in the DP camps, not only the one near Nuremberg. I went to a lot of DP camps looking for names and hoping to find some names. I had a lot of very, very moving experiences with the survivors. I could talk about that for hours. For example, every night they put on a play, and what were the plays about always? About all the terrible things that happened to them. I couldn't understand, "Why would they torture themselves?" Now as a psychologist, I understand that this is one way we learn to master the trauma, by actively writing the script that you once passively endured. You know what I'm saying? It's an attempt at mastery. To write a play about Jews being killed in a concentration camp is like taking control of the situation. I can understand now as a psychologist, but I couldn't understand it then.

I remember having dinner with two 16-year-old girls. They talked and they sounded like 40-year-old women. They had just grown old prematurely. It was very eerie. They just had to grow up very fast to survive.

At the trials do you think justice was done?

I didn't, no. I felt that they should have all been hanged, number one. I thought a lot of this was political, that some had to be acquitted. Schacht was as guilty as any of the others, but there had to be a few who had to be acquitted. I think Speer should have been hung and not given 20 years. I'm sorry I wasn't present at the hangings, but when they were hung I was already going to college in the United States.

On the other hand, I felt that this was something unique, that this was a new era in international law and I felt that on the whole it was a good thing.

What's your feeling about hunting for war criminals, even up to this day?

Oh, it should go on indefinitely. A hundred percent. I recently spoke to Simon Wiesenthal on the phone. I was in Vienna and wanted to meet him. Unfortunately, we couldn't arrange it, but he told me to go to Waterbury. He said there were Ukrainian war criminals in Waterbury. I regularly support the Wiesenthal Center. I'm actually more concerned about the evil that's going on right now. The neo-Nazis, and I think there's a form of ultraconservatives in the United States that I find very scary. Right now, the irony is that I consider Germany a better working democracy, much better than what's here. That's really amazing. To be very honest with you, I felt more at home in Frankfurt in March than I do here right now. It's just amazing. I don't know how long it's going to last, but right now there's a different kind of morality there and a different political atmosphere than there is here. I'm very concerned about what's going on in the United States, the swing to the right.

When did you leave Nuremberg?

I'll tell you exactly. I was there from October 1945 until June 1946. That's when they offered me the job as a civilian at colonel's pay.... Frankly, I feel that the only worthwhile thing I did in the army was my work at Nuremberg.

When you came home as a veteran, wasn't there any curiosity about what was happening, the trials? Did anyone talk to you about it?

I can't say that anything stands out in my mind that people were particularly curious. I think that occurred much later. There was a time when hardly anyone talked about the Holocaust until about the 1960s or 1970s. Then the interest started and now I talk quite often. I've given several talks at the Jewish Community Center and at various synagogues. An Israeli friend of mine often asks me to give a talk to teenagers in Sunday School about my experiences as a witness. So I've given occasional talks about it and there's much more interest now, particularly in Germany and Austria. I've talked to several of my colleagues there. Some of them have wives who teach public school and they regularly teach [about the] Holocaust and they take the kids to concentration camps. When they talk about it, they have tears in their eyes. It's just amazing. Many of them are not on talking terms with their parents and grandparents. There was a big silence they kept and anger they keep towards their parents for having kept silent. One young man talked about his grandfather as "that Nazi son of a bitch." It was quite an experience for me. That was the first time back in Germany for 50 years.

Is there any single incident or individual that stands out in your mind from the Nuremberg Trials?

I think that the one that stands out most was my interrogation of Höss. The other thing is I was there when they all pleaded "innocent" or "not guilty." I mean I couldn't believe my ears. I remember Kaltenbrunner. He was a very tall, nasty looking man with a huge scar. "Scarface," I called him. They all said they were not guilty because they acted on orders.

There was one incident that I witnessed in the courtroom where Keitel denied that he ever gave the orders for the infamous massacre of American

A chart and photos of the concentration camps and other evidence shown at the war crimes trials.

"The other thing that impressed me about the trial is the quietness in which it was going on. There was sort of a droning, quiet sound that went on and on about millions of people being gassed and cremated and tortured, and nobody raised his voice. I felt that people should have been screaming, but there was an uncanny quietness." —Harry Fiss

GIs. The American prosecutor delivered the document: "But General Keitel, here is an order signed by yourself not to take prisoners and have them all killed." He said, "That's not my signature," and everybody was laughing. People were laughing in the courtroom. I thought that was annoying, too, because it shouldn't have been a zoo.

The other thing that impressed me about the trial is the quietness in which it was going on. There was sort of a droning, quiet sound that went on and on about millions of people being gassed and cremated and tortured, and nobody raised his voice. I felt that people should have been screaming, but there was an uncanny quietness.

What would you say was any lasting effect of your participation?

Well, I found out more about the Holocaust than I would otherwise have known. I found out what I escaped. It's almost like I was at the brink of it twice: Once at the very beginning when I was in Vienna after *Anschluss* [and again at the trials]. It just gives me goose pimples to think how narrow it was, just a matter of a few months or maybe a year. It was a very short window and I'm sure I would never have survived. I was much too young. I was in good health, but I wasn't very strong.

I'll tell you very frankly, until very recently if I saw a documentary like *Playing for Time,* that probably upset me more than anything in the world. I couldn't sleep for weeks after that. It's almost like being at Nuremberg, getting more of this post-traumatic stress disorder. So it was a very scary experience. To see the films and the footage, the documents—I mean I could show you documents that would make you cringe. The horrible things in this document are unbelievable.

Did it have any impact on your becoming a psychologist?

I don't know. I'm always for the underdog. I've always been very sympathetic to blacks, to the civil rights movement. I'm very sympathetic to Native Americans. At work, I'm always in favor of hiring minorities. I suppose that may have a connection with why I'm a psychologist, to help people.

I have a colleague who went through a hell of a lot more than I did. She was hidden by a Polish family and raised as a Catholic in Poland and this way escaped with her life. She still sees her Polish foster parents every year and she's working on an Indian reservation with the Navajos as a psychologist.

There are two ways you can go: You can identify with the victim or you can identify with the oppressor. If you identify with the oppressor then you become someone like a *Kapo* [a concentration camp prisoner in charge of another group of inmates]. For instance, I shared an office with a Czech Jew who wore a Czech uniform in 1945. I guess he was part of the Allied Forces, and he told me that he had been a *Kapo* in Flossenburg and I didn't want to talk to him after that. I was always wondering what did he do to survive. Then, on the other hand, people had to do things like that. I've become a little bit more accepting as I get older and it's not haunting me as much as it used to.

But it still casts a shadow over my whole life, there's no question about it. My wife still to this day, she can't watch anything having to do with World War II, whereas I try to deal with it. I try to expose myself to it, desensitize myself. I wanted to go back to Vienna and actually look at that wall where I knocked myself unconscious [and say], "This is the place."

Did your wife accompany you?

Oh, yes, she did. She went to Vienna. She's been back in Germany, too. She has much less hatred for the Germans than I do—for the Nazis—I have to make that distinction. In her hometown a lot of people helped them. In fact, one of the most amazing stories is that the person who got her father out of Buchenwald was the head of the Gestapo because he remembered that her father had done his family a good deed when he was a child. It was incredible. Nothing like this happened to me.

I had one non-Jewish friend that I grew up with in Vienna and he was my closest friend and we spent all our play time together, vacations together. As soon as the *Anschluss* came, he joined the Hitler Youth. He did once visit me at home and said, "How are you, Mr. Jew?" I said, "Hermann, don't call me that. My name is Harry." He said, "Okay, okay." Then the next time I saw him, he wore a Hitler Youth uniform and when he saw me, he walked to other side of the street. This is a guy I grew up with!

I didn't have any positive experiences. I can't think of anybody. My wife has a much more positive attitude.

How did the film Judgment at Nuremberg *affect you?*

It didn't affect me one way or the other. Now, *Schindler's List* affected me very deeply, and *Playing for Time*. Those two probably. And the Holocaust Museum. The fact that I was able to go through and be able to sleep the next night proved to me that I must have overcome a lot of this.... I was one of the lucky few. I didn't experience anything compared to what these people did. It is unimaginable what it must be like.

Do you think that Nuremberg was the trial of the century?

Good question. I can't think of any comparable trial. I hope that they will try that Serbian son of a bitch and some of the Serb war criminals. It's unbelievable. I'm very angry about Bosnia, especially the Europeans who just sit there and talk and talk and talk. In the meantime, what's happening to the

Moslems is exactly what happened to the Jews, except at least they have guns in their hands and they can shoot back. But it is a form of genocide and Europeans are watching and doing absolutely nothing and it really makes me very angry.... I'm convinced that because the Bosnians don't have anything of value to us that we aren't doing anything.

I think that if it hadn't been for the Nuremberg experience I would probably have been less haunted by my experiences. The thing that I suffered from most as a child was fear, just being terrorized. It wasn't so much the fact that I was beaten up a lot, although it wasn't really a pleasure to be beaten up, several times unconscious. It was mostly the terror, this terrible fear and this feeling of being utterly helpless, like a deer being hunted. The government itself was your persecutor and that feeling is indescribable, this terror. I think as a result of it I've been a very anxious person all my life. I've suffered from a generalized anxiety disorder all my life. I always expect the worst. Whenever something comes up, I expect the worst scenario because it did. In a world in which the Holocaust can happen, I can't feel very secure.

I remember I was in Amsterdam last year and I went to see Anne Frank's house, which affected me much more than the Holocaust Museum because that's where it [actually] happened. What you see in Washington didn't happen in Washington, but what happened at Anne Frank's house happened at Anne Frank's house. After that visit, I couldn't feel safe in Amsterdam anymore because everywhere I was saying to myself, "Is this where they were deported? Was it over here?" It just kept haunting me.

I wanted to write a book. I wanted to interview Holocaust survivors who were exceptionally well adjusted and were well intact. I wanted to find out something about people who are called "supercopers," who can go through something like that and function well. We always study sick people; let's study people who are healthier than normal. [Sigmund Waller] was willing to talk to me about Auschwitz. I only got to the point where he was arrested by the French police and turned over to the Germans because he tried to flee over the border. At that time I started getting insomnia and I said, "I'm not the person to write this book. Let someone else do this." It was fine for him; he got it off his chest. But I started getting insomnia. So I'm not going to do it. It's easier for me to write about dreams.

JOSEPH MAIER

*Chief, Analysis Section,
Interrogation Division*

Although his parents and siblings had migrated to the United States by the 1930s, Joseph Maier stayed in Germany to finish his schooling. However in 1933, when "left and right my friends disappeared and I was afraid I would be next somehow," Maier found the means to join his family in New York. Maier went to Nuremberg as a civilian. "I had a vision of coming back to Germany and executing judgment. I had to be in on that trial; that was a holy mission." Maier later went into publishing and eventually teaching. He is a professor emeritus at Columbia University, and chairman of the Social Science Seminar there.

"I was born on January 24, 1911, [and] raised and schooled in Leipzig, Germany. Let me say at the outset how squeamish I feel about playing historian of my own history. Nobody's recollection and knowledge is sound enough for that sort of thing. What I can tell you in response to your question is based on one man's feeble memory at this time. It is a small item in one of the most important stories ever told. No other empire bequeathed to historians such veritable mountains of evidence of its rise and fall as did the Third Reich of the Nazis. To begin with, I clearly remember the day of Hitler's ascent to power.

Note: Professor Maier prepared a written statement before the interview, parts of which he read during the interview. Those parts are contained in quotation marks.

It was on January 30, 1933, a few days after my 22nd birthday. I was lying in the clinic of the University of Leipzig, recovering from an appendectomy. Not a piece of cake at the time. As the nurse came in to look after me, the führer's voice came bellowing over the radio. When I close my eyes I can still hear the roaring of the beast, and still feel what I felt. Namely, that sad and bad days were ahead, not only for Germany, but for the world. My most fervent expectations had been betrayed. President [Paul von] Hindenburg, backed by the army and the conservatives had made Hitler chancellor."

Now you want to know "Why and how I did leave Germany? How did I come to the United States? By the time I left the hospital and returned for the last of my three semesters at the University of Leipzig, the transformation of Germany into what was to become the Nazi hell, had begun with breathtaking rapidity, aided and abetted by wealth and stealth. In February, at Göring's and Goebbels's instigation, the Reichstag was set on fire. In March, Hitler ordered the so-called Enabling Act passed, taking the power of legislation, including control of the Reich budget, approval of treaties with foreign countries, and the initiating of constitutional amendments, away from Parliament, away from the Reichstag, and handed it over to the Reich cabinet for a period of four years. On April 1, the anti-Jewish boycott was decreed. Jewish stores were broken into and looted, and their owners beaten and dragged into concentration camps or Gestapo prisons. On May 10, 1933, the book burnings began at the University of Berlin.

"Even before the semester ended in July, I wrote to my parents in Brooklyn that I was now willing, nay, anxious to join the family in the United States, and would they please help and send me the affidavit and the boat ticket."

How did your parents get here, and you were still in Germany? Sometimes it's the opposite, that the younger children go to America first.

"My father, an orthodox rabbi, had left Germany and settled in the United States in the mid-twenties, and my mother and youngest brother joined him shortly thereafter. In 1930, my younger three brothers and two sisters followed them to New York. I stayed behind because I wanted to finish my Gymnasium schooling and get my diploma. But 1931 saw me with my folks in Brooklyn on a visiting student visa. In the spring of 1932, I returned to Germany to begin my studies in philosophy, sociology, and comparative literature at the University of Leipzig.

"Why not? True, there were plenty of Nazis. But Hindenburg had defeated Hitler, and been elected president. The Schocken Foundation had granted me a beautiful fellowship, and I was convinced I had a real chance to help prevent the worst from happening, a real chance to defend the Weimar Republic against its mortal enemy.

"I loved my country. I loved Germany. I didn't want to abandon it to the barbarians. The myth of the wandering Jew is just that—a cruel myth. If they had left us alone, most of us would never have migrated anywhere, but would have stayed where our people had been for centuries."

Was this your first visit to the United States?

That was my first visit to the United States. My father was very much interested in seeing me become a rabbi, and asked me to enter a theological seminary—an orthodox one. I was very unhappy about this, but I did agree to follow the tradition. You see, our family was a family on both maternal and paternal sides, where the first-born was always landing in the rabbinate. I broke with that tradition eventually. My father was never quite reconciled [with my decision], but my mother thought a professor was just as good as a rabbi. I fulfilled my mother's expectations more than my father's. But the learning didn't do me any harm, and I was glad I did acquire it.

I spent one year in this country [taking courses at the seminary]. I was ordained eventually, much later, by a private group of orthodox rabbis. But I hardly made use of it. It was when I came back to the U.S. eventually, and had become a citizen of the United States.

"In September 1933, when I fled Germany in fear of my life to join my family, the Nazification had proceeded with a thoroughness unparalleled in German history. Within nine months Hitler had put an end to the Weimar Republic, established his personal dictatorship, destroyed all political parties but his own, abolished all the state governments and their parliaments, and defederalized the Reich, smashed the labor unions, abolished freedom of speech and of the press, and driven the Jews out of public and professional life, and made them the preferred victims of his wrath."

How easy was it to get out of Germany in 1933?

I had to go through the American consulate and declare that I was in dire jeopardy and in fear of my life, that I wanted to emigrate and join my family in the United States, and I got a visa at the time. It took a couple of weeks. My father was already a citizen, and my mother was a citizen by that time. My brothers and sisters were all citizens, and I was the only one who wasn't. By that time I had been taught a lesson. I felt betrayed, and I had no chance of fighting, because left and right my friends disappeared and I was afraid I would be next somehow.

A lot of people were staying. Do you think that they didn't see the dangers that you saw?

I was politically interested. I was a member of the Socialist Youth Party, the student organization, and all the socialists were the preferred enemies of the Nazis. I was afraid that since some of my friends and colleagues had disappeared, that I would one day disappear into a concentration camp or Gestapo cellar, myself.

"By September of 1933, when I arrived in New York, until 1939, I was a student at Columbia University, where I earned my M.A. and Ph.D. degrees. I was also working as a research assistant at the Institute of Social Research, with all the principals of the so-called Frankfurt School, including Max Horkheimer, Theodore W. Adorno, Herbert Marcuse, and Eric Fromm."

The Frankfurt School was a group of thoroughly independent Marxist scholars. They were friends, academically highly respected, enjoying an international reputation all over Europe and the United States. President Nicholas Murray Butler of Columbia University had invited Professor Horkheimer and his institute to come to the United States, and a number of luminaries at Columbia University, whom I knew as my own teachers, supported that invitation, and became life-long friends of the institute.

I also had the advantage of becoming exposed to American advanced thinking, especially John Dewey, who was still alive at the time, and whom I consider America's most representative philosopher of democracy, *the* American philosopher for my money. On the other hand, of course, the Frankfurt School, for me, represented German philosophy at its very best, *late* German classical philosophy, especially during the periods of the eighteenth and nineteenth centur[ies], from Kant to Hegel. As a matter of fact, my own dissertation which became, I thought, [laughs] a revolutionary work, is still being used, for which I still get royalties. It was on Hegel's critique of Kant.

One important event, of course, was my becoming an American citizen, a proud American citizen and patriot. And another was that "I got married in 1937 to Alice Heuman, who was an assistant to Professor Max Horkheimer for his entire professional life in America and Europe as the director of the institute. In 1938 I became the father of a daughter—our only child—Doris. And from 1940 to 1973, I was assistant editor of the German-Jewish weekly newspaper, *Aufbau.* In World War II, that is from 1943 to 1944, I served as propaganda analyst in the Office of War Information in New York, and from D Day 1944 until V-J Day 1945, as propaganda analyst in the Office of War Information, American Embassy, London, while actually attached with a small group of American officers to the hush-hush BBC monitoring service in Caversham near Reading."

When you came over from Germany, what were people's attitudes toward what was happening in Germany? Were people aware?

Only partly. But I was one of those who felt a mission to make them aware. I was passed around to give lectures at all kinds of places, mostly Jewish places. Of course, even the Jewish audiences found it difficult to appreciate the fact that until 1933, German Jews had not escaped. Only those who were politically endangered had felt a need to escape. But those who were middle-class or wealthy and felt they had a stake in Germany thought, "We've been here for more than a thousand years; we've been more German than Hitler," who was an Austrian and didn't speak with a proper German accent, but spoke some sort of dialect. [They believed] he wouldn't survive; he would be booted out before long. But they were in error about that. They didn't take him seriously enough. If Hitler was in earnest about one thing it was about his Jew hatred, and that's what I had felt—in time—and I tried to make people in America aware of [that] whenever I had an opportunity to do so.

I had to convince them of my own experiences and of my own fears. I said, "Look, what is good and true about Germany is its classical literature and philosophy as it is represented by those who have fled the country, like the Max Horkheimer group at Columbia. They represent what's best about Germany. They're publishing their own magazine in German because they want to try and preserve the classical German of literature and philosophy, as opposed to the subhuman lingo invented by Hitler and his Nazis."

When you were in Germany as a young man or as a child was there any evidence of anti-Semitism that you experienced?

I personally experienced, of course, adverse things. Many times I was in a position of having to defend the Jewish God against those who tried to insult the Jewish God and make me responsible for what happened to Jesus. But it never occurred to me to feel that this was not my country, and that one day I would be driven out by the root. I couldn't believe it. Oh, yes. Why shouldn't people have enemies? I don't mind having enemies, but I don't want to destroy them by the root, lock, stock, and barrel, until the 10th generation, to obliterate them, even their memory. It never occurred to me that the Germans would be capable of that, until, of course, Hitler came to power, and I realized that this was potentially the case, and the only ones who would preserve what is good, the only people who would preserve German culture for a better future after Hitler would be the German Jews, who had been driven out, and preserved in language and in behavior, the best that was German.

So now you have become a citizen of the United States, and you entered the army.

I volunteered. I still have my papers. I wanted to be commissioned as an officer right away. And since that was not to be, I said, "I'll wait until I'm drafted." The commission didn't come. I volunteered to go overseas for the Office of War Information in London, actually attached to the BBC monitoring service, writing the German Report for the commanders in the field and the policy makers in New York and Washington.

The German Report was the intelligence that the BBC Monitoring Service collected by monitoring what Goebbels's Propaganda Ministry transmitted by teletype to the German newspapers and radio, what the German people were allowed to read and hear. The British Monitoring Service provided the raw intelligence and I analyzed this with respect to what points were emphasized. I tried to make out where the weaknesses were, or which points we ought to stress in our counter–psychological warfare. I was among the first to write the German Report, since German was my native language, and I knew every trick you could think of both linguistically and psychologically, and since I was imbued with sufficient fervor about it. I thought we did a good job and were so praised for it by our superiors.

I was in charge of the German Report because I was the most competent to write it. I was [34]. I was already getting on in years, and they were drafting 20-year-olds. I stayed in Caversham, near Reading. The BBC Monitoring Service hush-hush organization was there. Fortunately the Nazis didn't know where to bomb us. I had, of course, my problems with V-1 and V-2 [rocket bombs] in my frequent visits to London. V-1[s] and V-2[s] were the secret weapons of the Nazis. If it was a direct hit, you'd be lost. V-1[s] fascinated me because I could still see it. V-2[s] [were] faster than sound and light. I had a heightened feeling of life at the time. It made more sense to me, and the British felt the same way. I became an almost professional Anglophile at the time.

To see these men and women withstand with such courage and fervor these horrible attacks on their homes and their families was marvelous. It never subdued us. I made lots of British friends. The Americans became preferred friends. Those of us who were attached to the BBC Monitoring Service, as I was, were billeted near there, in villas. The U.S. Army truck came by every week, and supplied us with food. We learned to cook, and I invited many of my British friends, and gave them candy rations for their children.

And then what happened after the war?

After V-J Day, I wanted to be part of reeducating Germany. But before doing that, I wanted to go back and see if everything was all right with my wife and child, so I came home. And just at the time, the International Military Tribunal was being prepared, and recruiting by our War Department took place. So I thought I had better go to Washington and volunteer for that. I did. I was interviewed by Colonel Dostert, who recruited people capable of simultaneous interpretation, for Project Jackson, named after Supreme Court Justice [Robert] Jackson. I spoke several languages. I could pray and curse, speak and write in German and English better than any Nazi or anybody else. I was the right person for the job, and Colonel Dostert agreed with me. And before long, I was sent to Germany, to Nuremberg. I expected to see it in ruins and I felt it served them right. It was an uncanny situation. To the left and right were heaps of rubble. Nuremberg was a famous old town. It was also the seat of [Julius] Streicher, the *Gauleiter* and publisher of [*Der*] *Stürmer.*

Had you been to Nuremberg as a young man?

No, never. [This was] my first time. You know, I had not traveled very much in Germany. I stuck to Leipzig and Dresden, my hometowns.

Did you have any desire to go back and see your home?

It was in East Germany, and we were in the west. The East had been occupied by the Russians, and the German Communist Party, the so-called Socialist Unity Party, had become part of the Stalinist outfit in East Germany. Eventually I did [go there, in the 1960s and 1970s].

You were hired originally as an interpreter?

I was hired as a simultaneous interpreter. I was supposed to speak in German what I heard in English, and vice versa. It's very difficult because in German, the verb sometimes comes at the very end. Yes, I had to do the interpretation from English into German. I had to do both, but preferably from German into English.

Was this during the period of interrogating witnesses?

That was in the pretrial period because I got there pretty early. I think I was there in September of 1945. And the trial started a little later.... Let me tell you one thing that was a disappointment for me. "Colonel Dostert preferred the regular army officers, not an academic intellectual like myself, for the star interpreting assignments. I was thoroughly miffed, and requested immediate transfer to the Analysis Section of the Interrogation Division, where I felt more appreciated and welcome, and eventually ended up as chief.

"Now, the duties of our section consisted of examining documents and interrogation transcripts and protocols for any admissions, confirmations, or denials by defendants and witnesses, of their involvement in the commission, ordering, or execution of crimes. For example, when did Göring give the order to proceed with the so-called Final Solution of the Jewish question? Did Keitel or Jodl, the military men, issue orders to shoot Allied POWs? Yes or no? What did the poison gas industrialists say to Höss, and he to them? Höss, the concentration camp commandant of Auschwitz was our witness. He was not among the defendants. The analysis reports were then sent over to the principal prosecutor in charge of the case before the tribunal. And that included, of course, Mr. [Thomas] Dodd, as well."

What was your impression of Mr. Dodd?

I would say favorable. I was on his side. I was his boy, and I tried to do my job. Not that I was a buddy-buddy. I was too respectful, and he likewise. We did our jobs as conscientiously and courteously and efficiently as possible. We both had our jobs to do and we wanted to do the best with them.

Were you able to witness the trial?

Oh, absolutely. Every day. I couldn't have done without it. Every single one of the sessions. Anyway, I wanted to say that the prosecutors, including Supreme Court Justice Jackson and Mr. Dodd found the stuff we produced quite useful.

"Most of the interrogations would take place in a small interrogation room with huge windows, right next door to my office on the third floor of the Palace of Justice. There was a large table and some 10 or 12 chairs. Behind us—the interrogator, interpreters, court reporters—was a tiny unseen push button, which would summon armed MPs waiting outside. The door opposite us would open and an MP would step inside and motion the culprit to enter. The latter would sit down, and the interrogator would make him aware that he was testifying under oath. . . .

"You'll be surprised and disappointed to learn that while I was present at many interrogations of Höss, most of them were actually conducted by my friend and colleague in the Interrogation Division, Sender Jaari; also, by my immediate superior, Colonel Brookhart, and by the chief of the Interrogation Division, Colonel Amen. Höss signed and/or initialed a lot of these confessions in the presence of those listed on the face sheet of the interrogation transcript. The statement I gave to the Holocaust Memorial Museum in Washington, which was signed and sworn to before me, was actually nothing new. Höss admitted to the facts time and again. It was in the course of one of the many interrogations conducted by my colleague, Alfred Booth, with no other person present except the lady stenographer, that I suddenly asked him to write on a piece of note paper I gave him, the text of the confession. It was during one of the many interrogations that Alfred Booth conducted on Höss's relations and conversations with the poison gas industrialists."

What was your impression of the defendants?

"What a motley crew. What a motley crew. They struck me as a sad and drab assortment of mediocrities. The only bloke with an above-average, no, with a very high, IQ was Hjalmar Schacht. Hjalmar Schacht was the financier/conservator of the Reich funds. Hjalmar Schacht always behaved as if by a mistake of the prosecution, he got placed with an odd crew he didn't really belong with.

"As for the whole crew, they all whined and insisted they were mere 'executive organs' of the führer. They did their duty. Only Göring was occasionally willing to accept responsibility for the orders issued over his signature. But the tip-off that betokened his inferior being was his attitude toward the Allies. To the French, weakest of the Big Four, he was patronizing and scornful. To us, he was the hearty, free-booting buccaneer he thought might appeal to presumably naïve Americans succored on Hollywood films. To the cold, skilled British, he was quiet and respectful, anxiously attempting a gentlemanliness he thought might appeal to the British. Only when a Russian officer entered the room during an interrogation did Göring wince and cringe slightly. He knew of no pose that would intrigue a Russian. He was frightened to death of every Russian he saw. And that was true of the whole crew.

"As for Höss, the concentration camp commandant, our witness, the lord over life and death of millions, he considered himself a little man, a very little man, a very, very little man, a good father and family man, and a brave and obedient servant of his führer. That is what all these supermen tried to impress us as.

Hermann Göring was the highest-ranking Nazi to stand trial at Nuremberg.

"To the French, weakest of the Big Four, he was patronizing and scornful. To us, he was the hearty, free-booting buccaneer he thought might appeal to presumably naïve Americans succored on Hollywood films. To the cold, skilled British, he was quiet and respectful.... Only when a Russian officer entered the room during an interrogation did Göring wince and cringe slightly. He knew of no pose that would intrigue a Russian. He was frightened to death of every Russian he saw. And that was true of the whole crew." —Joseph Maier

"I had to get out after interrogations time and again. And because I felt sick, and I didn't want to show my weakness in front of the culprits, I cut off the interrogation, went to the bathroom, vomited a couple of times, and then resumed my duties again."

You asked me what other things I was interested in. "I had some theories at the time about issues that were being pursued—namely, the whereabouts of [Adolf] Eichmann, the [Grand] Mufti [of Jerusalem, who collaborated with the Germans in Jewish extermination], and any others that I knew of. But I don't think I had any grand theories about any of the supermen. Naturally I was trying to be helpful to Gideon Ruffer when he came to my office, as the first man who sought information about the whereabouts of Eichmann. He and I interrogated Dieter Wisliceny, Eichmann's immediate subordinate. We had no court reporter or interpreter in our lengthy interrogation of Wisliceny. He confirmed that Eichmann was indeed in charge of the Final Solution, so-called. He said that Eichmann told him he would gladly die in the knowledge of having executed the führer's order to that effect, but he could only speculate about his present or possible whereabouts. To my question, why the Germans took the trouble of transporting all the Jews from the west to eastern Europe at a time, when it made no military sense at all and transportation difficulties were great, he replied that the German authorities were convinced that the destruction of the Jews would find greater sympathy and more understanding and appreciation in the east, among the peoples of the east, that is, among the Poles, than among the peoples of the west, including the Germans themselves. That's a very interesting point to me. Of course, there is always somebody in your own camp—some people in your own camp—who have their own agenda, and you have to be mindful of that, too.

"As for the Mufti, I was personally interested as a Zionist, to find out to what extent he had collaborated with the Nazis, and actually tried to participate in the extermination policies, or in the planning of the extermination policies that were carried out by the Nazis themselves. My main source of information was an SS general by the name of Walter Schellenberg. This fellow was, in many respects, a guy who succeeded in teaching me an important lesson. He was a university-educated gangster. Absolutely charming, good-looking, and intelligent. For those of us who are brought up in the belief that Latin and Greek, if not Hebrew, were the unique garments of the truth—it was difficult to believe that such people could be other than humanist scholars, people interested in the well-being and happiness of mankind. This charming fellow, I eventually learned, was one of Himmler's closest and most promising disciples. He had almost succeeded in persuading me of his own goodwill and good intentions from the day he joined the SS, until the time he became the chief of Amt. IV of the Reich Security Head Office, in charge of intelligence and security. I learned through him that less than the whole truth can be revealed as easily in Latin and Greek as in German and English. He made me aware of the fact that even the *Horst-Wessel*, the official Nazi hymn, could be rendered in fine Greek verse."

Why wasn't Höss indicted?

He was a mere witness. He wasn't important enough. He was extradited to the Poles. They gave him a fair trial, and they hanged him right away.

What is your opinion of Nuremberg justice, as opposed to what the British wanted to do, or what the Poles did, in his case, of hanging them right away?

I had many discussions with the German lawyers. I thought the Nuremberg Trial was a most important event because the International Military Tribunal was not a mere "woe to the defeated," to those who lost the war. It was important in terms of giving statutory and visible dignity to international law. What we found as the victors—not as Americans only—as the Alliance—was a vacuum juris. That's what I said to the German lawyers who always tried to bait us for applying retroactive law; for punishing somebody for crimes which were not crimes in their books, but which we had created after the fact. I insisted that we had to give statutory character to international law. International law had to have teeth. That was my position, and I still hold to that. That was an important precedent, I think, that to this day it was important to set it both for Japan and Germany, and nobody in his right mind, including the Germans today, or the Japanese today, would question us. I never changed my mind about this.

"Did we mete out full justice?" Well, perhaps I would have been more severe in subsequent trials, especially involving the poison gas industrialists, and including the conservatives who had helped Hitler into the saddle. I thought we failed to do complete justice. We should have been stricter with them, held them to more account. But in the end, I was more interested in creating conditions for peace and prosperity, even for the defeated enemy, and not endless vengeance, which would have been against my conviction to begin with, even though I belong to those whose people had suffered most.

In my letters even before the end of the war, from wartime England, during the period I was attached to the American Embassy and to the BBC Monitoring Service in Caversham, and I didn't know whether I was coming back or how the war was going to end, I wrote to my wife, "We must never do what the Nazis did to us. It's against us." The British [bombed] Dresden, one of my own towns where I went to school, and Leipzig, almost to smithereens. I justified this in terms of "That's what the Nazis did to England." They paid no attention to civilian populations at all.

But then I thought I don't want everyone to suffer indefinitely. I want to create conditions of peace, including Germany. I don't want them to go back to the agriculture of the Middle Ages. I want to create something that's going to be good for Europe, and I want to be there to make sure.

Do you think that the trials helped to reeducate the Germans?

Partly. Some are not educable. Some people cannot be educated. Some are beyond repair, for whatever reason—envy, usually. Envy is an important emotion, very important. You invent your enemies if you don't have them. [Envy] makes them responsible for things they have never done. It makes them responsible for unemployment, for the lost war. It makes them responsible for your lost family. And you take the most proven "enemy," the most proven victim in a long history, the Jews. They can be hunted down and murdered without recourse. No, some people cannot be educated. Others can. I was interested at the time in building up West Germany, especially in view of what was happening in East Germany [during] the rule of Stalin [in the U.S.S.R.] and Stalinist East Germany. When finally the reunification took place, I felt very happy. Not that I was involved as a German, but I had some memories. I thought, "Now we're going to have peace. We're going to have reconciliation." And this struck me almost like what you would call the second coming of Christ.

There was Leonard Bernstein conducting at the Berlin Opera Beethoven's Ninth Symphony. You know the Ninth Symphony—the music and the text? I thought actually peace had broken out and reunification, and that would be one whole and wholesome Germany. Instead, once you have seen what the Nazis and the Stalinists have sown, what you reap is something other. The disappointment is something that we have to live with, even now. You know, there's rivalry within Germany. The East Germans are envious of the West Germans. The West Germans are "exploiting" the East Germans, both at the university level and the economic level. Right now we are in a situation which doesn't look very good, and maybe we'll never get into a situation where the world is perfectly ready for the second coming of Christ.

Of one thing I am more convinced than ever; anybody who promises heaven on earth and is willing to sacrifice half of mankind or more in order to achieve his political ambitions is like Hitler and Stalin: dangerous to mankind. If you promise heaven on earth, you promise too much you can't keep, and you have to reap what Hitler has sown. That's the lesson we have now, that we have to learn now.

What was your opinion of the film Judgment at Nuremberg?

Pretty accurate. Marlene Dietrich was one of my fanciful idols. And for me, "Falling in Love Again," in German, is one of those things that still touches me very profoundly. In German. That was the encouraging melody that I heard throughout the war, from D Day until after V-J Day and the British Eighth Army under [Bernard L.] Montgomery winning the war. Yes. She was one of my idols and heroines. My daughter learned how to sing that, too, both in German and in English.

When you were at the trial, did you have much contact with the ordinary German person?

I had some German friends, surviving Jews who had lived in mixed marriages, whom I took care of, and gave some of my rations to. I felt I had a mission to do that. I had to take care of them. You know, the funniest thing was, the skilled and educated people, were all former Nazis. The workers that survived somehow, were deprived and came out of concentration camps. They were not the ones that I could use for this job. So I had to be very careful whom I had to choose. These were difficult choices to make. I tried to be nice to my secretary, who was a German woman. I gave her some of my rations, which we weren't supposed to do. But I let her have it anyway.

Did you have any sympathy for the ordinary German person?

I didn't want them to be hounded anymore. I was suspicious at first. I think they all needed reeducation, and I wanted to make sure about this. The Nazis had done such an enormous amount of murder and mayhem, that I thought that can't be so easily forgiven, and that the whole generation has to be re-educated, and that we have to make every effort to do so. My brother, who was in the CBI, the other professor, he had a background just like mine, in Germanic languages and literature. He was sent to the CBI by the army. He was ready to come, he wrote in one of his last letters, to share with me the reeducation of Germany. We'd become part of the occupation because people like us had a mission to do so. But it never came to that. The army lost his papers, and he came way later, back to the United States. I was left in Germany alone, and then went home, and nobody went back to Germany anymore, except after the war.

What has been the effect of Nuremberg on your life?

I sometimes feel haunted by the memories of what I learned in Nuremberg in the course of my interrogations. [I have] nightmares. I'm still fighting the Second World War. [In my dreams] I get into the Nazi captivity, and they discover I'm a German Jew originally. And I get back to the United States and they find out I talk with an accent—I must be a German Jew. So I don't feel quite adequate here, either.

[Nuremberg] has been important for me. As I said, I still feel haunted. I'm still fighting the Second World War. At the opening of the Holocaust Museum there were only invited guests, you know? I couldn't go through on my own—my niece had to wheel me on the wheelchair—my daughter, too. I couldn't see. I broke out in tears. I was there. By the grace of God I escaped; I was one of the survivors. I came out of it myself. But I burst into tears, and I couldn't take it anymore. I don't need these museums. I know the story too well.

One more thing I want to tell you, one more thing I'm very proud of. I graduated from the gymnasium in Dresden; my first schooling took place in Leipzig, and then in Dresden. This is just a couple of kilometers further east. Dresden was the place I saw last before I left Germany. My uncle and aunt and my three little cousins were over there. And I said to my aunt before I left, "This won't stand. This will not stand, what the Nazis are doing. I will come back and sit in judgment. I'll make it my business. I'll sit in judgment. There will be a war; the Nazis will be defeated; and I will sit in judgment. This won't stand."

Of course my uncle, my aunt and my three little cousins were deported to a concentration camp in the east. After the war, three of them made it from the east from Stutthof, their concentration camp. They had been liberated by the Russian army, and they made it through, with the Russians, to the DP camp in Berlin. That was before the Nuremberg Trials had started.

My aunt in the DP camp remembered, and said to my little cousin Billy, "There's going to be a trial in Nuremberg. Go to the American Commander of the DP camp; ask him to be connected with Dr. Maier in Nuremberg. Joe is bound to be there. He will sit in judgment. He said so, and I believe that." And he did that. That little cousin is 19 years my junior. He called up and was connected with me in my office. I happened to be in my office, and I answered the telephone. I said, "Where are you?" [He said], "We are in Berlin, at the DP camp. My mother and my sister survived. We are the sole survivors." I said, "Stay where you are. I'm going to have my travel orders cut. I'll fly in and I'll get you out." What did I do? I had plenty of power, you know, as an employee of the court and in uniform. I never had such power in my life. I could travel anywhere immediately, or have the orders cut. I went to Berlin. I went to the DP camp. I went to the German authorities and said, "Please make out the necessary papers. Give them a birth certificate—German birth certificates—and I want everything to be in perfect order so they can come out when they have a chance to." I never spoke in German. I had a friend of mine speak in English, and I didn't speak a word of German. I just had a pack of cigarettes.

I said, "Offer him a cigarette of mine." I talked English to him. "Tell him in German he can have some more cigarettes. I want him to do this and that, and the papers, and no difficulties, or else I'll have other means of getting my will." He acted in accordance. I didn't speak a word of German, but I got the papers for the kids, and my aunt, and they came here. They moved to Poughkeepsie, where no word of German was spoken. I had some friends there who got them into an American school, and they became the best in their class to graduate.

You did have a vision of coming back and sitting in judgment?

Oh, yes. That was my mission. That I considered my sacred mission. I had a vision of coming back to Germany and executing judgment. I had to be in on that trial; that was a mission—a holy mission.

I even was willing to become the first American control officer in Berlin, in charge of radio and newspapers. That would have involved, of course, my family moving over to Germany, into one of those beautiful villas which we had left standing in suburban Berlin precisely for those reasons, as billets for American occupation officers.

After the main trial was over, I was offered a more permanent job. My wife was against it. She said, "I don't want any Nazi or hidden Nazi or any werewolf to take potshots at our child. Secondly, I don't want you to become one of those BTOs [big-time operators] of whom we hear so frequently nowadays. And thirdly, you're an academic. The G. I. Bill is in operation. "You always wanted an academic career. Your chance is right now. Come back and you'll have the young GIs as your students, the best students ever."

I said at the time, "I think you're right." My wife [had], as I believe, incidentally, all women have, an instinct, which is by far superior to scheme-making for ideas and patterns that you seek as a man. Women are better judges of character. That's my belief. A woman, unlike a man, is a better judge of character. She can't be that easily led astray. I think that's what makes women superior—different from men, who are led astray by all kinds of schemes and patterns they discover. I followed her advice, came back, was first very unhappy. But then I got a job with Hannah Arendt, in the publishing house, publishing Kafka in the original, and I wrote the dust jacket. Hannah Arendt was a very good friend of mine. We had conducted together a campaign while I was an editor of *Aufbau*. Yes, I was the editor-in-chief at one time, very early. Hannah and I had conducted originally a campaign to develop a Jewish army, because she said, "We are attacked as Jews, we have to fight back as Jews, and create an army." When we discovered that some right-wing organization was trying to make the most of it we dropped the idea, and I was drafted anyway. I said, "Let's forget about this." Now my last work is being done at the University Seminar at Columbia University. I'm still in charge, after more than 20 years, of an interdisciplinary Social Science Seminar called "Content and Methods of the Social Sciences." A very ambitious title. I'm looking forward to resuming my duties as chairman in the fall, if I survive that long. I hope I will. I hope that I even survive the appearance of the *Festschrift* that is being written in my honor. [laughs]

As I said, I never forgot [Nuremberg]. I thought it was part and parcel of my total experience and my life experience. It shaped me. It put a stamp on me. As I said, I am still fighting the Second World War. I'm still asking myself, "Who am I? What am I? What is my destiny?"

Nuremberg has been an experience for me of complete identification with the victim. I was made to feel I had been one of those who had been spared, and escaped by the skin of his teeth. Such hellish experiences nobody can forget, nor should forget. It should be a permanent remembrance.

ATTORNEYS

SEYMOUR PEYSER

Legal Staff for International Military Tribunal

Seymour Peyser prepared documents for the IMT prosecution from August 1945 to December 1945. One of his tasks involved collecting affidavits from the German police, judiciary, and press declaring the impact Nazism had on their lives during the 1920s through the 1940s. Another duty involved updating the Nazi chain of command charts with the assistance of defendant Robert Ley, who hung himself later that same day. Working with Ley provided Peyser with an occasion to realize that "I, an American Jew, hadn't been trained for that kind of intensive, long time, stick-to-it hatred." He recognized that Ley, with all of his human frailties, was human. Peyser continued with the same New York law firm he joined before going to Nuremberg. He is still of counsel to the firm.

I was born in December 1914 in the Bronx, which usually requires my jutting my chin out and saying, "Would anybody like to make something of that?" I grew up in the Fordham University Heights area, and went to public schools. I graduated from elementary school very young. I was just 11. In those days you skipped madly, which, fortunately for my own children and grand-children, is no longer the practice. I graduated from high school, Horace Mann Boys' School, in 1930. I entered Harvard and graduated four years later in 1934. I went from there to Columbia Law School and graduated in 1937.

My father was an accountant, a CPA. He was one of the earliest CPAs. He had certificate number 850 and we probably know almost 850 CPAs now. He had been a bookkeeper and worked to help support a large family of seven sisters and two brothers.

When he graduated from NYU in 1914, the year I was born, he started a firm which became reasonably successful in midtown Manhattan. It was at this time when his professional fortune seemed to be on the rise that he was able to send me to private school. I had two younger sisters, one of whom died about 17 years ago and the other is still very much alive and a retired New York City school teacher. She is married and has children and grandchildren.

In 1937 I joined the law firm of what was then Phillips and [Louis] Nizer. [I joined] immediately on my graduation from law school. There has been an unbroken relationship with the same firm. I'm still of counsel to that law firm. The term doesn't mean very much, except that I can use the facilities at the offices, but there's no pecuniary arrangement any more. All of the name partners have now died, three of them in 1994: Nizer, Krin, and Ballou all passed away last year.

Growing up in the Bronx in the 1920s, what was life like at that time?

Life for me in those days was a contest my father got me into. I was precocious and I'm not particularly proud of it now, but it became a good part of my life. Socially I was reaching to be with older children, really. It was a difficult time emotionally. I had no trouble with reading, writing, and arithmetic, but I did with the emotional problems of a young boy.

My father got more of a bang out of my successes in those days. Just to give you an idea what I'm talking about, I entered *The New York Times* Oratorical Contest. It was a national contest, actually. The *Times* ran it in the New York region; similarly, other newspapers [did] in other regions. It was a contest for high school boys and girls who had to write a speech about the Constitution and then answer some extemporaneous questions, either a general question or a specific question put to you by the judges. In the year 1930, my senior year at Horace Mann, I won the contest. It was a big deal in May 1930 for me to win $1,000, and a gold medal, and a trip to Europe to visit 11 countries.

I look back on those years as interesting because I was a featured player, if you will. I was something close to a parlor game for my parents, and I say that without any real resentment because I don't think they knew any better in terms of dealing with children. I used to divide fractions at the age of four and five. I can't do it now. [chuckles]

But otherwise it was a life in the Bronx. The area we lived in was half Jewish, half Irish, really, and now it's 98 percent black and Latino. Looking back on it, there were some good times. Where there are now old tenement buildings, there were empty lots where we built tar-paper shacks and huts and things of that kind. The runoffs of the reservoir, the brand new reservoir in the North Bronx, I remember actually going fishing in those waters.

So there were good times and a significant part of my childhood from the ages of 8 to 14 was summer camp. I probably gained more from that experience than I did the other 9 or 10 months at school.

The camp was called Granite Lake Camp in southwestern New Hampshire near Keene, run by a very charismatic New York school principal, who was a character. He built a whole army of young boys who looked up to him, worshipped him. As I got older, he seemed cornier, and he was, but he was a very important factor in the lives of a lot of my contemporaries and my friends in those days. It was where I played baseball and actually won a second place medal in running, which for me, because of my ease on the educational side, in math and English, was more important than it might be to others.

I remember being president of the general organization of the camp and running meetings under Robert's Rules of Order at the age of 14.

Having gone through college and law school from 1930–37, how much consciousness was there of what was happening in Germany at the time?

Very little. I've thought many, many hundreds of times, looking back, how could we—the people in my position—know as little as we then knew? How could we be that little aware? It was the other side of the world, but there was no excuse for it.

Due to the accident of the oratorical contest, I had been in Germany and had seen brown-shirted SA troops marching down the Unter den Linden in Berlin in 1930. These were the early, pre-SS Nazis. A few weeks later I saw Mussolini's thugs, and I remember actually being called to account that I wasn't standing at attention or I wasn't showing the proper respect for the Mussolini troops that were walking by and for their flag. It never dawned on me that this was anything more than a foreign way of doing different things. I didn't know anybody. I didn't know any German Jews. My forebears had come from *pogroms* in Poland in the time of the American Civil War—both of my grandfathers.

My father's father came over about 1870, I guess. He was 70 years old when he died in 1921, which means he was born in 1851 and he came over when he was 17, 1868 or 1869 on a sailing ship. It took three months, [with] cholera on board, he remembered. He died when I was only six years old, so I didn't really know him very well, but I remember hearing the stories and hearing the story of the name. When he got to Ellis Island after this traumatic voyage, they asked him his name. He said his name was Joseph A. Bardau. He came from the little town of Peyser in the Polish German corridor. They wrote it down backwards and every time anybody talked with him, he showed the card and they began calling him Peyser. He wasn't going to argue with that and it was made firm when his brother came two years later. They asked him, "What's your name?" "Bardau from the little town of Peyser." "Do you have any relatives in this country?" "Yes, my brother Joe came over two years ago."

They looked it up and said, "You just don't understand English. Your name is Peyser." He wasn't going to fight. So my grandfather and great uncle Max alternated as president of the association of refugees from the little town of Peyser in the Polish corridor all through my childhood.

But I was 15 years old and [the rise of the Nazis and Fascists] didn't make any sense to me. I don't remember thinking of this as in any way cataclysmic or something that would reach the history books. This was the way people acted in Germany and Italy in 1930, and my parents did not make a fuss about it. My father was a hard-working professional man, dealing with hard-working businessmen and didn't think in terms of the Holocaust. I'm sure that in those days there were signs of enormous prejudice, but you see, all my grandparents had fled Europe for the same reason and I'm sure if you had asked my father and mother the same question, they would have said it's the same as it was when their parents came to the United States. Both my mother and father were born in New York. Her mother and father came from towns in Poland just a few miles apart and met on the Lower East Side. The same is true of Joseph Bardau, also known as Peyser, who met his two successive brides in New York.

In 1933 Hitler comes to power. Were there no discussions at Harvard College and Columbia Law School?

It was the kind of discussion one would have about a distant country. Yes, I remember this clown that I had read about in the paper, [who] had suddenly become something to be serious about. Yes, he had this frightful anti-Semitism [which] was such an important part of his whole program and his whole being. Sure, Hitler was something that everyone learned to hate. He was the devil. But there was no intellectual awareness of the size of this and I have looked back on it many, many times. It didn't really ring true to me until Nuremberg, until I got actually involved in reading and preparing for presentation. The size of it was something that shocked me and millions of others.

There were a few articles in the American papers—not much—and there were other articles in other magazines that I would occasionally get to look at. My parents were not politically conscious. I guess they would have been regarded as middle of the road and probably as Jews living in New York would have been regarded as Democrats. I knew that there were concentration camps and that this was a recurrence of the *pogroms* that had existed in Germany, Poland, and Russia and the kind of things that my grandparents had fled from, and that it was getting out of hand and getting to be enormous.

What transpired that brought you to Nuremberg?

Lots of things. How did I end up on Justice [Robert H.] Jackson's legal staff? Number one, in my first three and a half years in the army, I had started as a seventh-grade private and by the time Nuremberg started I was a major in the Judge Advocate General's department. I had spent a year teaching at the Judge Advocate General's school in 1943 and '44, in Ann Arbor.

We took over the Michigan Law School. In 1943 there were perhaps a dozen regular students, maybe two dozen. More than a dozen were women and the men were, for various reasons, not qualified and not able to join the armed forces. I had therefore had a reputation as being a teacher. I was only a first lieutenant and then a captain in that role. I then was transferred to Washington to the Army Service Forces. Through the Judge Advocate General's department I knew a great many JAG officers who were prominent and some of them ended up with me on Jackson's staff. I then came to Washington and worked in the labor branch of Army Service Forces, and by lucky accident my commanding officer was William J. Rennan Jr., who became a close friend, as well as technically my commanding officer. I pinned his eagles on when he was promoted to full colonel in 1944. He still owes me three dollars for the eagles.

I also had been editor of the *Columbia Law Review* and a good many of my predecessors and contemporaries on the *Law Review* had already in a few years distinguished themselves and they had applied and been selected. So the people that I think whose influence got me accepted were the late Harold Leventhal who had been the editor-in-chief of *Columbia Law Review* a year before my year (and before he died was a most highly respected judge in the Circuit Court of Appeals for the District of Columbia) and Ben Kaplan. Ben was one of the closest friends of Telford Taylor. It was chiefly on the recommendations of people like Harold Leventhal, Ben Kaplan, and a lawyer long gone, Warren Farr, with whom I had served in the army for a few months.

This was early spring of 1945. It had originally been my plan and the plan of the people at the JAG school where I taught in '43 to '44 that I would be sent over as the judge advocate of an infantry division, but I had a bad back. A lumbar vertebra affected a disk and I still have the problem more than 50 years later. For that reason I stayed on to teach at Ann Arbor and for that reason I still was not overseas come V-E Day. I guess it was April or May of 1945. I had made an application before V-E Day, but it was just after V-E Day that it was accepted. I took off the brace that I was wearing on my back and passed a physical exam, put it back on, and went to London.

As a matter of fact, that same back injury was what got me off of the staff and out of the army in December of 1945. It was in early August that we flew to Nuremberg and the trial started on the 20th of November. I was gone by Christmas, back home.

What preparation did you have to go over and what was it like when you first got there?

Preparation to go over, there was really none. I didn't speak German. I can bluff a little bit in a number of languages, but I knew that we had on the staff all kinds of translators and interpreters. I did some fast reading about the Nazis in a matter of weeks before I got onto a plane. I remember the plane was a ferry command plane without seats. I slept on army blankets all the way from Washington to Prestwick, Scotland. Somehow we got to London.

We lived in a drafty old place in Mayfair. The office was equally drafty. It was June, I remember. I remember shivering in June in London. I remember what we used to call Willow Run, which was the Grosvenor House main ballroom, served 3,000 meals to American army officers every day, stationed in and around London.

It was a strange time because the war in Europe was over and there was a kind of sighing of relief. It was a time of difficulties and shortages. Nobody had seen an orange in years. Here I was in the company of people I looked up to. I shook hands once in London with Justice Jackson. I only talked with him a couple of times in Nuremberg. He was quite aloof from the staff, but it was an opportunity for me to renew my acquaintance with Ben Kaplan, who was older and Harold Leventhal, whom I knew well, and two or three others on the staff whom I had known, either in law school or at the JAG school or one way or the other, like Warren Farr.

We were planning our presentation, not knowing really very much about it. The only thing I could read in those days was the charter that had been agreed upon originally at the Potsdam Conference among Truman, Stalin, and Churchill. As Telford Taylor in his book explains, there had been various plans. It was a monumental job to take the legal systems of four different countries, particularly with the Russian and French system being so far from the Anglo-American, and creating a system to try the major Nazi criminals. It wasn't clear in the beginning what they were going to be tried for, until the charter was fully written and approved. There were all kinds of problems, some of which had an impact on me, problems like who was going to represent and defend these 22 major Nazi defendants. That became an issue that wasn't decided until mid-October of 1945.

In London, what I did was to read as much as I could of the work papers that had been prepared, many of them by the British, along with Telford Taylor, who had been one of the early leaders in working out the procedures. In many ways the fact that these four countries could work together was an achievement of great moment [in 1945], and that they could agree on a method of approaching the thing.

What most people still to this day forget is that these were military trials. This was a military tribunal and as far as the United States was concerned, it was convened by the president of the United States in his capacity as commander in chief, and the same is true of his majesty, King George VI. I don't even venture to know the origin of the authority in France or the Soviet Union.

I read as much as I could. Then I would get as much as I could of the translated writings of the Hitler group, so-called intellectuals of the Nazi movement way back to the *putsch* in Munich in the 1920s. And I read some of the so-called intellectual documents that had nothing to do with politics. This was the Aryan superiority. These were works of people like [Alfred] Rosenberg, like Robert Ley. Then I found myself in a plane on the way to Nuremberg.

In Britain, how large a staff was there?

It was a limited staff that changed every day. It was growing. I was not of high enough rank in the organization of things. I had no say in the planning. I followed along. I would say that when I was in London in the month of July and early August there must have been 20 or 30 lawyers. I would say 20 or 30 people. After all, we were just the lawyers. It was a group of lawyers that ultimately became as many as 75, I was told. But I think in London at the time there were 20 or 30.

There were a lot of housekeeping things being done, like hiring secretaries, many of them from the American embassy in London, hiring people to do nonlegal jobs, organizing the translation and interpreting, organizing the literature, and being in touch with the people who were in the field in Germany, compiling the documents.

Was there much interaction between the Americans and British?

I don't remember how much of this I got from Telford Taylor's book. Memory is a strange thing when you go back 50 years.

We were basically an American staff trying to fit into this mammoth, world-shaking experience that we were participating in. Everyone was pinching himself: "Are we really at this stage of the game?" Here we are, the war in Europe, at least, is won and we're going on this adventure, and a lot of it we have to learn as we go along. So the answer to your question is at that stage [there was] very little interaction.

You said you went on a plane to Nuremberg?

I remember that plane ride. It was a C-47, 20-odd passengers, and the pilot, who apparently had been in combat and here he was just ferrying a bunch of scholarly looking people, including a number of young British girls, along with a few American army officers. I remember we made a stop in Wiesbaden. It was one of the few times that I ever used my rank and threatened somebody with a court-martial. The pilot, with 25 people on board, including women and people who were a little frightened about being in a plane in 1945, buzzed the field. This was by way of greeting somebody in the air force on the ground. I said, "If you want to be free of any difficulties, get us to Nuremberg, please, as quickly as possible." I was senior in rank to him. He was a captain at the time.

We arrived and we were put up in the Grand Hotel in Nuremberg. They had not worked out all the billets as yet. This was about August 15 in 1945. I had a small room in the hotel [which] had been hit by a bomb at one point. I remember on [a top] floor, walking over boards and looking back on it, saying "How could I have had that much confidence in my sense of balance?"

Down below they had the café, and the nightclub, and it was a strange thing, and a bar serving bad German cognac. All of the drinkable beer, wine, and liquor that you could get was American or British. We would only occasionally go to the nightclub. It was the one place that was still open for gaiety. I remember distinctly a buxom blond German singer, singing the song, "Laura."

After a couple of weeks of that, they put us together in a house. The senior people generally had their own houses: Telford Taylor, Frank Shea, Sidney Alderman, General [William "Wild Bill"] Donovan. Each one of them had his own house with his own staff of caretakers. We were in a house with about a dozen [others]. The most senior was Ben Kaplan, and a lawyer from the mid-

The Grand Hotel, where Hitler stayed on his visits to Nuremberg, now housed the bulk of the legal staff during the war crimes trials.

"I had a small room in the hotel. . . . Down below they had the café, and the nightclub . . . and a bar serving bad German cognac. . . . It was the one place that was still open for gaiety." — *Seymour Peyser*

west named Sidney Kaplan and Bernard Milltzer, Tom Karstin, and James Mathias. I remember that Mathias and Karstin and I were in one room. We had a long, large room. It was an old house, a nice suburban house but no central heating, and by November it got to be awfully cold.

Two female servants served breakfast, and I don't even remember—I guess dinner. Lunch we got at some cafeteria in town. This was in the suburb in Dambach, which was actually part of the city of Fürth, the birthplace of Henry Kissinger.

Did you have much interaction with the ordinary German public?

Very little in any kind of organized fashion. I remember we started out two different ways. I don't remember how, but I did visit a couple of families who lived in Nuremberg and I got a picture of what life was like. It was bleak. These were upper-middle-class people, I would guess. They spent most of the time in my presence justifying their existence and explaining how they were really not Nazis. This got to be a standard refrain whenever you would talk with a German.

Did these people know you were Jewish?

Yes, I think they did. [There was] a rather famous person on our staff, Sergeant Stone. He was not a lawyer and he had no important function. He had some administrative function on the staff, but he had lost his family in the Holocaust. I remember Sergeant Stone because he spent most of his time not working on the trial, but gathering care packages for people in camps that were still existing. There were Jews in the camps still in the neighborhood of Nuremberg.

I visited at least one UNRRA [United Nations Refugee Relief Agency] camp and that was an experience, a frightening experience. I had a very close friend, a lawyer, a contemporary of mine who somehow got himself appointed the director of an UNRRA camp. [He was] a New York lawyer who had no experience of that kind, and I visited him at his camp, which was not immediately close to Nuremberg. I don't remember how I got there, but I had at least two visits.

Sergeant Stone sticks out because he was almost religious about his devotion and nothing could stop him from helping every Jew that was still alive. He had the kind of intensity of feeling about where he was, and what he was doing, and why, that was not duplicated by us or our counterparts.

What was the camp like that you visited?

It was a camp with barracks. It was not terrible in any way. It was just pedestrian. Everything was terribly pedestrian, terribly bland in terms of living.

135

They were barracks, and that's all I remember, and places where they filed off to eat, and where they were making speeches. The Jews were still fighting. They were fighting to get to Israel. That seemed to be the goal of everyone in these camps.

I also had gone through the experience of listening to my friend who was the director of an UNRRA camp, telling me about the Jewish gangsters in his camp who had set up a whole system of protection. If you wanted to live peacefully, you had to pay this gangster group. [I was shocked] when he told it to me, [but later] it was quite understandable. These were the survivors of some violent times and to have remained alive throughout the history of Nazism into 1945, you couldn't expect these people to be panty-waist and proper and prayerful types. These had lived in a rough world and I remember being somewhat frightened about the Jews that I saw in the camp near Nuremberg. They were still fighting and I was sympathetic and I wondered how they were going to get to Israel because that was a whole other kettle of fish.

Seymour Peyser (left) poses with two young German boys and two American colleagues in a light moment at Nuremberg.

"I met very few [ordinary Germans]. They sought us out and tried to explain and justify themselves on occasion. I remember ... tea and cookie[s] at a home in Nuremberg.... I didn't meet many Germans and I had some serious doubts as to whether I would want to." —Seymour Peyser

I met very few [Germans]. They sought us out and tried to explain and justify themselves on occasion. I remember having a little meal—not a meal, but a tea and cookie kind of thing at a home in Nuremberg on the main drag.

Nuremberg itself physically was something that had great effect on me. I don't know how much you have seen of the pictures of what Nuremberg looked like in 1945. It had been the target of a bombing attack on two nights [by] American and British bombers. The old city, which I had visited in 1930, [a] beautiful medieval city, was in ruins, just a mass of rubble, and people were living in that rubble. It was unsanitary, I'm sure, but these were Germans. These were not long-time homeless people. They were Germans and very proud of their ability to cope, and they had managed to create a little city in the ruins of the old buildings.

I didn't meet many Germans and I had some serious doubts as to whether I would want to. I don't know how many Jews were still around. I would think there were practically none still living in Nuremberg at the time.

It seemed to me to be appropriate [as a site for the trials] for a variety of reasons. For one thing, the big stadium was there, which had been the site for many of these enormous rallies that Hitler had. It had been the place for the so-called Nuremberg Laws, the [anti-Jewish] edicts that came out in Nuremberg at that time.

It was a small city and from that point of view was difficult. It was not as big as Munich or Berlin or Frankfurt. It was literally a small town compared to them, and there weren't hotel facilities for all the visitors we had. Of course, nobody sat down to figure out this thing as a tourist attraction, but suddenly the tribunal found itself the center of all the media. God knows what would have happened in 1995, but in 1945 we had enough reporters to fill a whole castle, and that's where they lived, Walter Cronkite, Andy Logan who still writes for *The New Yorker*, a few others still around. The Faber Castle was where the press was located. The total staff was estimated to be almost a thousand, including 75 American lawyers.

Incidentally, [it was] as capable and as skilled a group of young lawyers as you could imagine at any time. For people like Donovan and Alderman and Jackson, what they had already accomplished made their reputations. In the case of the others, consider what they were going to accomplish. Among 75 lawyers you had deans of law schools, many professors, many judges, presidents of the American Bar Association. [It was] quite a group. I had a gag that I used on another occasion: Of all these eminent people, I was the only one I never heard of. [laughs]

Was there a particular incident or an individual that stands out?

Yes, I'd say there were a couple of incidents in my few months in Nuremberg that stand out, so much so that whether I talk to my grandson's Sunday

School class or the Phillips and Nizer law firm, they both come to mind. Let me tell the two incidents that keep repeating themselves in my mind.

One was in either late September or early October—I think it was September 1945. I worked directly under Ben Kaplan. My assignment was to deal not with the aggressive war path, but to paint the whole picture of the Nazi state and the Nazi party during the whole period before the war, beginning in the early 1930s until the time of the war, and gather in manageable form some evidence about what Hitler and what the Nazis had done to the judiciary, to the bar, to the press, to the police, to medicine, etc.

I remember sitting at a very early stage with Ben Kaplan in his office at the Palace of Justice and suddenly realizing that here we were as lawyers before a tribunal of judges who couldn't be assumed to know all of the things which we knew. It's the old problem of judicial notice that trial lawyers deal with regularly. We still had to prove what was the structure of the Nazi state and the Nazi party. How do you do that? To whom does box A respond, and when you get to that box A-1, where do you go from there?

The first job was, in effect, to draw a chart, find out what the whole organization was. We were helped immeasurably by the German mentality because they have always been so methodical and so precise about these things. They had the need to know, I guess, who each of them was responsible to. I had the assignment, given to me by Ben Kaplan, to draw a chart or to find a chart that we could present to the tribunal showing how the whole thing looked.

We learned right away that everything was in twos. There were the state and the party, and they were separate organizations, both, of course, led by Hitler. In the party he was the führer, in the state he was the chancellor. But he and his henchmen maintained this dual existence all along the line. So we looked it up and found, yes, the Germans did have charts of the state and the party. Trouble was that they were losing the war by 1943, 1944, and 1945 and they didn't bring their charts up to date. So how were we going to do that? How were we going to have it authenticated?

Someone came up with the proposition that Robert Ley, who was the head of the Labor Front, also had the title of vice president in charge of vice presidents—in charge of organization. Who better than he?

So we got him out of prison and following the required rules of the game at that time, I was in the Documentation Division, not in the Interrogation Division. Somehow or other the legal staff was divided between litigators and documentary organizers. I was in documentation. So we got Ley and arranged a meeting in a room next to the prison, and this is a day that stands out in my memory. It was in late September of 1945. I wasn't allowed to ask the questions, even though it was my job to prepare the chart. I had to bring along a lieutenant colonel from the Interrogation Division and I told him what questions to ask. He asked them and we sat next to each other.

Why this division of labor?

I think it was a political thing dictated by the people who ran the two different sections: Colonel Robert Story, who was the head of the Documentation Division ... [and] later became president of the American Bar Association and a professor in Texas somewhere, and John Harland Amen of New York, who was a trial lawyer and a prosecutor [and head of the Interrogation Division]. They were both bucking for their stars; in other words, bucking to be made brigadier generals. It was a fight for the next position of power under Jackson and his originally appointed assistants, who were Frank Shea, Sidney Alderman, and General Donovan. I think that was the origin of it.

Justice Jackson was an eloquent man, who could make any kind of state paper into a state paper that people would put in anthologies. His opening statement to the tribunal is in many anthologies. But he was a complete flop as an executive and frankly he had been so many years out of litigation that he made many errors in the way he dealt with the facts of the original Nuremberg Trial. I had great regard for him, but most of us had some serious doubts. You never had a meeting with Jackson; you had an audience. It was that kind of thing.

He did stupid things like give his son special access, and his son was an ensign in the navy at the time, and that rubbed everybody the wrong way. Anybody who knew his female secretary would get all kinds of priorities. There were 50 demonstrable errors in his opening statement to the tribunal, but in the path of history that's really of less importance.

Getting back to Robert Ley: We traipsed into this room. Ley was 55 years old at the time. He had a bad cold, wore an off-white sweater that was unraveling at the elbow, and as we each came by, he clicked his heels and bowed. He immediately understood the insignia on my shoulder and he clicked his heels and bowed and said, "Herr Major." I had spent the night before reading some of the stuff he had written about the blood of the Jews running in the streets, incredible things, and I hated the son of a bitch. I remember that I had organized my intense feeling against him and he looked much older than 55 because he was ill.

So we sat down and started and we showed him the 1942 or 1943 charts. It was a series of the same questions. "Is that correct?" pointing to a box. Translated into German. "*Ya, das is richtig.*" Yes, that is correct. This went on. "*Nien, das ist nicht richtig.*" He said, "Well, because in 1944 we changed that and we put that department under this department."

We spent a good three hours with him because [there were] two big charts. The charts ended up on the wall of the courtroom. They were bigger than this whole wall and we ended up by being able to say that these had been authenticated by the top specialist in the Nazi hierarchy.

After we were with him two hours (everybody smoked in those days so he was getting a little bit flaky in his answers and you could see that his mind was

Nazi Labor Minister Robert Ley was one of the original defendants of the International Military Tribunal at Nuremberg. He killed himself before the trial began, the night after his interrogation by Seymour Peyser about the organization of the Nazi Party.

"I had spent the night before reading some of the stuff he had written about the blood of the Jews running in the streets, incredible things, and I hated the son of a bitch. . . . [But after several hours of interrogation], I realized suddenly that this was a human being." —Seymour Peyser

really not all there), I handed him a cigarette, which he took immediately and lit, grateful for it. That cleared his mind so he could answer the next series of questions.

I realized suddenly that this was a human being. This guy was breathing badly because he had a bad cold. He wasn't a good specimen, but he was human and I no longer had that intensity of feeling that I had when I entered the room. I hadn't been trained for that kind of intensive long-time, stick-to-it hatred, and I have never forgotten that.

It's not a feeling that I read about other people having, but everybody understands it. That's where Sergeant Stone came back to me. He would have had no problem maintaining that same pitch of intense personal feeling.

Just to finish the story of Robert Ley—that night he killed himself. He hanged himself on a GI towel in the bathroom and the then-colonel in charge of the prison was transferred to a beat in Staten Island.

How did you feel when you heard that he committed suicide?

I wasn't sad. My immediate thought was, "Is that in any way going to affect the work we put into this?" I didn't have that kind of a feeling of concern for him; it's just that I wasn't good at this business of intense and continuous hating, which underlay the entire war for so many of us. I had a strong disgust for Ley, but here was somebody who was alive and then suddenly was not. In a human way I sympathized with this despicable man and said, "Well, he's better off." The remainder of his life was certainly not going to be a pleasant one and he would undoubtedly have been one of those with the most severe punishment. He would have been executed along with a number of them.

But that was one story. The other, you asked generally for human stories. I guess that is one of the reasons for this process. The other was an interesting one. It had to do with the lawyers for the defendant. This being a military tribunal, if you took the standard operating procedure in American and I suppose British military law, the court-martial is convened by the commanding general, whoever that may be. In the case of the Nuremberg Trials it was Commander-in-Chief Harry S Truman. The prosecutor, known as the trial judge advocate, is appointed by that commanding general. Generally speaking, in military tribunals the defense counsel is also appointed, and under the Articles of War of the United States (and I assume similar rules in Britain), the defendant has the privilege of requesting civilian counsel, if civilian counsel is immediately available. It's a matter of convenience, again the decision [is] to be made by the commanding general, who is in this case the one who creates the trial.

The Americans and the British wanted to use the method used in our military tribunals because they were concerned that lawyers for these 22 characters, 22 defendants, would themselves be Nazis and we would be giving people prominence, simply as a professional matter, that they were not entitled to, and that it should be something that should be decided on a case-by-case method. There should be defense counsel and if the defendant makes a case for why he wants a civilian lawyer and a civilian lawyer is in other respects satisfactory, okay.

So the Americans and British went to a meeting in Berlin in October—early October, [or] late September. I was not there, obviously. This would only be, I think, the very top level of the organization; not only the chief of counsel, but representatives of the judges met with them on that occasion. The French and the Russians were violently opposed to this. They wanted the Germans to have their own lawyers because from the French point of view and to some extent I guess the Russians', they wanted to avoid the possibility that if the defendants exercised their choice or indicated their choice, they would invariably pick an American or a Briton and never a Frenchman or a Russian. So it ended two to two and that meant that the Americans and the British didn't feel that strongly about it.

It was decided that the defendants would retain their own counsel. They had, in many cases, the preeminent lawyers who were still alive. I remember the lawyer for Göring and for Schacht [was a] distinguished, elderly gentleman. All counsel wore the normal robes of a German lawyer, except for the lawyer for Admiral Dönitz, who was the assistant chief judge advocate of the German navy, who wore the uniform of the German navy into the courtroom until October 1946—one of the things that the Americans and British wanted to avoid. In any event, that's what happened.

What interested me was that we knew, sitting in Nuremberg, that this was a subject of dispute and had not been fully decided. It occurred to me that I might be facing a problem. One of the first things I had done when I reached Nuremberg, before I got onto this business of the structure of the state and other interesting jobs which I had, [was] to go over the list of all the roles that Hermann Göring had had and prepare a definitive list of them and have him sign off that these were the jobs that he did, which I did. He had some 25 or 30 different roles during the Nazi period, during that 15-year period. Therefore, I was a little bit more up on Göring than some others of us, [although] certainly not as much as those who had studied this as a life work.

Here I am late one evening in the bar at the Grand Hotel considering what would happen if Göring said, "That's him. I want that lawyer. I want an American Jew representing me." It might have been an offbeat kind of thing, but it was conceivable. He was clearly the brightest of the defendants, nobody ever doubted that. He didn't doubt it and none of the other 20 who were there doubted it.

Krupp, of course, was not around. Then by the time of the trial, Ley was gone.

Anyway, what would have happened? It wouldn't have been possible for me to say, "Well, I'm sorry but I won't do it." I'm in the army. This could be an order. As it happened, I thought about it considerably because in Manila at about the same time or a little after, an old friend of mine, Frank Riel, had been ordered by General [Douglas] MacArthur to defend [Japanese General Tomoyuki] Yamashita and he had not wanted to. He had been told by his senior commanders, "What you want to do is not relevant here. Do it." And he did.

As a matter of fact, he came to the conclusion that many of the crimes with which Yamashita was charged, he was not guilty of. The major thing in that case was his awareness of the atrocities being performed by his soldiers against Americans. Frank Riel was convinced that Yamashita was in no position to stop the atrocities, that there was no line of communication. He went so far as to fly all the way from Manila to Washington to argue an appeal before the Supreme Court of the United States on Yamashita's conviction, which was confirmed by a seven to two vote. Riel got two justices of the Supreme Court to dissent.

At any rate, it was a purely theoretical thing and never did happen, but many times I thought to write something along those lines, a fictitious treatment.

Again, by lucky accident, I was general counsel of United Artists Corporation in the 1950s and in that capacity served as a kind of technical advisor to Stanley Kramer on *Judgment at Nuremberg*.

The character played by Richard Widmark is Telford Taylor. My wife and I took Telford Taylor to the opening of the film, after I had discussed the script with him and gotten Kramer to accept a few minor changes in the script to avoid difficulty. But we were still very worried that Taylor would take some action because he was being portrayed by name.

Do you remember the judge played by Spencer Tracy, who actually has a meeting in the fictitious script with Marlene Dietrich? Taylor was shocked by that. He said the actual judge would be horrified and he may cause trouble. He said, "I come off pretty well in this Widmark character, but the judge is going to be scandalized that he should be talking and making eyes at this gorgeous [widow of a Nazi]."

It turned out that the judge, who was still very much alive and living in Florida, was delighted with it. He took all his friends to show them how Marlene Dietrich came to him in the film. So it didn't work out as a problem.

I remember it because I had thought what would have happened if I, in real life, had been ordered to act as defense counsel?

The policy then was that they chose the German defense attorneys. Were the German lawyers willing to come forward?

They seemed to be. Yes, they were and they were there and argued.

Had any of them been Nazis?

Yes, certainly some. The lawyers for people like Streicher and Sauckel could not have been anything else. But we didn't do a separate investigation of each lawyer to see. What good would it have done? Each one would have said he wasn't on trial and so it would be a waste of time and effort. In fact, [it] might even raise some defense arguments, if we persecuted the professional team. They still were lawyers.

The only other thing that I haven't mentioned that was interesting in terms of the jobs that I did in my few months in Nuremberg: I was sent on a trip to get affidavits from representatives of the police, the judiciary, and the press during the period from the 1920s to the 1940s, and what happened to them as a result of the Hitler period. Why affidavits? Because it would be just too difficult to dig out these people and transport them. We would try to do this in a somewhat summary and casual way—not casual, but a shortcut to evidence that in most cases would not be acceptable in American court. But here you're trying 25 years of a history of a whole people, so obviously the rules have got to be softened in some way.

I was very fortunate to have with me Colonel Stuart Hughes. He's the grandson of Charles Evans Hughes. Stuart had been the OSS Chief in Germany, operating out of Wiesbaden, and we borrowed a car assigned to Telford Taylor. I got his car because it was easier on my back than the ordinary Jeep of those days. Stuart and I traveled to Wiesbaden, Stuttgart, Frankfurt, and interviewed and got affidavits from these people. Stuart spoke fluent German and I was there to help suggest questions.

I remember we talked to a newspaper editor, who later became chancellor of post-Nazi Germany [German Federal Republic], Theodor Heuss. We had a couple of people who had been police chiefs, one guy who had been the police chief of Berlin until he had been fired by Goebbels. Another guy had been a judge, one of the judges who eventually ended up a defendant in the subsequent trials.

Was there any interaction with the Russians?

The Russians were under strict orders not to have anything to do with us. I remember very vividly a party. There was a great deal of partying. As a major I had the right to an enormous allotment of liquor. You could buy scotch for a dollar and a half a bottle. There was a kind of lonesomeness here and some frustration at the conflict between Documentation Division and Interrogation Division. The fact that there wasn't real planning. A lot of things happened because of politics.

We were at a party and there was a lot of drinking and suddenly in front of me, in our house, is a Russian major, a nice young fellow. I was 30 then; he must have been 30. He spoke no English at all, no French, very fluent Russian, and very lame German. So he and I got along in conversation with the completely inadequate German of both of us and the bourbon that he was drinking. He had never drunk bourbon. It was not the same as vodka and he really went three sheets. But he was a nice fellow and we talked about the fact that we were both big city boys, that I had come from New York and he came from Moscow. I remember that much we were able to communicate in our language. He got lost and found himself at a party with us. We had never seen anybody like him.

The next day, in front of the Palace of Justice, he was walking with a couple of senior Russian officers. He walked right by me, looked straight in my eye, and didn't blink.

My feeling was that he had had his wrists very soundly rapped for getting involved with these dissolute Americans. [laughs] [Every] Russian there was [in the] military. Unlike the other judges, the two Russian judges were generals, and the chiefs of counsel for the Russians were military men. So there were uniforms on both sides of the counsel table.

Is it fair to say that the Americans were running the trial?

No, it's not fair. They were certainly the dominant people. I would say the Americans were the host country and they were the dominant operating group, but the British worked very much with the Americans, and the British had some very competent and very hard-working lawyers. The French lawyers were bookish, professor types who never seemed to be getting out into the real world. The Russians seemed impatient and wanted to get on with the hanging. Everything that they did thereafter made that clear.

There's one incident that you may not have heard of. I wasn't there, but it was told to me the next morning. We had a state visit while I was there in Nuremberg from [Andrey Yanuaryevich] Vyshinsky. Vyshinsky had been Stalin's chief prosecutor in the [Great] Purge trials and he was a big shot. There was a dinner in his honor. He had some title of deputy vice prime minister or something and he was also a general and he wore a light blue uniform with big stars on the shoulders. They had a state dinner before the trial started, attended by all of the judges, as well as the chiefs of counsel, and that meant a big group. So you couldn't get below the rank of colonel at the party.

There were a series of toasts. Somebody made a toast to his excellency, President Truman; someone to his Britannic Majesty, King George VI; another one to his excellency, President [Vincent] Auriol of France; and then somebody to Generalisimo Stalin. So they had all four covered and they called on Vyshinsky. He drank a toast "to the prisoners and their march [from] the Palace of Justice to the gallows."

Mind you, this is a trial that hasn't begun yet and you've got not only Francis Biddle, the chief American judge sitting there, but his alternate, Judge [John J.] Parker, a very judicial character. He's holding the wine and I'm told his hand shook and then he spilled some of the wine drinking a toast to the conviction.

Was there in general a presumption of guilt?

Yes, sure there was. A presumption in feeling, but you got American and British lawyers who are trained to think otherwise. The fact that three of the defendants were acquitted is an indication that that meant something. The Russians certainly didn't vote for acquitting Fritzsche. He was the head of the radio section of the press under Goebbels. You know why he was one of the 21 charged with being principal criminals? Because he was one of the few people that the Russians had captured. He was captured in their zone and they had him physically and everybody else had been dug up by the victorious people from the other countries.

How could the four powers stand in judgment when the Russians were already starting their takeover of the Balkan States and the French had violated the Geneva Convention by mistreating prisoners?

It was more than just that. We knew of particular incidents where the Russians particularly had been involved. Yes, there was a sense of unease, but not very much we could do about it except go through with it. We couldn't stop in the middle and say, "Well, one of our victorious countries is also guilty. Would they please stand in the dock?" Yes, we knew about it.

It would not, to my mind, be a paradox if we discovered that the judge at a major capital case was himself guilty of crimes. It doesn't mean anything to me. I mean, so what if he was? That's a separate problem. It was an embarrassing problem to us at Nuremberg and it's embarrassment to the United States and Britain as nations to have to join forces with peoples and governments who are themselves responsible for some of this.

We also were aware at the very beginning—and everybody is aware. People to this day still talk about the *ex post facto* Nuremberg Trials. I don't know whether people take a poll on such subjects, but there are many perfectly respectable professional minds that felt all along that we should have just lined them up against the wall and shot them, get rid of them, that this whole business was a mockery of the true feeling of at least Anglo-American legal principals.

What's your feeling about Nuremberg justice?

My feeling, very frankly, was that I was persuaded there was enough of a background to justify a trial and that it was much better to go through this process. Certainly there was enough evidence under the classic war crimes definitions, the rules of land warfare, as it's called. Nobody could object to the evidence that American prisoners and American hospital workers and medics, had been dealt with in violation of the old conventions going back to the beginning of the twentieth century.

The important thing is that they added two other basic counts. One was the planning and waging of an aggressive war. This bothered a lot of people who felt they were being more realistic saying that the victors in any war are going to claim that the vanquished were trying to wage an aggressive war. The Serbs are now doing the same thing, so I can understand that argument.

The final one, which is what I think has interested the people of the world and the media, is the crimes against humanity. There's no precedent for people being tried for this. There are enough words in documents like the Kellogg-Briand Pact, the Locarno Treaty, and things of that kind, and lawyers can play around with it and interpret language, but I can understand friends of mine who think that the whole basis of that part of the Nuremberg history is misleading and self-deceptive.

I don't worry about it because I think it serves a purpose. It serves a purpose in talking about the responsibility of individuals for waging aggressive war and crimes against humanity. It's a precedent and precedents are made with great difficulty. They're usually made without any prior passing of a law. In international law, you have more difficult things. International law is made up of incidental and anecdotal agreements between countries, relating to particular facts of the past.

Telford Taylor wrote a book on Vietnam and the Nuremberg background, and stated properly that he didn't see any relationship there. But I can see it in terms of the Serbs now, except for one major difference: we haven't got any defendants to try.

I started here today saying that I thought one of the major significances of the Nuremberg trial was that the four countries did something together—whatever they did. I think that helped make the United Nations a possibility. Whether that's a good thing can be argued, too.

You were at Nuremberg for four months?

It was a little more than four months. Actually, I was on staff for almost six months, but I was in Nuremberg only from August through December.

Your back is what led to your leaving.

Oh, I had a couple of reasons. I was in considerable pain and I also had enough points to get out of the army and go back and practice law. I had already seen the beginning of the trial and I'd spent hours, both in the Palace of Justice and offices and with Stuart Hughes; I'd traveled around Germany and seen a good deal. I had sat in the courtroom for a number of hours. Sure, life would still continue to be exciting, frustrating in many ways, and it seems to me the rest of it was acting out the rest of a play, of which I was a very minor participant. [In light of that], as against coming back to renew my professional life and my life, I made the decision [to leave].

When you returned to America, did you have the sense that people in the U.S. understood what was happening in Nuremberg?

No, because many thinking people were asking similar questions about *ex post facto* justice. I don't think that many of them knew about the Katyn massacre [in Russia in the spring 1940] that the Russians were guilty of. I don't think that was common knowledge, or that the French had been guilty of violations of the traditional war crimes conventions.

This was a pretty big show. It was not so much the importance of it as, you know, you've got this incredible guy, Göring. To be sure there would be nothing comparable if it had been on television. Can you imagine the Nuremberg Trials carried to the O. J. Simpson level? I'm tired already, just thinking about it. But you had Göring, with his jowls hanging down. He had lost 100 pounds, was very bright, listening and taking advantage of every question, every translation. He understood English very well and therefore had a great advantage.

I was told by people who were there and whom I respected that Göring toyed with Jackson. Jackson made the mistake of asking questions when he did know what the answer was going to be. You had him and you had this mask-like face of Rudolf Hess sitting right next to him, and you had a bunch of small, evil men like Rosenberg and Streicher and Sauckel, all of whom were really directly involved in genocide.

You also had the generals and the admirals, an entirely different cast of characters. You wondered how they allowed themselves to get into this thing and by the same token, you realized that they never had been trained to avoid it. They just did what came naturally to them. This is quite a cast, in many ways much more exciting as a theatrical attraction than *Judgment at Nuremberg*. Even more exciting than Spencer Tracy.

In your own life, how important was participation in the Nuremberg Trials?

Not very much directly. It was important for me, [but] not as a lawyer. Professionally it did not mean very much to me because I became very much the corporate lawyer, not a trial lawyer in any way. I was not a litigator and in that sense I think none. It gave me a certain distinction, a panache, if you will, that I had been thought of well enough to be invited to join the group.

On a personal basis it's a distinction to have as well as a remarkable experience. I don't think it affected me as a practicing lawyer, particularly. It was an experience that I'm happy I had because it meant being that close to something of importance in history—whatever validity you give it. I met and was close to some very interesting and exciting people. I don't mean the defendants, I mean the staff.

I've been very friendly with Kaplan until he died, with Leventhal, Mathias. I have seen Telford Taylor [from] time to time at gatherings and still am friendly with him.

Was the 1991 reunion the first time that you got together as a group?

As far as I know, yes. There were other partial groups. I know a party that was held in 1947–48 while the other trials, the subsequent trials were on. Some of the alumni of the original trial had had parties. I remember one in Brooklyn, Park Slope. I remember it particularly because one of the young women who had been very active as an executive secretary in Nuremberg, very attractive and bright young woman, had come to the United States intending to stay and was looking for a job. That week, my [law] partner, Bob Benjamin ... was looking for somebody to act as his executive secretary there. So I put them together and they were married a few years later. They have many grandchildren.

What is your opinion on continuing the hunt for Nazi criminals?

It doesn't interest me that much. It's certainly something I would turn the television on to look at, but the mathematical justice quotient doesn't interest me. That there's somebody that escaped and should be punished 50 years later, I don't really care. If Martin Bormann is alive, fine. I don't have that feeling of wanting to settle the account by punishing somebody who has managed to escape. It's like watching a television fictional program to watch this, even the fact that they found an Eichmann. Sure, he should be punished, but it doesn't worry me that there may still be an Eichmann that's free.

Was Nuremberg the greatest trial in history?

I don't think it was the greatest trial in history, but I think it was one of the great theatrical events of the judiciary in that area.

I think with all of its limitations, and it certainly had many, and all of the errors that were made there, I think the world is better off that these four countries did what they did, rather than shooting all the defendants.

Any human venture can be said to be futile in an absolute way. Of course the judges are people with feet of clay. Of course the judging countries are defective, as ours will always be. It's not by itself the greatest trial in history. It's not by itself going to prevent other aggressive wars or other unspeakable genocides, but it's something that can be used to mobilize people and persuade people.

ROBERT KING

Attorney, Justice Case

Inspired by the eloquence of Robert Jackson's opening address, Robert King determined that he would be part of the Nuremberg Trials. "So far as I was concerned that's what I had to do, so I made the arrangements [through Telford Taylor in Washington, D.C.] and on July 3, 1946 I was on the way." Assigned to the subsequent proceedings, King worked on the IMT trial for a few weeks before beginning work on the Justice Case. Working on the Justice Case excited King. "It was a great opportunity because here we were dealing with people who, in effect, changed Germany's legal system from a very respectable system ... to a completely Nazi system." King believes the Nuremberg Trials were an important milestone in the history of both international law and politics. After the trial, King edited the transcripts of the Justice Case. He retired after a long career as an attorney, which included service in the Connecticut state legislature, and died on September 25, 1998 as this book went to press.

I was born in Minnesota, in the southern part, in a city known as Worthington, on November 22, 1912. I lived with my parents for only a short period of time, roughly about 18 months, at which time there was apparently some family discord, and they separated. My mother took me to Sioux Falls, South Dakota, which is about 60 miles away. Then after about a month or so, she called my grandparents in Org and said that I was ill and that she couldn't take care of me, and someone would have to come and get me, which they did. I went to live with my grandparents temporarily, at least, and I lived with them for the next 14 years. Org is four or five miles south of Worthington, very close to the Iowa line.

When I was 15, I left my grandparents' place for a job in Sioux City, Iowa. I worked at several jobs. The last one that I had was with a paint company, and I was involved in an automobile accident while with the company. I fractured my back and was in the hospital for quite a while, and wore a full-body cast for six months or so. I was not able to do much of anything.

I was 19 at the time. One neighbor, Mrs. Erma Prescott, urged me to go back to high school. I only had two years in Minnesota, at Worthington. There was no high school in our area. I went to a country school through eighth grade, and then two years of high school in Worthington. This neighbor urged me to go back to high school. It seemed to me an impossible situation because I had no job and no place to live. I did find somebody who would give me a room, and provide some of the meals, and I got along that way for the first year. The second year I had no idea what I was going to do, and this neighbor said, "Well, our girls are in school now. Come and live with us," which I did for a year. I finished high school and then went on to college, at the University of Iowa.

In high school, I had the very good fortune of working with a professor of English, John F. Schmidt, who was also the debate instructor. We did very well in the state debate contests. As you might know, the Midwest has more thorough curricula on debate and speech than here in the East. It's spreading now, but at that time, particularly Iowa, was great. A. Craig Baird was largely responsible for the program at Iowa. In any event, I won a four-year scholarship to Iowa. After I finished my B.A., I then went on, again in the speech department, and got a master's degree, and that led to a job at Purdue University. I met my wife there and we were married in December 1939, and I entered Yale Law School the following year.

What made you go to law school?

I think I always wanted to be in law. That had always been in the back of my mind, for a number of reasons. Now that I think about it, I recall once when I was particularly obnoxious to my grandfather, he told me that people like myself were going to either end up as criminals or lawyers, and he didn't see much difference between the two. [laughs] I don't know whether he was being prophetic, or I'm reading things into it. But in any event, I had always wanted to do that, in the back of my mind.

I had the opportunity to apply to Yale. I had a good friend who was teaching law at Iowa, by the name of Frank Strong, and I think he was probably the person that most likely had the influence to get me into Yale Law School. He had been a member of the *Law Review* there, and had very good connections with the school, so I felt very much indebted to him. Yale Law School then, as now, is very difficult to get into, and I felt very privileged to be there because I was a country boy with no great educational background. Adequate, but no great educational background, compared to some of the Eastern people. So I felt very fortunate in being there.

After that, I went directly to New York with a corporate law firm. It was then Root, Clark, Buchner, and Ballantine. It's now Dewey, Ballantine, which is one of the two or three more prominent law firms in the city. I was with the law firm for roughly three years. Part of that time I was managing or in charge of the Washington, D.C. office of the firm.

While I was in Washington, I heard Justice Jackson's opening remarks to the Nuremberg IMT—International Military Tribunal. It was really the most fascinating and thrilling experience I had in listening to public speeches for a long time. He was addressing the problems. The opening statement grasped the problem: "What should be done with the defeated Germans?" The eloquence of the speech was just overpowering to me. I then read it later, and so far as I was concerned that's what I had to do, so I made the arrangements and on July 3, 1946 I was on the way.

U.S. chief prosecutor Robert Jackson's opening remarks to the International Military Tribunal inspired Robert King and other lawyers to head for Nuremberg.

"While I was in Washington, I heard Justice Jackson's opening remarks to the Nuremberg IMT.... It was really the most fascinating and thrilling experience.... The eloquence of the speech was just overpowering to me. I then read it later, and so far as I was concerned that's what I had to do, so I made the arrangements and on July 3, 1946 I was on the way." — *Robert King*

Was his speech broadcast on the radio? Is that how you heard it?

Yes, it was. I'm not sure it was simultaneous, but somewhere along the line, it was broadcast.

At that particular time, the second part of the trials [was] being organized, called the subsequent trials. The IMT—the original International Military Tribunal—heard only relatively few of the total number of people who should have been tried. So it was necessary to get additional trials to handle not all, but some of the big shots that had committed such atrocious crimes. So the subsequent trials were being organized, and Telford Taylor was actually looking for prosecutors to come over and represent the various trials. So I made arrangements with him. I didn't know that there was a recruiter. I guess I can safely call him a recruiter. I didn't know that there was a recruiter around. I had to make an inquiry in the next few days to see what was going on, and I learned at that time that [Colonel] Taylor was in Washington, so we didn't have much problem getting together.

He didn't tell me then that I was going to be on the Justice Case because he didn't know. [The trials] were being organized, and I don't think he even knew at that time how many there would be, or what particular group each of the cases would be trying. But as it worked out, I wound up with what was to be called the Justice Case, which was the trial of the German judges and prosecutors.

Did you have a choice of what case you'd be put on?

I may have had, but I was thrilled to be on that case because it seemed to be of great interest and importance, which it turned out to be, in my opinion.

There was a period, perhaps, of two months, maybe three months, between the time that we agreed that I would go before I actually went. He was in the process of organizing things and that couldn't be done overnight. He had indicated when we first talked that it would probably be the middle of the summer before we'd be in operation. As it was, I arrived there in July, and the International Military Tribunal was still going on. The subsequent trials were not ready yet. So I worked for a few weeks on the international [trial]. There were all these things to do. I wrote a couple of briefs for one of the prosecutors.

Then our own case, the Justice Case, had to be organized, selecting staff, and documents, and so on. The first thing, of course, was to determine who was to be tried, then to prepare the indictment based on a very large number of captured documents that were available. We had to go find them, but they were available. We had a tremendous research staff, [including] two very interesting German Americans whose individual stories were both terrible and fascinating. They put their heart into what they were doing. That's for sure.

One by the name of Henry Einstein lived in Germany, before the war. His father was taken to a concentration camp early on. His mother was ill at the time, or in some way avoided being taken in the first bunch. She avoided it up until about three months before the war ended. Henry found out where she was, and he went to the area, and through his efforts, she did not go. After that he spent the rest of his life in Germany, until she died. She never came to the United States.

He happened to be in the United States because his father and mother knew what was coming, or at least they thought they knew what was coming. As a boy of 16, they sent him to the United States to live with some relatives. When the war came along, he enlisted as a private, but with his knowledge of German and English, he drifted into the Nuremberg area, and that's how he came to work with us. He was not what we might call a cultured person, in terms of having all the graces of society, but he was one of the finest people that I ever knew.

The other gentleman was a fellow by the name of Peter Bouvais, who was a sophisticate. He had Hollywood friends, and he was also ambitious to get into the German motion picture production business. But the war interfered with that, and he went into the army and [they] picked him out because of his English/German knowledge. He was great, too. He seemed to have a knowledge of what we wanted without telling him too much of the detail, you know? He sensed what the heart of the thing was, and [was a] tremendous interviewer. I sat with him a number of times when he was interviewing, and I hadn't seen anything quite like it.

Henry Einstein was a very interesting interviewer, not quite as forceful as Peter Bouvais was. I remember one time we had a general who was coming in as a witness. We'd had documentation on him. Henry came in one morning and said, "The general is not going to support that." I said, "Henry, he's got to support it. Here are the documents. You go back and tell him that I'm going to make it tough on him unless he agrees." Henry came back in about 20 minutes. His phrase was—it's quite a household word now—"Well, the general says 'yes' now." [laughs] Peter Bouvais was not quite that blunt. [laughs]

We started the trial after the indictment was out, and worked with the research people much more than we ever had at that point.

Did you get to meet or see any of the defendants in the IMT trial?

Oh, yes, I met quite a few of them. As a matter of fact, the last interview I had was with Göring about a week before he was scheduled to be executed.

Peter Bouvais did the actual interviewing, and the question that I wanted answered was, "What interest [did] the German air force or Göring [have] in the South American airline called SCADTA, which operated in Colombia?" The United States [had been] afraid that SCADTA was poised to hit the Panama Canal, and Pan American finally took it over. I was with the firm that represented Pan American at that time. The Americans arranged for Pan Am to take over all the operations of the airline. I believed Göring. He said that there was no connection whatever. He didn't even know SCADTA, and just his manner indicated that he was not making anything up. I interviewed a number of others, too. I sat in with somebody else while we were interviewing four or five of the main defendants in the IMT.

What was your general impression of those defendants?

Well, there were some rats. There were two or three that I wouldn't recommend to anybody for anything. [laughs]
On the other hand, there were some brilliant men there. I think Göring was probably one of the most brilliant. There were, as I say, two or three that were just the scum of the earth, and they drifted into the party because that's where they belonged. They were that sort of scum. But with the exception of that group—which is small, four or five at the most—I would say the rest of them were intellectually extremely bright. Somewhere [they had] taken a wrong turn, but they could accomplish almost anything on their own if they had been permitted to do so.

The IMT and the other subsequent trials were based mostly on documentation, rather than on witnesses. Was that true for the Justice Case?

Well, both, documentation and testimony. The testimony resulted from the documentation. When you confront somebody with a document with his signature on it, it's very difficult for him to deny that it happened or that he said it. And that, of course, produced the oral part of it, and that was very effective. Without the documents we would have no way of knowing whether they were telling the truth or not. With the documents, we were pretty sure that they were telling the truth. Thanks to the nature of the German people, they recorded just about everything they did. [It was] a very thorough record, not only militarily, but also legally and medically. It's just their nature. Fortunately, the Allies were able to capture most of it, I would say, in some cases, 100 percent.

What was your impression of Nuremberg?

Nuremberg is a very old area, and it was a walled city, to give you an idea of the age. The central city, was almost completely devastated. It was a shambles. Miraculously, the courthouse, the so-called Palace of Justice, which was not very far from the old city, hadn't been touched at all. So that part of the city was livable, and the residential areas out a mile or so hadn't been touched either. It was just the center. The railroad station and some of the very historic monuments in the center, the principal hotel, were not completely demolished, but badly damaged. They were repaired enough so the U.S. forces could be accommodated. But as far as the central part of it—it was gone.

Now, the interesting thing to me was, what do you think the Germans were rebuilding first? They were rebuilding the walls and the towers in the old city. By the time we left in 1950, the old city had been almost completely rebuilt, and a lot of industries and a lot of commercial buildings had not been. So the emphasis was placed on that part of it.

Did you have much contact with the ordinary German on the street?

Quite a bit because we had German secretaries. Quite a few German secretaries. There were a lot of other Germans who were employed in the whole process, and we got to know them and some of their families very well. We had domestic help, for example, who were all German. They were very, very nice people.

Some did not like us at all. Some felt that we were saviors who had come to do them some good. It didn't seem to make too much difference about what we were doing or how we happened to be there. If they had an attitude, that was it. Fortunately, all the household help that we had were not anti-American. So we got along fine.

They were pretty well screened before they came out. In other words, no ardent Nazis with a record were hired by the Americans. I'm sure that there were some that did get hired, but that wasn't the intention.

How aware were the ordinary Germans of the trials?

Not very many ordinary Germans came to the trials. The trials were open to the public, but I don't recall ever seeing more than a very few Germans at the IMT. I saw even fewer at the Justice Case trial. Once in a while, yes, and there were probably some that I couldn't identify. But I didn't see a great many people coming in. I think probably the average German had some resentment about the trials on the grounds that they didn't do anything worse than a lot of others, and in some respects, you know, they're right. I think the Germans erred in that they got into the Jewish question. The concentration camps and the extermination centers were not general knowledge to German people. Many had an inkling that something like that was going on, but I am convinced that many did not know. Therefore, when they were defensive of the Nazi government, many of them were without the knowledge of some of the terrible things that were going on because there was no way to get information during the war; that is, the kind of information that they would have to have. Certainly the Germans weren't going to give it to them. There was foreign broadcast, yes, but the penalty for getting caught listening to a foreign broadcast was more than most people wanted to take. So they were simply not as well informed as you might think they would be. Plus, there was also the other thought that the government wouldn't do things like that.

By and large, Germans have always been a very highly respected people, scientifically and every other way. Many of them were very proud of the fact that they have a long history. One of them told me once, "You know, we were a democracy before America was discovered," and to some extent, he's right. They had a lot of popular participation by the people in many ways. That goes way back; whether it was before 1492 or not, I don't know. [laughs] But at least that's a possibility.

On the Justice Trial, how many of you were involved, and what kind of interaction was there among the lawyers?

So far as the German lawyers were concerned, all the defendants had their own lawyers. Some of them had more than one, and they were, with a few exceptions, very adequate lawyers. They knew very little about American jurisprudence, and a lot of our proceedings were pretty strange to them, but eventually they understood what we were doing, and I think we had a better understanding of their system. In any event, they worked very well with us. They were not as aggressive as American lawyers would be, but they gave their clients, I think, the best defense possible. There wasn't too much that they could do. [If] you confront the defendant with a series of documents which outlined starkly the things that he did or recommended, or whatever the action was, it's pretty difficult to defend that even if you're a good lawyer. That was the situation in almost every case.

They brought in a lot of witnesses, most of them, I would say, in mitigation. A lot of them were believable. One particular story would be, "Well, I knew what was going on. I knew that I didn't like to do it, but I also knew that if I left, somebody worse would come, so I felt it my duty to stay." [laughs] Well, you can take that both ways, but in some cases I think it was true. We got that argument quite often. On the whole, I thought the German lawyers did a very competent job. It was an impossible job for most of them; they did it under conditions that weren't exactly ideal. The Americans did help them out a little bit, in terms of giving them supplies that they couldn't ordinarily buy—soap and coffee and cigarettes and I don't know what else. They were paid a pretty decent salary on behalf of their clients—paid by the Americans. Simply because there was no way for their German clients to pay them. They had no source of income. Marks were [practically] worthless. So that was the only way it could be done.

The Justice Case seems like the ultimate case for a lawyer—trying other lawyers and judges.

I don't think there's any question about it. As far as I'm concerned, it was a great opportunity because here we were dealing with people who, in effect, changed the Germans' legal system from a very respectable system under the

Robert King (extreme right with earphones) listens to an English translation during the closing arguments of the Justice Case.

"[The Justice Case] was a great opportunity because here we were dealing with people who, in effect, changed the Germans' legal system from a very respectable system under the Weimar Republic, to a completely dominated Nazi system." —Robert King

Weimar Republic, to a completely dominated Nazi system. The people we were trying were those who provided the machinery to do that. All Germans, we found, were very law conscious; that is, they didn't like to do anything— and, that's still true—that's not provided by law. That is the average German citizen. The Nazis were the same way. They didn't do anything that wasn't covered by law. The concentration camps were covered by law, a series of regulations called the Final Solution. With the law, you know, you have a little more freedom to act than you do if you're not operating under a law.

Did you feel that they as lawyers were more culpable than others?

I don't think so. No, I didn't detect that at all. Many of them were very prominent German lawyers before the war. They, I think, because of the prominence, were more easily adaptable to the Nazi regime. There were some things that were totally unbelievable. One of my defendants was the prosecutor for the People's Court [*Volksgerichtshof*], which is a very notorious institution in Germany. It was a court of final resort for a lot of people, in the real sense of the word. He had drafted or participated in the drafting of many of the more horrific programs, and I remember once we were talking about a particular program that he had drafted. I asked him if he felt any remorse in having participated in it. And he said, yes, he had. But he said under the conditions at the time, he felt he had no choice. His name was Ernest Lautz, and I felt perhaps more so than any other defendant, that here was a chap who was perfectly honest with himself. I think [that] not all of them were. I think he could look back and say, "Well, this is what I did, but I shouldn't have done it."

Was he the person that the Burt Lancaster character was modeled on in Judgment at Nuremberg?

You've seen the picture. I'm not sure that the defendants were identified. I don't believe Lautz was. I think the answer to your question is probably no. We'll get into the picture a little bit later. [It's] good entertainment, but it's not history.

How did the trial proceed on a day-to-day basis?

Well, there was a primary difference between the subsequent trials and the international. The international was [run by the] four powers, and there had to be [simultaneous translation in] four different languages, and that is a big job. It wouldn't have been done at all except for the ingenuity of IBM engineers. They made possible the simultaneous translation system, provided earphones for every seat in the courtroom.

The subsequent trials, although they were international trials in the sense that they were done under international law, were all American, so that we only had the simultaneous translation of German/English and English/German, and that simplified things a great deal from an administrative point of view.

I suppose the routine was pretty much like American courts. The judges were American, without any previous German experience, to my knowledge. They, too, had to be educated into the byways of German law because we were dealing with that almost every day. So far as cross-examination and direct examination was concerned, it didn't vary a great deal from what you find every day in American courts. You simply asked the defendant or the plaintiff, whoever it is, what the answer is to certain questions. That's basically what direct examination is.

Cross-examination is something else. Cross-examination is unknown in continental law. [There] the judge asks the questions. The defendants are never directly questioned by either attorney, that is, after the main presentation. They're questioned only by their attorney in presenting their case. If there are any questions to be raised, the judge raises them. It took the Germans some time to get used to that because obviously they had to do the same thing with American witnesses, if there were American witnesses, or witnesses who would testify counter to their own case. Cross-examination is a very potent weapon, of course, for the American attorney. That's how you bring out information that you wouldn't otherwise get, and I don't think some of the Germans ever mastered that. Others did.

Had you done criminal law previously, as a litigator?

No, I did not. I had only done corporation law, and that involved a lot of hearings in which there were presentations, but very little cross-examinations, as a matter of fact. I think most of my hearings were before government agencies of one kind or another, and only relatively few were [in] courts of law.

So that was a problem for the German lawyers. They probably tried the patience of the judges and some of the American attorneys when they tried to cross-examine, because they didn't understand the limits, and the American judges were always turning them off and telling them, "You can't do that. That's beyond the scope," and so on. That was more or less a constant problem throughout. Some of them, as I say, mastered it quickly; others did not. There was no way that we could transform the system to the continental system and have the judges ask the questions. That just wasn't in the cards, and no one ever thought of doing it.

Could you talk about your cross-examination of Kurt Rothenberger? Was that the turning point in the case?

Yes, he was an interesting person in the sense that he was very ambitious party-wise. He was a district court judge in Hamburg, and he made himself known to the party officials by starting a circulatory publication which he called *Judges' Letters*. In that, he took upon himself the task of finding cases in the German court system that were very good examples and very bad examples of what a Nazi judge should do. Naturally, all the cases he cited were pleasing to the party, and as a result, he made progress up the ladder. [It wasn't] always, I think, favorable to the rest of the judges because I detected immediately at least a lukewarm attitude toward him.

What he was saying at the time was simply repeating what he had said in the *Judges' Letters*. One of the questions was, "You say you didn't encourage this sort of thing? You said you wanted all judges to judge like the *führer*." I asked him then, "Well, if you wanted all judges to judge like the *führer*, aren't you saying that you wanted everybody to be a Nazi judge? You can't imagine the *führer* not being a Nazi judge, can you?" [laughs]

There were a number of questions like that. It was an amazing thing to me that he did not seem to have ever thought of that before. It just seemed from his attitude and his expression and so on, it was an absolutely new thought to him. Why would anybody question his intention? The emotional effect was far greater than anybody realized because that night after cross-examination, he attempted suicide.

Fortunately, the guard noticed it in time and he was taken to a hospital. [There was] no particular lasting damage, but after that, so far as the other defendants were concerned, I noticed a change in attitude, almost as though "the guy got what was coming to him." But nobody ever said that. [laughs]

How did you feel when you heard about the attempted suicide?

Well, it never makes one feel good, but what can you do?

Were there other defendants who stood out in your mind in that particular case?

From a virtuous point? No. There were some that stood out, but for other reasons.

This is one of the true incidents in the film [*Judgment at Nuremberg*]: It's called the Katzenberger Case, in which this Jewish merchant in Nuremberg was brought into court because of allegations that he had relations with a German girl who was 16. He had an apartment above his store, and somebody said that they saw her sitting on his lap, and that led to his arrest and trial, and [he was] charged with defiling of the German people.

She said that there were no sexual relations at all. I don't know whether that's true or not. In any event, he was eventually executed because of it. To me, there was never any proof that it happened, but then, I was never in a very good position to note that. But the way it was handled by the court in Nuremberg by Judge Rudolph Oeschey was pretty typical of what happened in many other cases throughout the country.

That is the one incident in the film that is true to life and dramatic and probably as authentic as anybody could get it. I don't think the names are the same, but Judy Garland played the girl.

Were the real trials more dramatic than the film itself?

No, I don't think so. I don't think it's possible to do that, because [in film] you can take an incident and condense it; you can concentrate on it. Take the Katzenberger Case. It was possible to do that because it happened in a fairly short period of time; it happened in one place; it happened locally, where you had local judges. The screenwriter did exceptionally well in getting the spirit of the thing. I wish he had done as well on some of the others.

In the first place, [in the film] you're dealing with one judge. The actual trial had three. And the actual trial had eventually 14 defendants. The film—what was it? Four or five. By-and-large, the film is drama-conscious. It doesn't really take into consideration anything that is not dramatic, and it adds things that never happened, of course, [like] the sequence in which Spencer Tracy meets Marlene Dietrich. Of course, that never happened. [laughs] I don't know exactly why that was put in. It may add something, but I would have preferred that it not be, because it was completely accessory to the film itself—to the actual facts themselves. As I say, the film is good entertainment, but don't ever think that that's the way it was.

I had absolutely no connection with the film. As a matter of fact, I had one call, and it may have been from one of the people who was working with a screenwriter, but he was never identified. He wanted information. I still get lots of calls. I didn't even know the picture was being shot. When it came out, I recalled that this particular caller wanted information about—I've forgotten now what it was—probably on sterilization. Some part of the picture that was prominent. I think maybe that was it, but I can't say for sure. So I didn't have any part in the picture.

How did you feel about seeing yourself portrayed?

Not very well. [laughs] I thought it was terrible.

I think we looked pretty stupid. Maybe that's the way it should be. [laughs] I also felt [it was] very unfortunate that Henry Einstein, who presumably was in the picture, was not given the sort of treatment that he should have been. I thought he was made to look very stupid, and that wasn't the case.

Did you think that the outcome of the trial was fair?

Yes, I did. The problem in selecting defendants in the situation that we had [is] you don't have very much solid evidence. All you have is rumors and possibilities. You don't have a track record on very many of them. Some of them you do, but most of them you do not, so that when you get around to the proof, which was our job, it's pretty hard to come by. In some cases, we may have missed crucial evidence against them, but I don't think so. I think the people that were acquitted actually did not take the part in what the indictment said they did. That was unfortunate for them, of course, but I don't know any way to avoid it, because it happens in American trials, too, where you have better access to evidence before the trial begins. We had to draw the indictments, actually without any information at all, except documents. Some interviews from the IMT were available. I think in one or two cases we probably used them, but for the most part, we just used documents. We had to make our selections on that basis.

The film brought up the issue of sterilization, but the actual trial didn't. Do you think that that was a double standard since our Supreme Court had ruled in favor of it, in some cases?

That was our mistake. Sterilization was a big factor in a lot of the German treatment of the feeble-minded; sometimes [for] people with the wrong political ideas, too. How sterilization would help that, I don't know.

There were so many cases of [sterilization] that we felt that it was an indictable offense, not knowing, at that point, what the American courts had said. There was a Supreme Court case [*Buck v. Bell*, 1927] in which Justice [Oliver Wendell] Holmes decided that sterilization was perfectly legitimate in some cases. If you have a long series of feeble-minded offspring, it's about time to end the whole thing. We got into that, and we were wrong.

The film, of course, makes a big point of that, too much of a point, I think. Nevertheless, they were right and we were wrong, because there wasn't, so far as American jurisprudence is concerned, American court decisions that upheld it. Would it be the same today? I don't know. Probably not.

Did you stay for any other trials?

No. After the trial there was necessarily some clean-up work to do. They appealed, they had the right to appeal. They did appeal, and we had to get those out of the way. They were more or less formal appeals. They had the right, but there wasn't very much that they could appeal from. I think probably the degree of fairness in which the trial was conducted is the main basis that they would have had. And nobody could ever question that because it was a very open trial—all of them [were]. The subsequent trials were very open trials. So [there was] no question of unfairness.

In the meantime, I was asked to make some selections for inclusion in the book on the case. I did. I tried to pick out representative defendants, and— well, I think I covered all the defendants in one way or another, and the highlights of testimony and cross-examination. Also, I included the indictment, the opening statement, the judgment, and, I think, possibly a statement on the appeals. But other than that it was testimony, representative documents, and the three major items that I mentioned.

How much contact did you have with Telford Taylor?

Telford Taylor is a very smart man. He's a Harvard graduate. He was an attorney for [the] FCC—Federal Communications Commission—before the war. And [he had] a tremendous personality. But for one reason or another, he was not interested in the Justice Case, and I did not realize why until recently.

Actually you guys were responsible for it because my youngsters never had much interest in Nuremberg until this dedication [of the Thomas J. Dodd Research Center] came up. One of my daughters, an administrator at Manchester Community College, said that she wanted to find out what happened. So she got a pamphlet by Telford Taylor, which was written in 1949. I had not seen it before, and after she finished, I picked it up, looked through it, and I came across his description of his reaction to the Justice Case. He said it was of very great interest to the lawyers. But he said the people that he really wanted to see tried—the chief justices of the People's Court—either had committed suicide, were killed in the war, or died naturally before the trial. He said because of that no one had much interest in the case. So that was a mystery, you see, that I had always wondered about. I know he was there for the opening statement. I know he was there for the closing statement. But I don't remember seeing him very many times in the meantime.

You have to remember that there were other trials going on, and he certainly had more interest in those than he did in the Justice Case. There were two or three military trials, trials of military generals, in which he was very much interested; also a trial of the doctors, which he had an interest in. He spent his time with those. I'm sure he was aware of what was going on, but he simply was not a frequent visitor.

Who did you report to?

My immediate superior was a chap by the name of Charlie LaFollette, who came from Washington. At first I was very disappointed because Telford had told me when we had first talked, that I'd be handling a case. After I was assigned the Justice Case, he told me that Mr. LaFollette would be in charge. I'm not the sort of chap who kicks over the traces that easily, but I was not very happy about it.

When Mr. LaFollette came I was even less happy because his legal background was certainly not that great. He was a congressman who had been defeated in the election of 1944, and he wanted a job, and with his political background, he got one. So I figured we had to put up with him. Actually, he turned out to be a very all-right guy.

One thing above everything else, which is so often untrue of people in situations like that, he knew what he didn't know. When he knew that he didn't know it, he didn't try to bull his way through. "You guys handle this. I don't know about it. I don't want to know about it. That's it." So a very easy guy to get along with, and I am very respectful of him.

You mentioned that you knew Tom Dodd at that time, but not very well.

Yes. It came about in this fashion. He was there for IMT, you know, and when the IMT was over, he disappeared very quickly. Incidentally, he and Taylor did not get along at all. If you ever read Taylor's book [*The Anatomy of the Nuremberg Trial*], you will find a number of scathing references to Tom Dodd. No question. [laughs]

But I met Tom Dodd almost immediately after I arrived. I was invited to join a group which had been organized and called themselves Yale-in-Nuremberg. Tom Dodd was a member of that group. We met several times—oh, three or four anyway—usually at the Grand Hotel for dinner or some other sort of festivity. Tom was there. He was always very dour, sometimes preoccupied, and not a hail fellow well met, that's for sure. I felt that I didn't really know him very well.

With respect to Nuremberg, have you ever looked back and thought about the justice that was done or not done there?

I think anyone who was at Nuremberg has to do that because, one way or another, it has become a very important milestone in many ways. Human rights and international pacts are all somehow tied in the public's mind now to Nuremberg, actually probably more so than the facts justify. But one has to look at it in terms of the kind of importance that Nuremberg has assumed since the trials. I think the ideas that have been generated are ideas that will remain. Certainly human rights and [opposition to] genocide are something we believe in as a nation. They are part of Western civilization, at this point, and we certainly embrace them. But I think in doing so, there is a real danger.

The danger is that there are some individuals who feel that because we are a powerful nation and we believe these things, that we should be a policeman to the world, and go out and defend them. I've heard that from two or three very prominent American people. I grant it does pose a bit of a dilemma. We believe it, and yet I'm saying we shouldn't go out and defend it willy-nilly, unless we have some other interest. How do I justify that? I just think that we should not be policeman to the world on those grounds. Then who does it? If you have a law, you have to enforce it; it's not worth very much unless it's enforced or enforceable. Who's going to do that? Is the United States going to do it? I don't think we should. I think that's the job of the United Nations, if it's going to be done at all. But the experience thus far has not been very good with [the] United Nations. They have not proved to be superior diplomats in dealing with these problems, nor on the battlefield, even worse. So what do we expect? Do we just mark time until something happens? Or do we say, "Well, we don't really believe that?" I agree that it's a moral dilemma for the country and for many people. That's one of the consequences that I think Nuremberg has generated, and maybe we haven't seen the last of it yet.

What lasting impact do you think Nuremberg had on your own life?

It's hard to describe, but for one thing—and whether this came solely from Nuremberg or whether it would have come otherwise—to realize how beastly people can be, the bestiality that we saw there. It's simply something that almost defies belief. And there are far too many people who say it didn't happen. But anyone who was at Nuremberg knows it did happen. You can talk to the people, see the documents, see the films. Actually, we showed some of the films in the trial of the concentration camps after the troops came in, and I saw one particular film which has been shown many times elsewhere now. I saw it briefly, and then I couldn't watch it anymore. I was just overcome. How people could do that? You know, when you see these bodies rolling like so, as a bulldozer goes along, pushing them to a mass grave, you have to wonder.

When you returned to the United States in 1952, were people impressed that you had been in Nuremberg?

I think somewhat, but not a great deal. That field was pretty well mined by Tom Dodd.

He ran for Congress [based] on [his fame from] Nuremberg when he got back, and I don't think there's a person in the state of Connecticut who didn't think that Tom Dodd ran the IMT. Not that he ever said so, but the impression certainly was that Tom Dodd was a very important person there, and he was. [There is] no question about that, but he didn't hide his light under a bushel, that's for sure.

I think [Nuremberg] was becoming [a] dormant [issue by 1952]. I am not able to judge the publicity that the trials were given. I assume that it was quite a bit. I think probably the public was saturated with it, and I can understand, like the O. J. [Simpson] trial, too much is too much, and that leads to boredom. The situation now is that almost no one knows about Nuremberg. I've had a couple of occasions to talk with high school people, and my guess is that probably two-thirds of them—maybe even more than that—never heard the name Nuremberg and connected nothing whatever with it. I don't think history people teach it. I've talked with a couple of my youngsters in college history courses, and they had nothing at all about it. It's a dead subject so far as most people are concerned. I don't think it should be, but it is.

Why do you think that's happened?

It's hard to say. It shouldn't happen because so many things have been built on it. Human rights, for example. [Opposition to] genocide. These are things that certainly everybody knows. Currently you talk to high school people about human rights, and they understand what you're saying. Although there was never anything specific about human rights that I know about spelled out in either the IMT or subsequent trials, the evidence and the documents were there, and the ideas have arisen from those, plus the fact that people wanted to have something to base their ideology on. [There is] nothing better than Nuremberg for that, because you have the full story laid out, both sides.

HENRY T. KING JR.

Prosecution Staff

Henry King gave up his job at a prestigious New York law firm to become a prosecutor at Nuremberg. His impetus was his wife's vision of sharing "a great human experience." That experience of Nuremberg became "the most important thing I ever did.... It gave me a blueprint of the world as it should be." King has continued to work for international human rights and world peace. He is also a law professor at Case Western Reserve University.

I was born in Meriden, [Connecticut] on May 27, 1919. At the time, my father was mayor of the city. He played an important role in the government of Meriden and also on the state level. In the growing-up years, my father was mayor and he was known as "Mr. Integrity." He was the only public official I've ever known to refuse a pay increase.

On Sunday nights we would discuss the major issues of the day. He would ask for comments from my mother, sister, and myself. One of the issues we discussed was, "How do you stop wars?" We were stumped for an answer. My father, having asked the question, gave his response, which was, "The people don't want wars; it's their leaders. To stop wars, you have to punish the leaders." I never forgot the answer. It's always been with me, ever since.

I was 16 at that time. I was going to Choate School which I went to for five years, and then to Yale University, and Yale Law School. So I had a Connecticut education, basically. I did law school in two years instead of the regular three.

Then I was down in New York, in the canyons of Wall Street, with the firm of Milbank, Tweed, and Hope, which was a "silk stocking" firm, meaning it was one of the best firms of the day. It certainly was one of the largest. It was very prestigious.

I was there for a year or so, and my wife said, "You'll be the world's greatest authority on corporate indentures, but there's a world out there, and we should be part of it. What we need is a great human experience, not just the legal experience for you—a joint human experience, which we can share together." With her vision and my qualifications, I was soon en route to Nuremberg. I had reasonably good qualifications because of the standing of Yale Law School.

A classmate of mine from Yale Law School came out to dinner one night, and he told us he was going [to Nuremberg], and so I wanted to share the experience. He touted it. He was very happy about going. And I was envious, until I was on the ship with him.

That law firm—I believe it's where William Jackson is. Was he there at that time?

No. Bill was a classmate of mine at Yale, and I got to know him very well at Nuremberg. He's the son of the chief prosecutor, and I played tennis from time to time with Bill. I was president of the "Yale Club in Nuremberg," and he was a member.

[The club] used to get together frequently at the Grand Hotel, which is where Hitler and his minions had stayed and played. I remember our dinners.

Was your wife part of the trial, too?

When I got there, no wives were allowed to go with us. I moved heaven and earth to get her there, and finally succeeded. The problem was that they were short on billets, and they didn't want to be responsible, I suppose. But I did talk the authorities into allowing my wife to come. But [it took] six months.

She was at the proceedings every day. She's one of the few wives who did; perhaps the only wife who attended all the sessions. I can't document what the other wives did. But she was there far more than the average wife.

I got to Nuremberg in March of 1946. The major trial was going on, and it went on until October. I was working for Telford Taylor; he was responsible for preparing the General Staff and High Command Case. I worked on the tail end of [the IMT] and I worked on the brief and documentation for the General Staff and High Command Case.

The tribunal was concerned about what the people did, but it said that they were not a cohesive group. So it found them not guilty as an organization, but there were plans for trying them individually, and I was given—by Telford Taylor—three cases to develop.

One was the case against Walter von Brauchitsch, who was the commander-in-chief of the German army. Another one was against Heinz Guderian, who was the founder of modern tank warfare, and also subsequently, a chief of staff of the German army [head of the *Panzer* forces]. And [Field Marshal] Erhard Milch, who was deputy commander-in-chief of the *Luftwaffe*, and who led the *Luftwaffe* in the Battle of Britain.

Now, two of these cases were turned over to other people. It was decided that the British would try von Brauchitsch rather than the Americans, and it was projected that Guderian be tried by the Poles because he'd done lots to destroy Warsaw. He got as far as Berlin, and we got into a dispute with the Poles on the proper boundary between East Germany and Poland. So he never got transferred anywhere. He went back to North Germany and organized a neo-Nazi party. He was not tried.

I was a primary developer of the case against Erhard Milch, and the Milch case was started in December 1946, and then tried in the winter and early spring of 1947. Milch was found guilty and was given a life sentence at Rebdorf Prison, outside of Munich. He appealed his case to the Supreme Court of the United States, and on a four to four decision, they refused to consider overturning the Milch verdict.

I also worked on other cases—the Ministries Case and other cases. But my real focus was on the Milch Case.

Why was the Milch Case, with only one defendant, one of the first of the subsequent trials after the IMT?

Telford Taylor gave a lot of people assignments. Then, after a month or two, he said, "Which cases are ready?" I raised my hand. I said, "The Milch Case is ready." And James McHaney said that the [Medical] Case was ready. He [Taylor] needed to get some cases going, and mine was either the first case or the second.

It's between McHaney and myself as to who went first, but certainly those are the two cases. I remember raising my hand and saying that my case is ready. So that's why it went on right away.

I have several recollections [of that trial]. One of Milch himself, who was a person who looked like you and me. I saw him every day in court. He knew that I had prepared the case against him. He was very intelligent. But the documents showed that he had been involved in some terrible crimes in the slave labor area. Milch was one of my vivid recollections because he was the only defendant, and the whole focus was on him. He had a very able defense counsel: Friedrich Bergold, who defended the Jehovah's Witnesses in the Hitler era, and who also defended Martin Bormann in the first trial. Bergold and Milch are my most important memories from the courtroom in that case. Obviously I have memories of meeting Hermann Göring and Albert Speer, particularly Speer. I am working on a book about Albert Speer.

I think that it was a hard-fought case because sometimes it's hard to connect the defendant with the crime, even though you have reason to believe he's guilty. The Central Planning Board ran Germany's war economy. Now, Milch's remarks at the meetings of the Central Planning Board, of which he was a member, were documented for permanent historical record. Basically what we did was use his remarks to convict him. One judge quoted parts of these minutes from sections of the closing statement that I worked on and prepared. Basically, I did the first draft of this statement. Another judge, Judge [Michael] Musmanno, wrote a long concurring opinion. He used the very quotes from Milch in the meetings of the Central Planning Board, which we had cited, against Milch.

[Milch] would say, "Let's punish slave laborers in a certain way"—usually in terrible terms—or, "We used Russian prisoners of war in the armaments industry," which is a straight prohibition. There's a straight prohibition against that under the conventions governing the conduct of warfare. So we really convicted Milch with the documents.

My section of the case that I prepared and worked on was the *Jaegerstab*, which was concerned with labor for the underground aircraft factories, where thousands of Hungarian Jews were used. The conditions were very bad in the underground aircraft factories because they were underground, the cold was penetrating, they were poorly fed, poorly clothed; the most unfortunate conditions. That was my section of the case. I think he [Milch] was convicted with good reason, both by the documentation and what we could drag out of the witnesses.

Did you meet Albert Speer in connection with this case?

Yes, because Speer was the chairman of the Central Planning Board, and Milch was a member. The reason I met Speer was I tried to get evidence against Milch from Speer, but Speer said that he took full responsibility for everything and that Milch's role was secondary. But the problem for Milch was that we had his remarks at these meetings, which showed that he fully participated. But Speer was not going to avoid responsibility. That was his approach in the whole trial.

He could have testified, but I didn't use him because he didn't say the things I wanted to have him say against Milch.

We sat there, in the room, about five o'clock in the afternoon. Speer was drawing a silhouette of a woman with a black shawl, sitting in a chair against the sky. She looked as though the world was coming to an end. I complimented him on his artwork, and I told him that my mother was an artist, and my mother-in-law was an artist, and thereupon we started a major dialogue.

We would discuss his relationship with Hitler. I found him to be a window into Hitler's soul. He was the only one who really took an analytical view of Hitler. Göring, when I saw him, seemed to think that Hitler had the answers,

170

Albert Speer, Hitler's minister of armaments and war production, served a prison sentence of 20 years for war crimes and crimes against humanity. Henry King developed a long-term dialogue with Speer after interrogating him in connection with the Milch Case.

"I found him to be a window into Hitler's soul. He was the only one who really took an analytical view of Hitler." —Henry King Jr.

and in the long run Germany would discover that he had the answers; maybe 50 years down the pike, but that there was no question that Adolf Hitler was right in what he did. That's a different approach from Speer, who said, "I'm responsible for some terrible crimes that have been committed. Here I am."

A recent book about Speer says that he would accept responsibility in a general sense, but not in specifics, and that he was not a compassionate person.

I don't know. I found it different. For instance, I had a running series of letters with him, dealing with my son who was autistic. He was very sympathetic toward him. I remember during our last visit, just before [Speer] died, he was quite thoughtful.

We were en route to Heidelberg, where he was staying. We were staying at Nuremberg to revisit the courtroom with my son. Speer told me he had been forgotten by the German populace; that he was a nonperson. We visited the courtroom and then came back to the hotel, and the telephone operators were in a turmoil: "Mr. King, Mr. King, Albert Speer has called you." They said, "You've got to call him at 5:30." When I called him he said, "Where are you staying in Heidelberg?" I said, "Well, we're staying at such-and-such a hotel." He said, "When you come to Heidelberg, you need a sense of the history there. It's a thousand years old. You have to stay at a hotel where you get a sense of that history." I said, "Well, that hotel is the Hotel Hirsch. We tried it and couldn't get in there." He said, "Well, I have no influence, but let me call you back in about a half-hour." He called us back in about a half-hour and he said, "I've got you a suite at the Hotel Hirsch. I want to have you sense the antiquity of the place, so that you soak up the atmosphere." So I'm not sure that I agree with [the author]. I haven't read the book though. I would have to read it.

You went back to revisit the courtroom. Why was that?

I wanted to give my son a sense of what it was like to see the physical set-up and to revisit something that was very important in my life. Of course, Nuremberg at that time, wanted to forget. It's changed now but for a while there wasn't even a postcard mention of Nuremberg.

Nuremberg was selected for the trials because this was the location of the [Nazi] party headquarters, and also where the party rallies were staged. [The Germans] are coming to grips with the fact that it was not an indictment of the city as such, but just a point in history where the blueprint for the future became a reality, or at least a projected reality. That's why I wanted to have him [my son David] see Nuremberg.

There was only one waiter at the Grand Hotel who waited on me earlier, and I had a nice talk with him. I used to get up very early—about five o'clock in the morning—and then I went down the minute the dining room opened at six, and then I would walk to the courthouse.

One of my colleagues said, "You drove the secretaries crazy because you did so much writing," and that's true. I made heavy demands on secretaries because I did write some of the closing and opening statements for the United States of America at Nuremberg—the first drafts anyway.

Did you have much contact with Germans?

In Nuremberg at that time, contact was quite restricted because, of course, you had the army around all the while. Obviously they wanted to make sure that nothing happened, and they wanted to make sure the trials came off.

I would say that my primary contacts were with people in the international sector—the Russians, the English, not much with the French—and with Americans. We had a cadre of people who were living at the Grand Hotel, and because of the fact that there weren't many other places to go, your social life would be restricted to the Grand Hotel. After the courtroom, you went into the bar and had a few drinks, and then after that, everybody went into the Marble Room at the Grand Hotel, with a magnificent orchestra under Koenig, which is "king" in German, and had dancing every night. That was quite an interesting context in which to do this.

But I did quite a little talking to German youth groups. I tried to convince them that it was important to have the trials. Obviously, Germany was going to be very strong, and you had to have some people who understood what it was all about; that we were not just the victors trying the vanquished.

I went to the Special Services [to arrange these talks]. I remember giving a talk right across the street from the Grand Hotel. I don't know how many talks I gave, but I tried to explain it to them.

What was your general sense of the Germans' attitude towards Americans?

One of the things you have to keep in mind was that in the first place, the German people were not anti-American as such. They didn't like the Soviets and we got the benefit of that. The other point was that no matter who you talked to, there were no avowed Nazis there. In other words, nobody ever admitted that they were a Nazi. So you wondered about these huge crowds, tremendous crowds, who made Hitler what he was, who wouldn't let him drive on the street, who made him a public figure without parallel in Germany. How did he get these huge crowds when the people we saw said, "Well, I had nothing to do with it"? I think there was a lot of denial there. They were not coming to grips with what the reality was.

Is that why you wanted to do the talks?

Yes, but that's a hard proposition, when you're also responsible for these cases. I don't know whether it had an effect, but I tried it. The thing that impressed me at that time was that everybody would whisper in your ear, "Well, I really was opposed to Hitler, and I did this and that." But then you have the fact of life that Hitler carried off some very important activities which required at least public acquiescence. To me, that represents a denial. Now, it may be they feared possible prosecution.

Germans respect authority, and the trials were authority. I think given the German mentality, they did have some [educational] effect. I'm not at all sure that it was as comprehensive as we would have liked it. The reason Hitler got so far is that when he was *führer*, he represented authority, and nobody would challenge him. That's a very important aspect of the German social context. So I think they did have some effect. After all, some of the principles of Nuremberg are incorporated into the constitution under which current Germany operates today.

When you got back to the States, how was that, after being in this proceeding?

I had trouble getting a job because Robert Taft, who was a senator from Ohio, had muddied the water on Nuremberg. He said it was *ex post facto*, that these Nazis didn't know that what they were doing was criminal when they did it, and that it was the victors trying the vanquished. And that hurt me. I finally got a job, but he had muddied the water a lot. I don't think of Taft as an authority on international affairs, although he developed a lot of competence in domestic affairs. I think his credibility in the international [arena] is very, very circumscribed.

How often do you think of Nuremberg?

Every day. No day goes by that I don't think of it.

I think the important thing is that this was a golden moment in history, to try to get something done. The Cold War has ended, and we've seen some terrible crimes in [the former] Yugoslavia. I think it's very important that we seize these moments of opportunity to create institutions which will outlive the lifetime of any individual, and make for a better world. I cite the EEC—European Economic Community—which is an institutionalized arrangement on an economic basis of the continent of Europe. You have a court over there; you have administration. They've given up some sovereignty, but it doesn't make that much difference.

The bugaboo beating the advocates of an international system whereby a rule of law would be established in the world is sovereignty. I think sovereignty is an illusion in today's world, brought together by trade and communications as we are. We ought to be realistic and say, "Well, we are interconnected with other nations. If we give up a limited amount of sovereignty we'll have a structure for peace in the world." The international institutions can't exist without some cession of sovereignty from the United States and other countries. Now, I don't think this is bad. I think it's very good, obviously. I think that then you can eliminate some of these surprises that we have, whether it's Bosnia or Rwanda, or potentially Korea, or certainly in the Middle East, with Saddam Hussein in Iraq.

What about the effect that Nuremberg has had on your career or on your own life?

It's the most important thing I ever did. It's been my guiding light. It gave me a blueprint of the world as it should be. I have that every day in front of me. I know what has to be done. I want to do it. The main problem is I've also had to make a living.

But I've done an awful lot in that direction. When I was head of the international section of the American Bar Association, which is the brass ring in the international legal profession, in the United States at least, I worked towards the adoption of the international human rights conventions by the United States. I believe also that a way to stop wars is to develop arbitration provisions which enable countries to settle disputes peacefully between each other and with others. And that's the route that I'm working intensively on.

I developed an initiative of the American and Canadian Bar Associations, and later the Mexican Bar Association, whereby we would make proposals for the settlement of disputes between the three countries, and many of these proposals went into the free trade agreement with Canada, and also in the NAFTA [North American Free Trade Agreement]. I'm U.S. chairman of that group.

I found another thing is that to move the dialogue on, you have to be part of large organizations that have clout, that have a constituency, like the American Bar Association. The United States Senate takes very great heed of what the American Bar Association says on international issues. What I wanted to do was to help to shape the context by getting inside the ABA and getting my ideas across. And not be on the outside looking in.

What do you think about President Clinton's proposal for a world court?

Marvelous. It was a 10-strike for the University of Connecticut to get President Clinton up here [for the opening of the Thomas J. Dodd Research Center]. It was a magnificent step to a more secure world for him to endorse the current war crimes trials at The Hague. That's the first time an American president has ever done that, outside of Harry Truman, who endorsed the concept of Nuremberg. Harry Truman was one of our truly great presidents.

At the same time, we also had the president of the United States endorsing the concept of an international criminal court, which is very important. We now have a number of people such as Ben Ferencz and myself, who are really pushing the concept very hard. You have to institutionalize peace initiatives so that they're extant for future generations. They can't be totally dependent on the momentum created by particular individuals. That's the value of the European community institutions, which have been with us for a long while.

It's very important to capture the vision of Nuremberg as [Justice Robert] Jackson had it, and institutionalize it now, when the time is right. That's really what has to be done to immortalize Nuremberg. It's the most important trial that's ever been held. Over and above the twentieth century, it's the most important trial ever.

I think there's a lot of potential good that can come out of Nuremberg for the future. But the time is now to get something going. Even if you don't bite the whole bullet, you bite a piece of the bullet and you put some crimes in, see how it works, and then you feed more in. Like, you start with genocide, which everybody agrees is a crime. Then you can put more in, after you see how that operates. Or you start with whatever crimes we're most unanimous about.

I think that's the future. Slow, progressive dealings with the problem of sovereignty, meeting it in such a way that you feel as though you got something going. Then look at it on the basis of experience. How does it work out? Maybe later on you want to put additional crimes in, but only after you see how it works out.

Why has it taken 50 years after Nuremberg to talk about proposals like a world court?

You had the Cold War, where the United States and Russia—the two superpowers of the world—didn't trust each other, and one country would try to institute trouble with the other in the undeveloped world, and the other would do the reverse. The importance of the here and now is that we don't have that type of thing going on. You have mutual trust between these two superpowers, and now's the time to strike. We couldn't do it for 50 years because of the Cold War.

Do you have any other thoughts about your experience at Nuremberg?

I think the important thing is that there's meaning to my experience. My wife had the vision that you could live a life in the here and now, you could be a very, very good journeyman lawyer, but if you wanted to see the stars, you had to climb the mountains. At Nuremberg, I got a sense of the blueprint of the world, the future, the way it ought to look, and I became an idealist because I had the vision. I knew what had to be done. I had time to see the stars, and to have some vision myself, and to try and work for the achievement of the goal, with a sense of mission.

JOURNALISTS

HAROLD
BURSON

*American Forces
Network Radio
Correspondent*

Harold Burson began his journalism career at the Memphis Commercial Appeal. Inducted into the army in 1944, his first assignment involved demining fields in Normandy. After the war ended, Burson was transferred to the American Forces Network for which he wrote a daily radio program on the International Military Tribunal (IMT) trial. "Certainly before the first week was over I recognized that [straight news of the Nuremberg Trial] was not going to be able to sustain 15 minutes every day." To encourage listener interest, Burson added feature interviews to his news format. After leaving Nuremberg, Burson founded the public relations firm of Burson-Marsteller, where he is still chairman.

I was born in Memphis, Tennessee, 1921. My parents had come to the United States from England just prior to my arrival. My father had been in the British army for five years, during World War I. To say that I came from a family of modest means would be to overstate it.

I grew up in Memphis. Either good or bad, my father taught me how to read by the time I was four years old, so I started school in the third grade, and graduated from high school at 15.

At one point, [my father] had a hardware store that during the Depression went bust. He had various odd jobs. He was really not very successful, from a financial standpoint, although he was a very good father. My mother was really the support of the family. She sold clothes and the family eked out a living. That's about all. I started working when I was about 13 on *The Commer-*

cial Appeal in Memphis—the morning paper. I started as a copy boy, worked summers filling in, doing different odd jobs, writing obituaries, covering the wrestling matches, and things like that, that no one else wanted to do. The reason I went to [the] University of Mississippi is that I knew that if I went there, I could be the campus correspondent to *The Commercial Appeal,* get paid 14 cents a column inch. I could, on 59 or 60 dollars a month, literally go to school, back in 1936, when I entered Ole Miss. So that's my reason for going there to school. I was able to pay my way through school. At one point, in the middle of my junior year, I also became the acting director of the college news bureau, which started pointing me [toward] public relations.

I graduated in 1940, and immediately went to work for *The Memphis Commercial Appeal* as a reporter—25 dollars a week—and was hoping that someone, at some point, would rescue me and get me out of Memphis. At that time, anyone who felt that he or she had writing ability wanted to go to one of two places, either Hollywood or New York. New York appealed to me more, and eventually, I interviewed [with] somebody—a head of a very large company—who offered me a job, and I came to New York in early 1942.

The war was on at that time. I was with a large engineering building firm, which started getting me deferments because this company was engaged totally in war work. As an indication of how times have changed, I went to my boss in the latter part of 1943 and said, "I don't want this war to end before I'm in uniform." I literally asked to be drafted. The efficient classification system that the army had at that time, seeing that I was working for an engineering building firm, put me in a combat engineer group.

I was inducted in early 1944, and was in Normandy about eight weeks after the invasion. The group that I was attached to—its original job was to de-mine the hedgerows and the fields in Normandy so that the army could bring in troops. Having done that, we started going across Europe, across France, into Belgium, up into Holland, and finally into Germany.

I was able to, as the war was ending, arrange for a transfer to General Bradley's headquarters in the Press and Psychological Warfare Detachment. A month or so after the war was over, the commanding officer of that detachment, who was a colonel (I was an enlisted man) said to me, "This outfit is probably going to Japan before long. You don't have enough points to go home. So if you want to stay in Europe, you've got to find yourself a job that will keep you here."

I said to him, "Well, that means *Stars and Stripes* or *Yank* or American Forces Network." He said, "You got it. I'll try and help you." He helped get me some appointments in Paris. I went to Paris, and actually went job-hunting. The most immediate job I was offered was on the news staff of American Forces Network, which probably was the greatest radio network that ever existed, including the commercial networks in the United States. The reason for that is that we were able to draw on all of the network shows in the United States, and also from [the] BBC. We also had a very talented staff of people who had had a lot of news and radio experience.

So I was in Paris for about four months, through the summer of 1945, into the fall. The early part of November, the commanding officer of the American Forces Network, a man named Colonel John Hayes, who later became ambassador to Switzerland during the Johnson administration, called me to his office.

He said, "There's a special assignment that is very sensitive that I'd like for you to undertake." I said, "What is that?" He said, "I'd like for you to go to Nuremberg and cover the trial. We want to give this as much time as it needs, so what we thought we would do is we would start out giving you 15 minutes at nine o'clock." It seemed to me that 15 minutes was a lot of time, but he insisted on starting that way. And he said, "This thing is of such importance that the general who heads up the Information and Education Section of the army would like to meet you. He wants to talk to the person who is going to cover the trial."

It was General Paul Thompson, who later became a senior officer at *Reader's Digest*. He has now passed away. General Thompson gave me what his feelings were. He said, "We've got two missions that we want fulfilled." He said, "The first is we want the troops to know what went on in Germany, and how the Nazis [conducted] the war. The second thing is, we have tremendous evidence that the German people are now relying on AFN as their principal source of news." He said even though a relatively small percentage of the people speak or understand English, many of the leaders do. They wanted the German people to get a full dose of straight coverage.

I have a feeling that the reason the general wanted to see me personally, and talk with me, and know what my background was, is that he did not want anyone who was bringing in any ideological baggage of his own to the issue. He just wanted straight reporting. "This is what happened in the courtroom today." He did not want any interpretation. And so that's what I provided.

Did you have a sense, at that time, what the situation had been in Europe, regarding the Holocaust?

My father was very politically sensitive from the standpoint that he did a lot of reading. I grew up in a household that was very much abreast of current affairs. And also because my mother and father had come from England, there was an interest in Europe that you would not expect to find in the average poor household in Memphis, Tennessee. So like many, I knew that there were concentration camps. I am Jewish. Not in my wildest dreams would I have imagined that it was going on on the scale that it was. But even before I went into the army, I was aware that there was persecution. So I was politically aware.

I wasn't ideological. I've always regarded myself as a middle-of-the-roader. So I evidently passed the test with the general, and I was at Nuremberg for the opening of the trial.

What kind of preparation did you do before you got to the trial?

The first thing I did was I went back and started reading all the news accounts. I went to the *International Herald Tribune*. They let me into their library, and I was aware of the Nuremberg Tribunal that had been set up. I did not know in detail how it came into being, what its mandate was, but I spent the better part of a week just reading everything I could about the mechanism.

The trial started November 22, 1945. I think I left Paris for Nuremberg about the 19th. I was an enlisted man; however, I didn't wear any stripes at all. I had a correspondent's patch. When I reported in as an accredited correspondent, the person who checked me in was a young lieutenant. Apparently, they had had an overflow of correspondents and housing accommodations were really tight. So he said to me, I later found out he had also told the *Stars and Stripes* correspondent, "We're going to put you in the enlisted men's barracks, with the truck drivers and the radio people, and other support staff."

I said, "I don't think I can do my job as I should if I'm not with the other correspondents. I want to know what these other reporters and foreign correspondents are saying and thinking. It will give me a perspective that I wouldn't get being in the enlisted men's barracks."

He finally said, "Well, we'll let you have dining room privileges." But I insisted, "That's not satisfactory." He said, "Well, you'll have to talk to the colonel."

The man in charge of the press camp was a fellow who was yachting editor of *The New York Times,* named Colonel Clarence Lovejoy. We used to call him Colonel Killjoy. I told him the same story. I felt that if I were going to report this to the troops and the world at large, I should have all the privileges of a civilian correspondent.

He said, "Well, I've got to think about that." I said, "Well, I have only one alternative. And that is I'm going to call General Thompson and tell him that I'm being discriminated against, and it's affecting my ability to carry out his orders." He said, "Don't do anything rash. We will work it out."

Also, I had already learned this colonel had riled enough reporters in the days preceding the trial for them to have formed a Correspondents Committee. I found out that the chairman was Howard Smith of CBS News. Howard Smith continues today as one of my very, very dear friends. I told my story to Howard, and he said the committee would file an official protest in my behalf. Well, the outcome was that I got full privileges.

But another thing—I was in a very unique position at the trial vis-à-vis the other correspondents. The courthouse was in Nuremberg. The press headquarters were in a little town called Stein, about eight miles from Nuremberg in [the Faber] Castle. That was Eberhard Faber, from the pencil company.

He had a magnificent place that was converted into the press facility. The uniqueness of my position was that I was the only correspondent at Nuremberg who had his own Jeep. So I was able to make a lot of friends among the press corps because the provider bus transportation ran at various hours, every 15 to 30 minutes. So I had any number of friends whom I would drive back and forth to the courthouse.

What was your impression of Nuremberg, as a place?

I had been in a number of devastated cities in Germany. I left my unit in the combat engineers in mid-April. We had already reached the Rhine. I had seen Aachen and München-Gladbach and Frankfurt. Nuremberg was one of the

The old city of Nuremberg was almost completely destroyed during the war.

"[People] were living in the rubble, in the basements of houses that had been destroyed." — *Harold Burson*

two or three most devastated cities in Germany, Cologne being another one that was really on the ground, flattened.

The thing that was hard for me to realize was Nuremberg was still a city of several hundred thousand people. They were living in the rubble, in the basements of houses that had been destroyed. It was a bleak, cold winter, that winter of 1945–1946. You saw very few men. You'd see women with string bags, carrying what looked like three lumps of coal, three or four sticks of firewood, food stuff wrapped in newspaper. It was really a very tragic sight to behold.

Of course, at the courthouse, they had done a fantastic job of building a setting that looked very imposing. They had state-of-the-art technology at that time: simultaneous translation into four languages. It was more like going into a theater than [going] into a courthouse.

We had assigned seats, and I had a front row seat on the balcony, overlooking the courtroom and the boxed area containing those on trial. And so every day until I left in about mid-March, I saw Göring, I saw Hess, I saw all the defendants.

What were your impressions of the defendants, the judges, the American prosecutors, and the prosecutors from the other nations?

To start with the judges, the chief judge, Sir Geoffrey Lawrence, was a character out of Dickens, just exactly what I would have expected from a lord chief justice. He ran that court with an iron hand. Even though he was relatively short and a little stocky, he projected a sense of authority when he walked into that courtroom. You knew who was in charge, and he did it in a very nice, even-handed way. He didn't yell. He wasn't boisterous. He had a very calm voice. I felt by far he was the outstanding person on the bench. [There were] two Americans—Francis Biddle, who was the principal U.S. judge, and then we had an [alternate] judge, named Judge [John J.] Parker from North Carolina. I felt Biddle was a bright, smart man, but very pedantic, although he wasn't meddlesome. He would get off the point with his questions every now and then. The other two—the French and the Russian judges took no active role in the proceedings. They just sat there.

Among the prosecution staff, the British team was the superior team by far. The person I regarded most highly was the number two person on the British prosecution staff, Sir David Maxwell-Fyfe. He had an advantage over the Americans. He knew the European history, and in his cross-examination, he couldn't be flim-flammed. Their number one attorney who didn't stay at the trial very long was Sir Hartley Shawcross, a very erudite British barrister, but he was not nearly as impressive as David Maxwell-Fyfe.

I think the American delegation was somewhat out of its league. They just didn't have the background they really needed when they came into confrontation. I got to know Justice Jackson. I always thought he was there because he thought bigger things were ahead for him, politically. I didn't regard him as any kind of legal scholar.

What about his opening statement, which was supposed to be very good?

It was a very good opening statement. Where there were prepared statements, the Americans did well. They even did well in making their case. Where the Americans showed their weakness was whenever they got into cross-examination, because they just weren't immersed in the history, not only of what had happened in Germany at that time, but what led up to the war.

There's a lot of criticism of Jackson's cross-examination of Göring, for instance.

Göring made mincemeat out of him. As long as Justice Jackson was making the case, as long as he had a lot of young lawyers preparing the written case which was, in effect, read, I think he did very well. But when he came head-to-head—Göring was a tough witness; the military people were tough witnesses; Keitel, Jodl, Raeder; Schacht was a tough witness—he didn't hold up as well.

Did you see Tom Dodd in action?

Tom Dodd, I thought, was one of our better people. I guess, you would have to say that he was the number two American lawyer. He presented a major portion of the case. Of the American lawyers prosecuting that first case, I suspect he acquitted himself with greater distinction than any of the other American lawyers.

There was a man named [Robert] Storey from Texas. He was a railroad lawyer, and I can remember the correspondents commenting he had better get back to his railroad practice before he forgets what it's all about. Telford Taylor had not yet entered the arena. My recollection—I could be wrong—I don't think he appeared in the first case.

After the first trial was over, a lot of correspondents had had enough of Nuremberg. They began to leave. I know I was anxious to get home, after only four months. The army had a point system at the time, so I could predict the week that I was going to be discharged. I knew it was going to be at the end of May. I had a lot of leave accumulated, and I wanted to travel around Europe before I went home.

What did you do in terms of the AFN broadcast?

AFN did not have a station in Nuremberg. Munich was the closest station that we could get to. As you can appreciate, telephone lines were at a real premium. When I went to Nuremberg, I took an engineer with me. I did not broadcast. I wrote the scripts. I had a reader who read my script because my Southern accent was even more than probably you detect today. I was never a trained radio announcer type. To my great surprise and discomfort, I found out that no preparations had been made to get us from Nuremberg to our Munich transmitter. We needed a telephone line to get us to Munich. There were relatively few telephone lines in service at the time, and a lot of demand for them. I [had] to go back to General Thompson to get the problem solved just hours before our first broadcast.

There was a priority system that the army had for the use of telephone lines and other utilities. It was army military government, and they were running all the utilities. I kept getting from them, "Sorry, soldier, we just don't have any open time to give you for this purpose." I needed about 25 minutes all told, starting at about seven or eight minutes to nine [o'clock]. I called General Thompson, and he immediately got in touch with his counterpart, and they suddenly found a way to give us a line from the Nuremberg courthouse to our transmitter in Munich. We had a broadcast booth in the Nuremberg courthouse. That was not a problem. And nine o'clock at night was a good time for us because the broadcast booth wasn't in use since it was two o'clock in the afternoon in the United States, and that was a dead news hour period. It didn't start getting heated up until the six o'clock broadcast, which was after midnight in Europe. That's when the studio was busy at the courthouse. So I was able to get the land line, and every evening we went on air. The first evening, we weren't sure we were going to make it because we received approval for the line at five or six o'clock in the afternoon. I found out later that evening, through the Army Signal Corps, that there was a message congratulating me from headquarters in Frankfurt, where our headquarters were. That's the first I knew we had gotten through.

Was there any censorship?

No. I wrote it, and there was no review whatever of my script. In fact, if it will help your cause I still have all my scripts. [See Appendix B.]

It was amazing for me as a 24-year-old. I literally was in charge. I started writing when the court was over, usually around four-thirty or five o'clock in the afternoon. It took me about an hour and a half to do a 15-minute script. Then I'd have dinner. I'd always go with the announcer, and he would read my script.

The first few days we reported straight what was happening in the courtroom because it was very dramatic. Certainly before the first week was over I recognized that it was not going to be able to sustain 15 minutes every day. It was going to get very, very boring. So we developed a format where we did about a six- or seven-minute report on the trial, and then we dedicated seven or eight minutes to an interview of someone. I tried to get as many military figures as I could, who had to do with the trial. For example, the prison psychiatrist, the prison psychologist, the officer in charge of the guards. I also had the first interview with Justice Jackson. Every now and then I'd bring in a correspondent whose name was well known. So the broadcast was a combination of straight news and a feature interview. I diligently followed what was going on in the courtroom. Radio news reporting back then was very expository and straight. Today, radio and television is interpretive. We did none of that.

Did you know how the programs were going over, either from those who were higher up, or from GIs or from Germans?

The most immediate reactions I got were from the other news people covering Nuremberg. Other than the BBC, the AFN was the only radio reporting they would tune in to. My report was the only American reportage they heard. They couldn't hear the major U.S. networks. At breakfast in the morning, a correspondent would say, "You know, you had a nice angle there," and, "Tell me how to get in touch with the psychiatrist. I think I'd like to do something with him."

Who were some of the correspondents that you became friendly with?

Howard K. Smith. Walter Cronkite, whom I still see. Walter Cronkite was a junior member of the United Press team at the time. The two top people with the Associated Press, Wes Gallagher, who became the general manager after the war, and Daniel DeLuce; Dan DeLuce became a very good friend. Mark Watson of the *Baltimore Sun.* Tania Long, *New York Times.* Marguerite Higgins, the *New York Herald Tribune.* Russell Hill of the *Herald Tribune.* My counterpart from *Stars and Stripes,* and I, became very good friends, and still are. A man named Allen Dreyfus. Pauline Frederick was another. By coincidence she later married a very good friend of mine. I got to know Thomas Mann's daughter; Erica Mann was her name.

What happened after trial hours? Did people go out and have a few drinks?

There were two places to go to relax. One was the hotel in Nuremberg, which I didn't go to very frequently because the hours that I would have been there were my working hours, up to nine o'clock. I didn't get there often because we weren't through at the courthouse until about nine-thirty. It meant arriving at ten, and it would be one o'clock before I'd get home. So I didn't do that.

The place where I socialized most was at the bar at the press camp. . . . There was a lot of drinking. Some of the funniest people were the Russian correspondents. Some of them spoke fair English, but one thing they could do a lot better than the Americans was they could drink more whiskey.

Was there trust or distrust between the Americans and the Russians, at the time?

There was some degree of trust. It was a camaraderie, and I think it was the feeling on both sides.

The Americans had two feelings about the Russians. Generally, they were likable people. And we felt that they were—when they were doing their reporting, slanting their story, giving it the Soviet slant—pro-Soviet, not necessarily anti-American at the time, but certainly pro-Soviet. They were very evangelical, as far as Communism was concerned.

At the same time, I think many, if not most of us, gave them credit for being smarter than to believe what they were writing. You could never get them to be critical of their system when anybody was around them who was Russian. If you would get them off in one-on-one conversations, they would ask questions about the United States. [They would ask questions like] "Is what they are telling me in Moscow about the U.S. really true?" "Are there great pockets of poverty and hunger in the U.S.?" and questions like that. Also, they raised the social issue. I think several I got to know were sufficiently independent of mind to know they were acting out a charade in the way they were writing about the Soviet Union. I always felt that one or two of the reporters was a commissar representative, but no one knew who they were. So they were always edgy among their peer group.

The drinks were ridiculously cheap. Ten or 15 or 20 cents, but the Russians had little money. After they bought the first drink, they were out of the game. They were dependent on the rest of the correspondents and we came through for them.

Did you have much interaction with Germans?

Very little. Mainly, the Germans I worked with were the technicians who put us on the air, the engineering staff. I sent our own engineer home, back to his base because the Germans were very skilled, so we depended on Germans to get us on the air.

There were a couple of bars not far from the courthouse, which were basically patronized by GIs. There would always be a bunch of German women in there, and very few German men. Our only contact, more or less, was with these German women.

Was there a lot of anti-American feeling at the time?

No, none whatsoever because the Americans were their source [of] anything tangible: extra food, blankets, soap, cigarettes. There was very little in their own economy—not only in Nuremberg, but all over Germany. At that time, the Germans felt very subservient. They were really a defeated people.

And again, it was a 70, 75 percent female society. The men, even after the war was over, were kept in [POW] camps for months. You just didn't see very many men in Germany.

What were your living conditions like?

As an American soldier after the war, they were usually pretty good. What happened was that the army commandeered the buildings that had not been damaged, and moved people out. So we lived in nice apartments, usually. At Nuremberg, I lived in converted servants' quarters that became nice bedrooms. There was a communal bathroom for the correspondents. The dining room was in a beautiful long room in the castle, and the food was pretty good.

Did you get into the prison at all?

No, I never did. I tried to, but I never did. What I wanted to do in one of my broadcasts was to pull a shift as a guard. Colonel [Burton] Andrus, who ran the prison, was just afraid to let me do it. He thought that no matter how delicately or sensitively I handled the broadcast, this would be a stunt. I was very upset at the time that he wouldn't let me do it. But looking back on it, with a more mature perspective, I think he was right. I wanted to go in and do guard duty—I think it was a two-hour shift—and then report on what the prison was like and how the defendants acted. But it was not to be.

When you departed, what were your feelings about leaving?

Well, I was of two minds. My going-in impression was, "This is mankind's opportunity to establish a rule of law that can be universal, and can serve as a deterrent against genocide, against people committing aggression and planning aggression, a deterrent against crimes against humanity."

As time went on, and by the time I left, I thought that Stalin and Churchill had the right idea. About the only thing that they ever agreed on was that they ought to have a quick court-martial for the defendants and then take them out and shoot them. This became very apparent when the defense started. I got to know a couple of the defense lawyers, and they were at such a handicap in representing their clients. They depended on the prosecution for every document that they needed. They did not have the staffs to back them up that the prosecution had. So here it was, the might of four nations, with all their resources against these 20 lawyers who, I think, were paid by the Allied Commission. But we didn't give them any real resources, we didn't give them any real places to work, and they had nothing themselves, no commercial facilities.

I think justice was done, but I don't think it should have taken the better part of a year—10 months—to arrive at the decisions they arrived at. Telford Taylor's book analyzed the deliberations that were going on behind the scenes, which I was not aware of at the time. There were a lot of trade-offs. It got very political. [The correspondents] were always speculating who was going to get the death penalty and who deserved to get it, and who [was] not going to get it. I guess the one that surprised me in getting [off] totally free was Schacht.

I think he tried to present himself as not being part of the cabal, that he brought expertise, which they used, but he never embraced what they did. But the fact was that he really provided the financing that enabled Hitler to carry out his atrocities. I don't believe Hans Fritzsche should ever have been there. He was there because Goebbels had killed himself.

You mentioned that you got to know some of those defense lawyers. Was there anyone special that you remember?

The lawyer for Speer. I can't remember what his name is. I talked to him several times.

He was not [a former Nazi] but there were several who were. The interesting thing is that those lawyers who had been active Nazi party members were pretty much ostracized by the lawyers who were clean. I'd say there were probably four or five of them who had strong Nazi records. The other lawyers would not consider themselves a part of this circle. And the lawyers also—the two or three that I talked to—felt that most of the people in that dock should be given the death penalty. They had very little compassion for them. Speer's lawyer got what he wanted out of it, and that was to save his client's life, and get him a relatively short sentence. But I think most of them were going through motions and felt they had to do this. They were public defenders.

You were going back home in March. What was closing up shop like?

They appointed a successor to me, actually, a soldier who did very well at NBC in Washington for a number of years—Herb Kaplow. I had had about as much of it as I wanted at that time. Göring testified; Hess, Ribbentrop, Keitel. But after Keitel testified, it was more and more of the same. Göring was a fascinating one. Many of us correspondents speculated if he had been running the show, the Allies would have had a much harder time because he was smart.

When you came home, how much consciousness was there of the Nuremberg Trials? Were people tuned into it? Did they have an interest that you had been there?

Who reads about foreign affairs matters in the newspaper today? You start out with a relatively small percentage of people. But that small percentage of the people usually are the upper-scale people, and there's a lot of interest in foreign affairs then. There was interest, most of my friends knew there was a

Nuremberg Trial, for the first 15 years, maybe. My business associates were in awe that I covered the Nuremberg Trial. So in the circle I moved in, it was a credential. But in the big scheme of things, I think it was just a little blip that happened.

What did you do immediately after leaving the army?

I got out of the army on May 28, 1946, and I went home to Memphis and spent June and July, and returned to New York in August, and started a [public relations] business that consisted of myself and a shared secretary. And that has ended up where I am now.

[We have] 2,000 people around the world, 35 countries.

You know, I wish that Nuremberg had had more impact as a precedent than it seems to have had. Every now and then, you know, you will hear Nuremberg cited, but to my knowledge it has not deterred very many people from doing what they want to do.

What has been your impression of fictional or historical accounts of Nuremberg, compared to your actual experience?

I think from a standpoint of physical context, they got it right. *Judgment at Nuremberg*, particularly, portrays a bit of pageantry in that courtroom. Well, there was. Right in back of where I sat was a visitors' gallery, and there were visitors from all over who were coming there every day, and they would find this scene awesome, to hear these people—they could almost touch them—who committed, perpetrated all these vile acts. So I think it probably served a purpose in exposing the guilt of the German hierarchy and the willingness of so many Germans that followed them. But I think it was short-lived, and now you've got people denying the Holocaust ever even took place.

But I think it's a story that has to be continually told. People don't like to remember unpleasant things, particularly about themselves. We, in America, have a feeling that the only revolution that was ever justified was the [American] one in 1776. And they totally forget what we did to the Indians. Would I have wanted to miss [the Nuremberg] experience? Absolutely not.

What lasting effect has it had on your life?

I guess I have to take that in two parts. One is very personal, as far as I was concerned. And that is, I was very gratified that at age 24 or 25 I could hold my own with the best correspondents writing for the best news media in the world. So it gave me a sense of confidence in my ability.

The other thing, as far as what I do for a living is it was a model for getting people to do what you wanted them to do through imagery, through direction, through sloganeering. You know, vile things that demigods can [make] happen, and they're sustained by effective propaganda. This can be very, very scary. If you've got the resources, you can move people almost anywhere you want to move them. This really is the basis of fascism as well as Communism. It goes through both ends of the political spectrum.

ANDY LOGAN

Correspondent for The New Yorker

Andy Logan's earliest job out of college was at *The New Yorker* as the first female "Talk of the Town" correspondent. She accompanied her husband, Charles Lyon, a prosecutor at the subsequent proceedings, to Nuremberg. Logan reported for *The New Yorker* on the devastation and drama of the events she witnessed. Logan found that "life became the courthouse" because there was not much else to do other than visit ruins and tolerate the antipathy of hostile Nuremberg civilians. Logan continued to write for *The New Yorker* for over 50 years.

I was born in Cleveland, Ohio, but I was raised mostly in North Carolina, western North Carolina, in the mountains, where the Blue Ridge meets the Smokies. I went to school there, mostly, and some in Ohio, and then went to Swarthmore College. And from there—the next day after I got out, I went to *The New Yorker*.

I was the first woman "Talk of the Town" reporter. So I broke new ground there, I guess. And I've been there ever since. Part of the scenery, I guess.

What brought you to The New Yorker?

In my spring vacation, I had come there and talked to William Shawn, who was then the managing editor. And he said, "Come to see me after you get out." I had done a short story that was in the O. Henry collection. A short story in one anthology keeps being chosen for others, it seems. Somerset

Maugham put it in his collection. But I never wrote much more fiction. At any rate, when I saw Shawn after graduation, he said I could start right away and mentioned that I would be the first woman. It wasn't that I was so brilliant, but it was June 1942, and America was in the war. All the men they would have hired in the old days, as was their practice, were in danger of being drafted. So I came along at what for me was a very lucky time. Actually, *The New Yorker*'s commitment to hiring women was quite tentative. I was the only woman reporter there for close to three years.

What did your parents do?

My father was in the aviation business, and a lawyer. And my mother, as was often the case in those days, did not work outside the home, although she did later. She was a college dean in Hillsdale, Michigan.

You came to The New Yorker *during the war. Can you just describe what it was like at that time?*

Actually, for Americans the war had barely begun. We were just adjusting, as was *The New Yorker*, which would never again, I think, be thought of as primarily a humor magazine. The staff was very small then. I was stunned later to realize *The New Yorker* was only 17 years old when I went to work there. It had started in 1925. We were all on one floor; it was great from the beginning.

[Harold Ross] was the editor for nine years while I was there. I knew him very well. He was always great to me. As, of course, was [William] Shawn, who then became the editor in 1952.

What kinds of things were you writing, and how did you get to Nuremberg?

Well, I was writing "Talk of the Town." Every old thing. Sometimes I would cover all the pieces in "Talk of the Town" because there weren't so very many people. And I did longer pieces including a profile of a man who had the crazy idea that cigarettes cause cancer. But how I got to Nuremberg is very simple. My husband [Charles Lyon] became a prosecutor there.

I said, "Can I go on and do pieces from there?" They said, "Sure." So I did. And that was the story. Not very ambiguous. [laughs]

When did you first get to Nuremberg?

July 1946. Charles went some months earlier. I did a short article in *The New Yorker*, on the trip over on the Queen Mary, which until then had been bringing war wives back with their babies. It was funny how easily the cruise director atmosphere took over again.

What was Nuremberg like when you got there? You did one piece where you were looking down from the hill and you said it sort of looked like the inside of a decayed tooth.

Oh, that was right. It was devastated. You had the feeling they would never get back. Of course they did. It must have broken their hearts, of course, to have the old city be bombed.

What kinds of things were happening?

The main trial, of course, was still going on. It ended in October. I was there when the hangings took place. I was part of the huge press corps. It wasn't large compared to [the coverage of the] O. J. [Simpson trial], but it was large. And, of course, even more international. And I was there watching the trial and going to the trial, going through the prison there, which was at the courthouse.

We lived in the Grand Hotel, and the bath mat said, *Gasthaus Reichsparteitag*. It was in Nuremberg that the Nazis held their big rallies, as you remember. Of course, the one in 1938 was almost sexual. Rudolf Hess with the sweat gleaming on his brow and so on. I'm sure you've seen that. Nuremberg was their center so it was entirely appropriate that they should be tried there.

All officers and people involved with the trial [were staying at the hotel]. There were no enlisted men living there, so far as I know. It was very elitist, I guess.

Was your husband in the service, or was he civilian?

He was civilian. I think, except for Telford Taylor, who was a brigadier general, almost everybody by that time was a civilian, I believe, whether or not they had been in the army [at one time]. But the army provided all accommodations. The Grand Hotel was hardly a barracks. There was the night club there, and you could have dinner there, and so on. There was every effort to make people feel at home. I didn't live in a hotel [laughs] with a night club in it, at home. But they provided, and we adjusted. And it was very, very segregated from the Germans.

Did you meet any Germans?

It was very difficult because it was right after the war. Their lives were in ruins, and most of them blamed not Hitler or their other leaders but the Americans, British, and Russians who had done the bombing, which was natural. I used to go on the *Strassenbahn*, and people were openly hostile even when I was with my child. I left him for a time in North Carolina with an aunt, but we eventually brought him over. He was born in August 1945. So when I would see children on their mothers' laps, I remember smiling at one of them, which is what routinely you do. And his mother turned his face away. On one occasion, we were in the [PX] of course, everything was provided by the army, and ... you would get clothes from the PX. I was in there with my little boy. He was maybe a year-and-a-half or two, and he ran toward the street. Well, you would naturally reach out to stop a child in such circumstances but the Germans in the street did not. It did not seem to disturb them at all to see an American baby running toward peril.

So there was a lot of resentment then?

Well, certainly these are people whose lives had been ruined, as I say. It's understandable.

How did your husband get the Nuremberg assignment?

I am not sure that there was a long line of people wanting to go there. A friend of ours had been over there. [He had] gone over very early, in the first trial, and he told him that it should be interesting. So he told him who to go to see.

It was fine with me. I had never been to Europe. Most Americans in those days had not. They were not as [well] traveled as they are now. Of course, it was before air travel, essentially. So people would go to Europe, and they'd come back, and show their postcards, just as they did in the nineteenth century. [laughs] And it's so different from the way it is now. So I was pleased. I thought it was a very interesting thing for him to do, and I was glad to have a chance to go myself.

In one of your articles, you talk about the Germans being fairly well dressed.

Yes. I wouldn't have remembered that, but I noticed that in much of Nuremberg they were, and they were [often] better dressed than the British, who had had a hard time, also.

Some of the cities, like Dresden and Nuremberg, and to an extent, Frankfurt, were bombed. But the towns outside were beautiful and untouched. I think the clothing was available there, I would assume. They did not suffer the way the cities did.

At the trial itself, who stands out on all sides? The Germans, the Americans, the British, the French, the Russians?

Well, of course, Göring was just so incredible. I've never seen anybody who was just as you imagined him being. And you would watch him, and when we went through the prison, we could talk to him a little bit, though he usually turned his face away. However, Albert Speer, the most sociable person on earth—he came right out, wanted to talk. It was as if it were a cocktail party, to which we'd all been invited. But Göring was incredible to watch. And so smart, you could see. When the prosecution went after him, Sir David Maxwell-Fyfe, the British prosecutor was, I thought, devastating in his interrogation. Then Göring would banter with him saying, "But Sir *David*." [laughs] "We're all in the same level. We understand each other," was the idea. He was very memorable.

Do you remember Justice Jackson's interrogation at all?

I was there for part of it. It was very good. He may have been more impressive as an eloquent writer and thinker than as a lawyer on his feet. I know that he was very distracted during part of his time at Nuremberg. There had always been speculation that he thought it likely that he would be the next chief justice of the [U.S.] Supreme Court. It was an extraordinary thing he had done, stepping down temporarily from the high court to prosecute the Nazi war criminals. While he was there, the post of chief justice fell vacant, and President Truman appointed someone else. Jackson took the news very hard. He held a very angry press conference, in which he spoke bitterly of this development, assuming—accurately perhaps—that if he hadn't been off in Nuremberg making another kind of history, what he saw as a miscarriage of justice might have been prevented.

You mentioned Speer and Göring and Maxwell-Fyfe. Do any other characters stand out in your mind?

Schacht. He used to sit like this. [sort of to the side] As if he was constantly making the point that he was not part of that crowd—Göring and the rest—and, of course, he wasn't. He was acquitted.

As a reporter, were you in the courtroom constantly?

No. I tried to keep track of what was going on in Germany beyond the courthouse. Until the end of the main trial, when I took over, I would cover events in the courthouse only if Rebecca West wasn't planning to. *The New Yorker* pieces on the early months of the trial had been by Janet Flanner. The idea that my coverage of the trials would follow that of Janet Flanner and Rebecca West, two of the great writers of this century, was naturally quite daunting to me. In fact, they were not daunting figures at all but wonderfully helpful. In later years Rebecca West would keep me up to date on her problems with Anthony West, her novelist son. And Janet Flanner became godmother to one of my children and left her money in her will.

In terms of the assignments of your writing, did you just pick up a theme your-self? Or were you asked to do a piece?

As I remember, they were mostly my ideas because back home they had lit-tle idea of what was going on where I was. For instance, that trip I made out to the camp, where the former SS men, now prisoners of war, were being made to dig up and rebury Nazi victims who had been buried too close to the surface. Dig them up and bury them deeper. I remember vividly the masks they wore over their faces because of the stench. That's not in the published piece.

Do you think it was edited out?

Yes. William Shawn was famous for his delicate sensibilities and could find all kinds of reasons for editing out repellent images. We communicated inter-nationally in those days, by the way, thanks to something called Press Wireless, which does not exist anymore. The messages to me were always signed "Love, Bill"—that is, Bill Shawn. Not a routine sign-off on Press Wireless, but Shawn was not only an encouraging but an affectionate editor. One of the earliest "Love, Bill" messages I got after I came to Nuremberg dealt with a piece I wrote about a trip on a German train with American GIs and how callous they were [toward the Germans]. And also corrupt. [laughs] Gathering up highly valuable souvenirs and shipping them home.

In one of your pieces you mention that every American soldier seemed to have a Leica camera.

Right. Always. I don't know that I wrote about it very much, but Kronberg Castle was the site of one of the big heists of American soldiers' jewel thefts. So I went to that trial [of the soldiers] in Frankfurt. [The soldiers on trial were] a man and a woman who eventually married each other. I don't know that they had the slightest interest in each other, but they then couldn't testify against each other.
So you'd go into the lobby of the Park Hotel in Frankfurt, and there would be the people who owned the jewels on one side, and there would be the rel-atives and lawyers for the American soldiers on the other. Close quarters, I would say. So one was constantly reminded. Incidentally, SS men were assigned to help rebuild the Palace of Justice in Nuremberg, so the trials could get under way. I thought that was appropriate. [laughs]

You described the courthouse in one of your pieces. You talk about the velvet green curtains, sort of going along with the justice of the time. Can you describe the courthouse, as you remember it?

Well, I wouldn't have remembered the green curtains. [laughs] It was a very impressive place, and there were the judges along one side. I remember Justice Francis Biddle, with his long, swanlike neck. [laughs] And the line-up of the defendants. Of course, that was so dramatic, to see the men who'd once had such immense power, now scrunched up together.

You mentioned Göring and Speer. Were there a variety of different reactions from them?

Yes. Sometimes they'd sneer and look contemptuous as the prosecution made its charges. And others would—was it Hans Frank who said that a thousand years would not erase the shame of what the Nazis had done. But the others—after all, it gets boring after a while, and they were kind of looking around for something interesting, as anyone would, because they were long, long days there. Meanwhile outside the Palace of Justice, in the American zone of Germany, Americans were conducting a de-Nazification program for far less prominent Nazis....

In the case of the Nuremberg Trials especially, there were people who kept asking, "Why should we be doing this? Why should we put a glaze of order and ethics onto this? It's the victors trying the vanquished." And so then I would always ask, "Well, what would you do with the really bad Nazis?" [laughs] I remember there was one reporter at Nuremberg who said, "Turn them over to the Jews." [laughs] I thought, "Oh, that's great." [laughs] I think Justice Jackson was right, that Nuremberg had to happen. At least with all the evidence, the terrible record, no one can say this never happened as some of the defendants tried to claim in the trial.

What was your feeling about the fact that three of them were exonerated?

Actually, I didn't think the evidence was so strong in the Schacht case. Fritzsche, I think, was another one, wasn't he? Was von Papen the other one? I'm not so sharp on Nuremberg as I once was. As I remember, Fritzsche replaced the elder Krupp in the dock after he was removed as a defendant. As it was described to me, they kind of needed another body. [laughs] But it didn't seem to me that the evidence was so strong against Fritzsche or Schacht. Of course, von Papen was a wily old fellow. From the first World War, of course, he saved all the incriminating evidence against him, and got tried then. On his own evidence. [laughs] And in the Hitler era he saved everything again. His son was one of his lawyers, and was around the courthouse a fair amount, and was involved with one of the British reporters. I think years later, they may have married. They certainly were closely involved for many years. The younger von Papen was very good company. What was his friend's name? Betty. I think she was in the *London Observer,* but I may be wrong.

She was a reporter. [The press camp] was the old Faber Castle, as in Eberhard Faber pencils, and it had a wonderful painting down in the front—as you came in the door there. It showed a war scene, and the conqueror, who won out over everybody, was a man holding the victor's weapon, a large Eberhard Faber pencil. [laughs] So that was pretty funny. [Walter] Cronkite was at the press camp early that summer. He was with UP [United Press] then.

I remember the night of the hangings. One of the women reporters from a British paper got news of this. She said, "I was sleeping with this sergeant, and he told me." So that was the way some of us got word that they had happened.

You mean you didn't know publicly?

Well, they didn't run through the streets proclaiming it at the time, for fear of the German response. But word got around fairly fast. She had the first word, as I recall.

Your husband was a prosecutor in the trial of the industrialists?

Yes. And in the case against Friedrich Flick, one of Germany's richest men, you see what Charles did? That was really extraordinary. He got convictions in the case against what was called the Circle of Friends of Himmler, who included Flick. They used to meet every few weeks. And Himmler would show them pictures of what was going on in the concentration camps, which had a special interest for them because they relied on the camps for workers— that is slave labor. The concentration camp scenes with which Himmler would entertain his guests were quite graphic. The industrialists could never say, "We didn't know. Until we came to Nuremberg, we never heard of this," you know? And conviction in that case was really quite remarkable because it's very hard to convict rich industrialists, I would say. [laughs] Because they'll say, "How would I have known anything [about] some matter that would be so insignificant to me?" Well, it was not insignificant, and Flick and the others went to jail, thanks to Charles. So that was quite an achievement, I thought. He did the industrialists. Also the Ministries Case.

In one of your pieces you make the contrast between the German lawyers and their robes, and the American lawyers who just wanted to be [called] "Mr." Was this your husband, or was this just your general impression?

He didn't have to tell me how things were; I was right there.

How old was he at the time?

He was born in November 1916. He was 29 when he went over there. On weekends we used to play touch football in the stadium where the Nazis had held their huge rallies. Many people were very young. That is why so many people have come back, I guess, to these reunions. As I said, there's going to be another one. I just got a notice about it.

With respect to the industrialists, you made some comments that if somebody had a defense, that they were just doing business as usual, this is a strange kind of defense.

Yes. But they could claim they couldn't have known what was really going on as high-level criminals so often try to do. After Nuremberg it was harder for them to get away with this. The [I. G.] Farben Case [trial of chemical manufacturers using slave labor]—I knew the prosecutors there especially well. My husband was deputy chief counsel, eventually, so we knew all of the cases quite well. The medical case, of course, had been one of the most memorable. Telford Taylor at one point planned to write a history of the second wave of trials.

Did you stay through the entire series?

It was still going on, but I think it was about done. [At] the end of 1948 it was dwindling down considerably. I think one problem was the level of judges that was sent. Some of them were quite good, but others were judges who ... were well connected politically, perhaps. But they also were not terribly interested in the remarkable things that were told to them, and were said in their courtroom, and it was very hard for them to grasp things well enough to write very wise decisions, I think.

Was this sort of Americana coming to Germany, after the war was over, to send these kinds of people over there?

The British—in the first trial—well, because they're Europeans it was all much closer to them. They had given more thought to it. Certainly more than had many of the American judges in the second series of trials. But some of them were okay. Some of them were sort of comical. [Michael] Musmanno, the judge in the *Einsatzgruppen* case, for example—I remember his talking about what was not, of course, then known as the Holocaust. It often comes to my mind that, according to the Nuremberg judgment, six million Jews and 12 million people were liquidated in that time, and not a great deal of attention is paid to that fact, but, in all, 12 million victims died at the hands of the Nazis, mostly in the camps. There was, in 1948, I think, a German-sponsored exhibit in Munich of what they could find of anti-Nazi publications during the Nazi era, during the war. Almost nothing. This is a German search. Jehovah's Witnesses had published a few protests. And, of course, many of them died. There were [the Roma, the gypsies], though I don't remember any publications.

Personnel organize the 4,000 tons of documents used in the trials, which were based primarily on documentary evidence.

"The Germans ... documented everything. The worse things they did, the more copies they made of the document." —Andy Logan

There was just almost nothing that they could come up with. A few anti-Nazi publications they displayed turned out to have been put out by the Nazis to see who picked them up, and they would be hauled away to the camps, presumably. But there was very little. I can understand why, in a regime where protest meant death.

You were 25. You were a young woman out of the United States. Did you have a sense of the gravity of what was happening, when you were back here in the United States?

Ben Hecht had held, late in the war, I think, at Madison Square Garden, a great protest against the atrocities in Germany. We had heard about them. But it was so remote, and you then thought, "Well, maybe that's exaggerated." They always talked, in the first World War, about the cutting off of Belgium babies' hands. We had studied that in school, and learned that it never happened. It was hard to believe that what happened in Germany really happened. But there certainly was—I remember this rally. I did not go, but I remember reading about it. So that we should have known more than we did, I think. Certainly the government should have known.

When you were there in the courtroom, and you heard about the atrocities were you shocked?

That was not a shock. We had heard about it by then. We had not run our fingers over the documents as we did at Nuremberg, but we had certainly heard about it before we came. I guess I was surprised at—the Germans, as usual—they documented everything. The worse things they did, the more copies they made of the document.

The films of the camps as the war ended had been very difficult to watch. I went to Dachau. Now it is a tourist attraction, I guess. It was—again, hard to believe when you actually saw it, saw the gas chambers. But it was early enough though, that—as I said, there were no tours or anything of that sort, I believe. Propped against one of the gas chambers was a little sign, a handwritten sign. It said, "This really happened." I asked somebody, "Who put that up?" It was one of the GIs.

The reporters knew about it. We had seen the pictures. They were played in the courtroom. There was, of course, never a discussion with the people we met in the streets—in Dresden, in Nuremberg. And in Munich. I spent a lot of time in Munich, out in the countryside, where all the Germans were so charming, some of whom we were learning had done such terrible things.

In the countryside, did you experience any of the anti-American feeling that you mentioned that you had in Nuremberg?

No. I think it was all there, but they were much too polite. You know, they had good manners, and you knew what they were saying probably. I think I wrote a little about that—how they were. I remember Karl Wolff, who was one of the Nazi figures, although I believe he eventually dropped out. I've forgotten exactly. But he was a witness at Nuremberg. He was a very imposing looking man, and I remember one of the GIs there—some reporter was trying to get in to talk to Wolff, or push through to talk to him—and the GI said, "Oh, you can't talk to him. He's a *VIP*." [laughs] The GIs didn't always get along well with the displaced persons—the citizens of conquered countries whom the Nazis had uprooted and brought to Germany as workers, whom the Americans took responsibility for after the war. There would be fights among them, with American GIs.

Was there much sympathy for the displaced persons at the time, or were they looked upon as a burden?

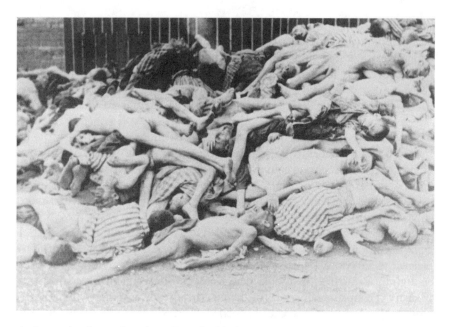

A photo taken by an American GI at the liberation of Dachau concentration camp.

"It was hard to believe when you actually saw it, saw the gas chambers ... Propped against one of the gas chambers was a little sign, a little handwritten sign. It said, 'This really happened.' I asked somebody, 'Who put that up?' It was one of the GIs." —Andy Logan

They could get jobs from the Americans, you see, and the Germans could not. So there was great resentment. Some of the Americans, including at least one of the American lawyers, married a displaced person. So many lives were changed because we went to Nuremberg. And sometime in 1947 the scene there changed physically. Everything had been grim and gray and dark among the ruins when we got over there. But then the Technicolor government-issue cars began to arrive from America, suddenly brightening up the scene. It was quite a sight seeing them glide, bright blue and crimson, through the still gray, still ruined Nuremberg landscape. Also, another thing I noticed that I see that I wrote about, was the German's fondness for quoting [Abraham] Lincoln. They do identify with the [American] South. They kept pointing out that Lincoln had said, "Forgive and forget," and so they would quote him a lot. Still do today, I am sure.

I was from the South. I resented the comparison, naturally. I wondered how Lincoln would have reacted to the defense in the *Einsatzcommando* case. I did write about that in May of 1948. One defense argument was that it was unfair to say they killed a million people. It was not *quite* a million. These defendants who had seen themselves as supermen, fit to preside over the deaths of not quite a million human beings, were not hopeless thugs but middle-class and upper-middle-class professional sorts. Fourteen of them were sentenced to death. At the sentencing, the Americans arranged to have stand on each side of the superman as he was sentenced the biggest, blackest GIs they could find. I don't remember the Americans doing anything like that in any other case. I approve of the way I ended that piece, saying of the black GIs: "They did not by the barest smile betray the dignity of the occasion, but one could not escape the impression that they were enjoying their work."

Did the Germans react to the blacks being the guards? Was there any "master race" business?

When we had the guns, when the GIs had the guns, there wasn't. There were not many black GIs at Nuremberg until, I would say, the second year. But there were some there. The pianist, Andre Watts, was born in Nuremberg. His mother is German, and his father, I believe, was a black GI. Then one time, one of the GIs told me of a wonderful thing that had happened. They had found some black girls. When they first got over there, it was very lonely. There were not very many black women. [Then] they had seen some black girls—children of GIs from the first World War. [laughs] I think, French, not necessarily Americans. It was a very happy ending.

You mentioned earlier that you had actually gone into the prison. Were you there to interview prisoners?

Not individual interviews. [In] two excursions that I was on, we were allowed in to go around the prison, and if any of the famous prisoners wanted to talk to us it was all right, but we were hurried along. I mean, we weren't allowed to just stand and talk for too long.

Was this when you spoke with Speer?

Yes, that's right. [laughs] Oh, what a piece of work. I only could see the cells. Conditions seemed reasonably good but I don't remember any signs of luxury or anything.

Was it heavily guarded, do you remember?

Yes. Not so heavily that Göring couldn't get what he wanted there. [laughs] ... There was a theory that it was an American guard from Texas who provided the cyanide [for Göring's suicide]. Whether there is definitive proof, I do not know.

You say you stayed there until 1948. What brought about your leaving?

It was three years, almost, we had been over there. Charles came back and forth from time to time, and in the spring of 1948 he and three friends founded a law firm which later became the largest in New York—Skadden, Arps, Slate, Meagher, and Flom. It was Skadden, Arps, Slate, and Lyon, originally. So he really needed to get back.

What were your feelings about returning?

Many of our friends had left. Telford stayed on, I think, through mid-1949, perhaps. It was a very important experience for the rest of our lives. I mean, we lived near Telford and his family always, and others whom we met over there, we would never have met otherwise, became our closest friends, who were deputy chief prosecutors, and so on. So it made a great difference. I was a little surprised, as I thought back on it because my husband and I both went to Swarthmore [College] five years apart, so presumably that would have been most influential. But I don't think it was. It was Nuremberg. We kept up with all of these people.

When you came back, did people in America care that there were Nuremberg Trials?

Very short attention span in this country, as you know. They were not terribly interested. There were people who wanted justice done, but they didn't know who they wanted to have do it. But they also, I don't think, cared a great deal anymore, by that time. A lot of other things [were] going on. The Cold War was coming.

I know that Telford did a lot of speaking, and people were interested. But most of them were Jewish groups. The interest naturally continued there. But otherwise, I don't think quite so much. We were getting into, as I said, the Cold War. And before long it was McCarthy time.

Speaking of the Cold War, did you have much relationship to the Russians?

They were there, of course, for the first trial. There were Russian reporters at the press camp at the Faber Castle. And one got to know them, somewhat. God, they could drink a lot. They were just incredible. [laughs] But except for the reporters, I didn't know very many [Russians]. They were very open. Did they go around saying, "Down with Stalin?" Of course not. But later in the evening, they would be reasonably open. They knew they could say the next day, "Well, I was drunk."

Did you have a feeling that the distrust between the United States and the U.S.S.R. was affecting the trial at all?

I did not have that feeling. It was certainly not anything open in the way of hostility. The Russians were very proud to be there, was the feeling I had. Because they should have been. They lost so much. But they were proud to be there, and I don't know of their misbehaving or doing anything hostile. But I was not on the inside.

Any impressions of the French?

They were their usual charming selves. [laughs] I don't remember their contributing so much to the trial. The British really did. They were very impressive. [Prosecutor Hartley] Shawcross, and so on. They were very good in court. You wanted to be there when they were cross-examining.

Did you have the opportunity to see Judgment at Nuremberg?

Well, I did see that. That was a ridiculous film in many respects. I mean, it meant well. But, for example, they had the GIs wandering in and out of the Grand Hotel and close encounters with Germans in the streets. And a lot of the things could never have happened. But they meant well. Americans were much more isolated than they were portrayed, I would say.

Are there any other accounts of Nuremberg, fictional or otherwise, that you have read that you think are accurate?

I don't think I've read any. I did get very interested in the July 20th uprising, and I went to Berlin, and I talked to Eugen Gerstenmaier, who was a minister who was involved in the uprising. So I did get into that a fair amount.

Of all the individuals or events that occurred during your time at Nuremberg, does anything stand out particularly?

I guess it was the line-up of those 21 defendants in the first trial. These historic figures. And some of them were terribly impressive, even sitting there in the dark and scrunched up together. These were very strong individuals. I guess that was really the main memory I have. Göring was by far the most fascinating. I can still hear his voice. And he knew the joke he was going to play on us, too. "They're not going to get me." Streicher, of course, was from Nuremberg. So Nuremberg was an appropriate place for his trial to be held. And Bavaria generally. That's where the beautiful scenery was, and the really bad Nazis. Up north, it is not quite so beautiful, and the Nazis seemed to be less virulent. I remember Hitler tried to get started in Stuttgart, and they threw him out. But Nuremberg was very welcoming.

Did you ever think of writing something about it after you came back?

I did not. I had a child while I was over there, and I had a good-sized family after I came back. And I kept writing for *The New Yorker* right along. [My second child] was born in Switzerland. So I maybe was a little preoccupied. There was not all that interest, I think. But there probably should have been on my part. I watched Telford's career with interest. He was the moving force in all the trials, as you know. I'm really very sorry that Telford did not go further as a national figure, because he was brilliant and very capable. But Nuremberg became not the prize credential it had briefly seemed. Still, I'm very proud of having been there.

...ch points to the reason why there was such a hard time finding ...think during the 1940s, most women didn't have the type of jobs ...pull together for reunions. They tended to hold more support per-...itions, and people don't celebrate jobs as support personnel. I ...e of the women that we interviewed said, "I was very disinterested ...k because they never told me why it was important." And I think ... why I think we were able to catch some of these women was ...ey were married to people who held more prominent roles, who ...of the reunions and rehashing of Nuremberg.

...in this sense, the women that we ended up interviewing reflect ...erns and social patterns of 50 years ago, rather than of today.

...re there any surprises in the interviews for you?

...ink early on we were very surprised because we happened to have a ...ish immigrants in the interviews, and I think we were very surprised ...ount of forgiveness—especially in the earliest interviews we did. ...re so many people who, from our standards, had such rough experi-...Germany or wherever they were when the war started, and to hear ...about the Nuremberg Trials, in terms of forgiveness or the closing ...rs in their lives, was a very surprising initial discovery in this project. ...ink that not everybody felt like that, but many of them did. And that ...was an element. I think simply finding a number of people who had ...entially involved in the Holocaust, who got out of Europe, and then ...k was of interest to me. I guess we should have realized that people ...that language facility, and perhaps the desire to go back, would have ...se working at the trials, but when we first started this, I didn't realize ...would be the case.

...ne of the things that surprised me was how little people knew of the ...st before the trials. They actually learned so much at the trials. This ...true of people who were born and grew up in Europe and could see ...happening. But even among Jews—American Jews—it surprised me ...y were in some kind of denial about it, or just really didn't have the ...tion, or really couldn't believe that that kind of thing could happen. ...ls seemed to be an educational experience for everyone, not just for ...s.

...hat may have been one of the reasons for the trials ultimately, to give ...d of experience. To educate people as to what happened during the ...in a sense you have a show trial element, as well as a trial that's ...ing to get justice done.

...rms of the folks that we interviewed, there were many fascinating sto-...e stories. Does anything stand out in your mind particularly? Any of ...rviews that seemed most unusual or most fascinating?

...I think one of the translators' life story [not printed in this volume] ...y was one of the most dramatic. He was born a Jew in Germany and

Conclusion:
Talking about *Witnesses to Nuremberg*

STAVE: What were we trying to accomplish with this book?

PALMER: We wanted to recreate what happened 50 years ago at Nuremberg by talking to people who were there in a variety of roles, so [the reader would see] it from different perspectives, and to see what lessons could be learned from them and from the whole Nuremberg experience.

BS: But what about the fact that there have been many books written about Nuremberg, and some of what we've been trying to do is to recapture the atmosphere in the community that existed at Nuremberg for the people that were there. This is somewhat different than looking at the legal questions on which much has been written. Do you feel that we actually got some of this community feeling and feeling of atmosphere?

FRANK: In the interviews there is a sense of capturing the experiences of what it was like at Nuremberg that is missed in the works that deal primarily with legal aspects. We were able to reach the notion of justice from a very personal perspective, a different accounting of justice.

BS: A different accounting of justice. What do you mean by that?

LF: With the legal studies, they're more concerned with how international law was formed, and whether it was done correctly. Whereas with the people that we interviewed, there's a larger sense that what we did had to be done. These people were part of a community whose purpose was to enact justice. Justice infused their lives, but it wasn't a legal sense of justice, it was a personal, moral sense of justice.

BS: But we're looking more than at the issues of justice itself. We're looking at the prosaic, in a sense, of what it was like to be at these trials on a daily basis, how people got there, and why they got there, and there are many different motivations running from very idealistic, to the most banal reasons for getting there. For instance, someone went simply for a job. Do you think that this colors the interviews that we get and the approaches of people, and their attitudes towards what happened?

MP: I think there were two lawyers at least who were inspired by Justice [Robert H.] Jackson's opening speech, who wanted to just drop everything and be at the trial. They retained their idealism throughout the trials and throughout the years. Other people who more or less got there because they were in the army and they were assigned to Nuremberg, might not have had the same interest or intensity in the beginning, but the fascination of the trials sort of swept them in anyway. And for some people, over the years they seem to have developed an interest, perhaps because they were very young at the time and didn't realize the impact of the event until they matured.

BS: Some of them say that they weren't quite sure what it was, but I got the feeling from our interviews that many of them knew that they were involved in some momentous element of history even though, I think, as one of them said, they knew it was a courtroom. They didn't know if it was a traffic court or something else. They did have a sense that this was a momentous time in the twentieth century, if not in the history of the world. And their role there, I think, over time, takes on greater importance for some of these people as we look back over 50-plus years and see the impact of Nuremberg on society. Although I think the folks that we interviewed are not entirely clear as to the impact of justice at Nuremberg, the impact on their own lives is very great.

MP: Yes. I think that most of them agreed that even though they were victors, and to some degree, just because of that, it was a kind of victor's justice, that the trials were fair, and that what was done needed to be done. But there is a sense for most of them that there was not a lasting impact, that the Nuremberg Trials didn't influence the world in a more positive way that they would have liked to have seen.

LF: For many of the interviewees, the timing of the trials coincided with very important formative years in their own lives. Many of the people that we interviewed were on the young side at the time of the trials. From 18 to probably about 36. In the long run, I think that really affected the way they internalized these trials and their senses of justice and the like. Nuremberg became not only part of the American myth of what happened during World War II, but part of their own personal stories of coming of age. Their sense that they were fighting for something that was right, or that they were participants in something that needed to be done and required that they make very strong statements at a very young age and increased the impact of Nuremberg on their personal lives.

BS: The way we got into this project in a sense helped shape what was happening because at the University of Connecticut the Thomas J. Dodd Research Center was going to open in October of 1995, and President Clinton was coming to the inaugural, and there were a number of activities attached to the opening. The year was devoted to human rights because Senator Christopher Dodd's father, Thomas J. Dodd, was one of the leading prosecutors at Nuremberg. So Nuremberg took on a central focus for the opening of the Dodd Research Center, and we became interested in the project as a

consequence of that initiative, and the happ viduals who attended reunions of those w That's very unusual for an oral history proje much harder to do this project had we not g ing with that list, in trying to arrange inte process was followed?

MP: We were limited to some extent, becau within the New England/New York area, but much of a problem because there were enou could interview. In fact, some were even local f positive responses from nearly everyone that w

LF: There was some word-of-mouth, too. some of the interviewees would tell us about th thought we should contact. There were defin that way.

BS: In the first list we sent out—25 or so body did respond on that list. And then we se ters. So I'm not quite certain of the proportio stantial number did respond, and one of the became clear that there were individuals who v that were not on that list. One day we saw an c the newspaper. It was talking about her as the Trials. And we had not heard of her at all. We there in the army who were not directly associat present in Nuremberg at the time. There seemed of people who had associations with Nurember imagined.

MP: Not only from interviewing people, but j Nuremberg, we found out that there were more "N than we realized.

BS: Do you think that we were faced with a ve consequence of who we interviewed and who wasn that they came forward, they were available?

MP: I don't know. Looking back, it seems that th sonality types and professions represented in the p cerned at first that lawyers would dominate the list, have a balance. I think that somehow things worked of our interviewees were men, while the trials thems ratio of men and women working there. I'm not exac find more women to interview.

BS: We did make an effort to seek women out whe der proportion was overbalanced towards the male, a viduals, but a number of them were wives of individu in capacities such as a prosecutor or something of tha

LF: Wh women. I that people sonnel po believe on in my wor the reasor because th were part

BS: So career pat

LF: Yes

BS: We

LF: I th lot of Jew at the an There we ences in them tal of chapte

BS: I t certainly been pot came ba who had been tho that such

MP: C Holocau wasn't a what wa that the informa The tri Germar

BS: T that ki war. Sc attemp

In te ries—li the int

MP: certain

Conclusion:
Talking about *Witnesses to Nuremberg*

STAVE: What were we trying to accomplish with this book?

PALMER: We wanted to recreate what happened 50 years ago at Nuremberg by talking to people who were there in a variety of roles, so [the reader would see] it from different perspectives, and to see what lessons could be learned from them and from the whole Nuremberg experience.

BS: But what about the fact that there have been many books written about Nuremberg, and some of what we've been trying to do is to recapture the atmosphere in the community that existed at Nuremberg for the people that were there. This is somewhat different than looking at the legal questions on which much has been written. Do you feel that we actually got some of this community feeling and feeling of atmosphere?

FRANK: In the interviews there is a sense of capturing the experiences of what it was like at Nuremberg that is missed in the works that deal primarily with legal aspects. We were able to reach the notion of justice from a very personal perspective, a different accounting of justice.

BS: A different accounting of justice. What do you mean by that?

LF: With the legal studies, they're more concerned with how international law was formed, and whether it was done correctly. Whereas with the people that we interviewed, there's a larger sense that what we did had to be done. These people were part of a community whose purpose was to enact justice. Justice infused their lives, but it wasn't a legal sense of justice, it was a personal, moral sense of justice.

BS: But we're looking more than at the issues of justice itself. We're looking at the prosaic, in a sense, of what it was like to be at these trials on a daily basis, how people got there, and why they got there, and there are many different motivations running from very idealistic, to the most banal reasons for getting there. For instance, someone went simply for a job. Do you think that this colors the interviews that we get and the approaches of people, and their attitudes towards what happened?

MP: I think there were two lawyers at least who were inspired by Justice [Robert H.] Jackson's opening speech, who wanted to just drop everything and be at the trial. They retained their idealism throughout the trials and throughout the years. Other people who more or less got there because they were in the army and they were assigned to Nuremberg, might not have had the same interest or intensity in the beginning, but the fascination of the trials sort of swept them in anyway. And for some people, over the years they seem to have developed an interest, perhaps because they were very young at the time and didn't realize the impact of the event until they matured.

BS: Some of them say that they weren't quite sure what it was, but I got the feeling from our interviews that many of them knew that they were involved in some momentous element of history even though, I think, as one of them said, they knew it was a courtroom. They didn't know if it was a traffic court or something else. They did have a sense that this was a momentous time in the twentieth century, if not in the history of the world. And their role there, I think, over time, takes on greater importance for some of these people as we look back over 50-plus years and see the impact of Nuremberg on society. Although I think the folks that we interviewed are not entirely clear as to the impact of justice at Nuremberg, the impact on their own lives is very great.

MP: Yes. I think that most of them agreed that even though they were victors, and to some degree, just because of that, it was a kind of victor's justice, that the trials were fair, and that what was done needed to be done. But there is a sense for most of them that there was not a lasting impact, that the Nuremberg Trials didn't influence the world in a more positive way that they would have liked to have seen.

LF: For many of the interviewees, the timing of the trials coincided with very important formative years in their own lives. Many of the people that we interviewed were on the young side at the time of the trials. From 18 to probably about 36. In the long run, I think that really affected the way they internalized these trials and their senses of justice and the like. Nuremberg became not only part of the American myth of what happened during World War II, but part of their own personal stories of coming of age. Their sense that they were fighting for something that was right, or that they were participants in something that needed to be done and required that they make very strong statements at a very young age and increased the impact of Nuremberg on their personal lives.

BS: The way we got into this project in a sense helped shape what was happening because at the University of Connecticut the Thomas J. Dodd Research Center was going to open in October of 1995, and President Clinton was coming to the inaugural, and there were a number of activities attached to the opening. The year was devoted to human rights because Senator Christopher Dodd's father, Thomas J. Dodd, was one of the leading prosecutors at Nuremberg. So Nuremberg took on a central focus for the opening of the Dodd Research Center, and we became interested in the project as a consequence of that initiative, and the happenstance of getting a list of individuals who attended reunions of those who participated at Nuremberg. That's very unusual for an oral history project, or at least it would have been much harder to do this project had we not gotten that list. Michele, in working with that list, in trying to arrange interviews and such, what kind of process was followed?

MP: We were limited to some extent, because of budget restrictions, to stay within the New England/New York area, but actually, that didn't present too much of a problem because there were enough people in that area that we could interview. In fact, some were even local folks. We sent out letters and got positive responses from nearly everyone that we approached.

LF: There was some word-of-mouth, too. Once the project got rolling, some of the interviewees would tell us about their friends or people that they thought we should contact. There were definitely some connections made that way.

BS: In the first list we sent out—25 or so people? I'm not sure if everybody did respond on that list. And then we sent out a second round of letters. So I'm not quite certain of the proportion that responded, but a substantial number did respond, and one of the interesting things is that it became clear that there were individuals who were involved in Nuremberg that were not on that list. One day we saw an obituary of a local woman in the newspaper. It was talking about her as the librarian at the Nuremberg Trials. And we had not heard of her at all. We did find people who were there in the army who were not directly associated with the trials, but were present in Nuremberg at the time. There seemed to be a much wider spread of people who had associations with Nuremberg than I ever would have imagined.

MP: Not only from interviewing people, but just generally talking about Nuremberg, we found out that there were more "Nuremberg alumni" around than we realized.

BS: Do you think that we were faced with a very self-selecting group as a consequence of who we interviewed and who wasn't interviewed, in the sense that they came forward, they were available?

MP: I don't know. Looking back, it seems that there's quite a range of personality types and professions represented in the project. I was a little concerned at first that lawyers would dominate the list, even though we tried to have a balance. I think that somehow things worked out. Unfortunately, most of our interviewees were men, while the trials themselves had about a 50-50 ratio of men and women working there. I'm not exactly sure why we couldn't find more women to interview.

BS: We did make an effort to seek women out when we found that the gender proportion was overbalanced towards the male, and we found some individuals, but a number of them were wives of individuals who had been there in capacities such as a prosecutor or something of that sort.

LF: Which points to the reason why there was such a hard time finding women. I think during the 1940s, most women didn't have the type of jobs that people pull together for reunions. They tended to hold more support personnel positions, and people don't celebrate jobs as support personnel. I believe one of the women that we interviewed said, "I was very disinterested in my work because they never told me why it was important." And I think the reason why I think we were able to catch some of these women was because they were married to people who held more prominent roles, who were part of the reunions and rehashing of Nuremberg.

BS: So in this sense, the women that we ended up interviewing reflect career patterns and social patterns of 50 years ago, rather than of today.

LF: Yes.

BS: Were there any surprises in the interviews for you?

LF: I think early on we were very surprised because we happened to have a lot of Jewish immigrants in the interviews, and I think we were very surprised at the amount of forgiveness—especially in the earliest interviews we did. There were so many people who, from our standards, had such rough experiences in Germany or wherever they were when the war started, and to hear them talk about the Nuremberg Trials, in terms of forgiveness or the closing of chapters in their lives, was a very surprising initial discovery in this project.

BS: I think that not everybody felt like that, but many of them did. And that certainly was an element. I think simply finding a number of people who had been potentially involved in the Holocaust, who got out of Europe, and then came back was of interest to me. I guess we should have realized that people who had that language facility, and perhaps the desire to go back, would have been those working at the trials, but when we first started this, I didn't realize that such would be the case.

MP: One of the things that surprised me was how little people knew of the Holocaust before the trials. They actually learned so much at the trials. This wasn't as true of people who were born and grew up in Europe and could see what was happening. But even among Jews—American Jews—it surprised me that they were in some kind of denial about it, or just really didn't have the information, or really couldn't believe that that kind of thing could happen. The trials seemed to be an educational experience for everyone, not just for Germans.

BS: That may have been one of the reasons for the trials ultimately, to give that kind of experience. To educate people as to what happened during the war. So in a sense you have a show trial element, as well as a trial that's attempting to get justice done.

In terms of the folks that we interviewed, there were many fascinating stories—life stories. Does anything stand out in your mind particularly? Any of the interviews that seemed most unusual or most fascinating?

MP: I think one of the translators' life story [not printed in this volume] certainly was one of the most dramatic. He was born a Jew in Germany and got out early, when Hitler first came to power. He ended up in England only to be transported out of there by boat because he was considered an enemy alien. The boat got torpedoed; he was one of the few rescued; and he spent the rest of the war in Australia, in a camp for enemy aliens, along with other Germans, including Nazis.

BS: We heard stories of all kinds of people. Some of these are not in this book because we've done more interviews than could be included. I remember the man whose father was the governor of Slovenia who was assassinated in his presidency by a Communist who was dressed as a priest. The attitude of the interviewee was obviously not very enthusiastic about the left [wing]. And on the other hand, there seemed to be some feeling that the trials themselves may not have been doing justice because the individuals who were on trial were individuals that other countries—at least the interviewee claimed—did business with before the war, with respect to diplomatic relations. So he raised some questions, "Why do you put them on trial if you're dealing with them beforehand?" Any other interviews that may stand out in your mind?

LF: I thought to some extent there were some interesting juxtapositions. We interviewed a man who was the lieutenant in charge of the division that took care of security outside of the Palace of Justice, and he was very impressed with the men under him, and he worked very hard to make sure his men were happy. I thought he was an interesting juxtaposition to another man who was a prison guard, who performed his job, but he did it according to his own consciousness, and had to break rules for his own self. And I think it's an interesting juxtaposition of having the person in command and the person beneath, and seeing how sometimes, when getting a job done, the people underneath are actually doing different work than the people on top realize.

BS: I think the particular prison guard that you're talking about is a fascinating example because he was talking about how he broke rules, how he permitted the prisoners to sleep with their hands under a blanket, and not to have to face the light that they were supposed to face. How he saw them as human beings, even though he had a sense that they had done something wrong. But their defense, of course—you get a defense of, "Well, we were following orders." So here's an 18-year-old prison guard who is an American, who is not following orders in dealing with them, and there is some irony.

One of the individuals that I found most interesting in interviewing was the architect of the courtroom who was part of the OSS, and designed the courtroom with the idea of wanting it to be orderly, unified, and dignified. He had a goal in putting together this courtroom. He even talked about how he didn't want to put backs on the seats of the prisoners so the defendants could be more comfortable. He was a fascinating man—this is Dan Kiley. He is a very well-known landscape architect, subsequently becoming world-renowned. But that time at Nuremberg had a major impact on him, and he remembers it. He also remembers going off skiing all the time while he was at Nuremberg.

So for him it had many kinds of memories. But asking him about how he related to, say, someone like Albert Speer, who was the architect for Hitler, as well as the overseer of supplies [armaments minister], he talked about how Speer did not design for democracy. I found that interesting. He didn't go beyond that and explain how he designed for democracy. I had tried to get him to talk about that. But implicit was that [Kiley] did design for democracy, and Speer did not. Speer came from the top down, in terms of the kinds of things that he did.

MP: Speaking of Speer, there was a general fascination with him, and the other defendants. Some of the prison guards, and army personnel who had access to the prisoners, felt compelled to get their autographs. They were celebrities in some way. Göring and Speer, in particular, had very strong effects on people. One of the interviewees, Joseph Maier, would be so upset when he had to interrogate them that he would leave and go to the men's room and vomit, which is a little different reaction than trying to get their autographs! But they seemed to make an impact on everyone who even just watched the trial.

BS: Of course, the one who made the greatest impact it seems—well, of the secondary literature that we read, and from the interviews—was Göring. He, apparently, was a very dominant personality. He also understood English. Everybody seemed to talk about him. He was like a magnet [drawing] people to him.

MP: Those who got to know Speer were of two camps: those who liked and trusted him, and those who didn't trust him. He seemed to be one of the most complex of all of the defendants.

BS: Of course, Speer is the one who apologizes and says that they were wrong, and people raised the question whether he was sincere or whether he was trying to save his skin. A number of books have been written about him recently to that effect. So he is a very complex personality.

One of the things about doing this study is our naïveté in beginning it. Perhaps it was our own innocence that allowed us to start the study because otherwise it would have been so intimidating to do so. So much material exists about Nuremberg. And in this sense, perhaps, a little bit of knowledge helped rather than hindered. At least it did not stop us from beginning this. The more you peel the onion, the more layers there are. The themes that we dealt with— I've identified several, and you might think of others. It was a defining moment for many of these people who were our participants. They talk about Nuremberg after the war; the role of nonlawyers; the relationship to the German people; the question of the impact of the Cold War, which was starting at the time of Nuremberg; the reaction of Americans at home to the trials, particularly when some of these people who participated came home and found little interest in what was happening in Nuremberg. Do you see any other themes emerging, and what about these?

MP: I thought their interactions with the Germans were interesting. They seemed to be divided along gender lines because the women had more of a distrust of the Germans, or felt more of their hostility.

BS: Would this be because of the kinds of positions that at least several of the women that we spoke to had? In other words, they were more subordinate—working in a PX or something of that sort?

MP: I think partly, women are more sensitive or intuitive about those things. Also, several of the women we interviewed understood German, and heard things that the Germans didn't realize were being overheard.

LF: To some extent this distrust or hostility was brought out by motherhood or more broadly by parenthood. Because at least a couple of the women who really talked about their anger towards Germans crystallizing once they came to Germany, talked about it in terms of—"You know, they wouldn't watch out for my kid if my kid raced out towards the street, they wouldn't pull my kid out of the road." The same sentiment came out also in another interview with a man who had his family there—a little bit more distrust. Maybe for some of these people who had more of a family context, they saw more interaction and maybe had more of a survival instinct for the group that made them more aware of hostilities or underlying hostilities.

BS: Was it more an everyday role in a sense, too, for some of the people? If they had families there, and they were taking care of the families, that they would interact with a butcher or someone in a grocery store or something of this sort? Whereas some of the other people who were tied up in the professional side of it really wouldn't have that interaction?

LF: I don't know if we can say from the interviews because we don't really know about their housing situations. Or we don't know uniformly, but I would say that it does seem that a lot of the young single people tended to wake up in government housing and go to government dining halls and go to work and have a very insulated existence. I don't know so much for the families—how that worked.

MP: I didn't get a sense that there was all that much interaction anyway between Americans and Germans. There was some, obviously, but there were restrictions against it.

BS: We were constantly talking to people who were told, "no fraternization." The soldiers were told that and they had to follow. But some of them followed it in the breach, rather than in the order.

What about the defining moment for these people? Long-term friendships. Fifty years later they still have reunions. Did you get much of a sense of that?

MP: I think for many it *was* the defining moment in their lives. As Leslie was saying, they were relatively young and this was the time in their lives when they would forge friendships that would last throughout their lives. The circumstances made it such that they were working together on a common project, and that common goal led to a bonding.

BS: It seemed to me that this was especially so—the journalists seemed to be very much affected by this, and I guess the lawyers, too. But there was something about the sense of history, and also, I guess, if you are in your 20s or early 30s, the war is over, America is victorious, you're playing a very significant role in a major historic activity, obviously it's going to have a long-term impact on you, and we get that sense. I know Harold Burson, who was associated with the Armed Forces Radio, talking about how he got to know all of the correspondents at that time. People like Walter Cronkite and Howard K. Smith and such. He kept this relationship on for 50 years. So people who become significant in American life are present at Nuremberg.

How about the descriptions we get? Some very vivid ones of Nuremberg after the war. Do you have a sense of that?

MP: Most of them arrived at Nuremberg by train and were quite distraught to see the devastation. Unless they had been soldiers who had seen active combat, it was a pretty startling setting. That may have contributed to some of the sympathy or empathy that the men especially seemed to feel for the German people.

LF: The interviews really do portray a very vivid picture of a war. Or the remnants of a war-torn country. Especially for somebody who just wouldn't consider—like myself—the material reality of the war experience. I think one of the women actually said, "Coming to Nuremberg was very stunning and devastating" to her because she had already seen devastation, but she had seen it in London, where she had been staying through the war. The difference was between living in a country that was victorious and a country that was defeated. Defeat really increased the impact of the devastation surrounding the Nuremberg Trials.

BS: You [Leslie] are younger than both of us. Did you have much sense of World War II? I remember growing up as a child during the war, and having some memory of it from the American side. But what about yourself?

LF: I had very little sense of World War II coming into this project. One of my grandfathers was flat-footed and was not allowed to participate. And the other one was part of the navy, but never really saw active combat. So the war didn't become part of my family's stories. Beyond what I would have gotten through public education, which is relatively little; I didn't get too much. The movies of my generation tended to focus more on Vietnam than World War II stories. So I came into the project knowing not that much about World War II.

BS: What insights do you get about World War II?

LF: I was surprised by the real sense of camaraderie, and the real sense of a higher purpose, a nation united towards a common goal. I guess in my life experiences, I recognize that as a nation, we have a sense of higher purpose, but we're not unified. We don't have an outside force that's threatening us, so we tend to look more critically at each other. So there is the sense that everybody was pulling together for the war and for the trials without divisions. Perhaps it wasn't so much actually stated in the interviews, but was brought out in the interviews. That people were coming together for this common goal really impressed me.

BS: Michele, did it give you any insights? You probably don't remember the war.

MP: I was born during the war, so I don't really have a sense of it. But I've always viewed Nazis as the embodiment of evil—and certainly their ideology and practices were horrific. But hearing the interviewees describe the defendants as sad, drab, and mediocre drove home the chilling realization that any person has the potential for evil.

BS: With me having some visions—and probably visions based as much on war movies as anything else—I'd seen movies during the war—I think this brought home, particularly the immediate postwar period, better than I had any vision of it. And a little more of an understanding of people going over there. I remember having a cousin who was in the occupation army in Germany, and I thought very little of it because he wasn't in the real war. I had other relatives in the real war. These people—some of them having gone through the war—a number of them in many of the major battles, and then coming out to Nuremberg—it's interesting to see their reaction in the sense of war and peace because I remember one or two of them went through many, many, many days of consecutive battle. And then they're finished, and then they get another assignment, and the assignment is to go to Nuremberg, and they sort of keep their sanity about them, and they're looking at it in a somewhat different way. I think it gave that perspective of the transition from war to peace, which I didn't have a good sense of. I was a little child at the time.

What about the notion of the Cold War? You had some commentary on that during these interviews. Did it seem to have much, do you think, of an impact on some of these folks? Does anything stand out with respect to that?

MP: I don't know how much interaction there was between Americans and Russians to start with before the Cold War set in, but there was some. There was some joint partying, I guess, before the Cold War. And then there seemed to be a very sharp differentiation with no interaction.

BS: Some of the interviewees talk about this kind of comradeship and the joint partying, and then all of a sudden it stops, and the distrust seems to mount. And, of course, distrust was there in terms of the trials themselves because when you have the International Military Tribunal and you have the United States, Britain, Russia, and France, the Russians' view of what should be happening in that trial and what the outcome should be is much different than the American and British view. Part of it stems from the different kind of approach to law, as well as the ideology of capitalism and Communism. But there was an element of the Cold War that obviously plays a role in what happens with the trials, and Leslie—while this project was on, you did a paper about what was happening post–World War [II]. Could you talk a little bit about that?

LF: In my paper I was discussing the changing American policy towards Germany during the postwar period. When the trials first began, Americans were definitely an advocate for punishment of Germans, which eventually faded into a policy of rehabilitation of Germany. This change in policies has been ascribed to political concerns with the coming of the Cold War, as well as the need for economic recovery. One of the things that I found with these interviews was that people's personal experience and the growing distance from wartime was prompted at the individual level—and reflected in government policy by a need for reconciliation, and to move on with people's lives. In terms of the Cold War, I think that many of our interviewees—the ones who spoke of it—there wasn't really a variation from the standard story of "we were chummy, we had friendships with the Russians, and then overnight it disappeared." But I think that for many of these people it didn't really have—at the time they were going through it, I don't think they knew that their relationships with the Russians were going to have the same sort of impact. They didn't really focus on it that way, so they don't really have this long-term impact. But these stories that they've collected and their experiences had definitely explained—especially with hindsight—or been part of the tale of the Cold War. The beginning, the root of it.

BS: So you were looking more at the private than the public?

LF: Yes.

BS: We were talking about the difference between the private and the public.

LF: I think oral history has the real power to reach the private. Traditional sources such as many that we consulted when we began this project on the Nuremberg Trials, emphasized written documentation. It's very difficult to get a personal experience or an accounting of human experiences from written sources. But that's where the oral history makes up the difference. Because through all these interviews you definitely capture individual human experiences that, when all added up, come up to the historical record that we understand as the Nuremberg Trials.

BS: I think that's well said, that the oral history really humanizes this whole era and humanizes history generally. But you can get at the story of many individuals which add up to the story of, in this case, Nuremberg. And obviously, you have hundreds of thousands of other stories. We have not had the opportunity to interview Germans, and I suspect we'd get a very different story. But what we were interested in here was the American participants in Nuremberg as opposed to all of the participants.

What about the feeling of these interviewees about coming home? Do you get a sense of the reaction that people have to them when they come back? Was it a big deal that they were at Nuremberg? What sense did you get out of this?

MP: Maybe initially people were interested to hear about their experiences. But I got the feeling that there was not that much interest in the trials at home.

218

Some of them did, of course, make a career out of talking about Nuremberg. But generally speaking, I think that whatever initial interest there might have been died down very quickly. People on the home front were more or less anxious to get on with their lives, and wanted to be finished with the war and the trials seemed to be dragging that out for them, so there wasn't as much interest in it.

BS: At the end of World War I there was the term that Warren Harding used—"normalcy." America wanting to return to normalcy, and I think the same thing probably occurred after World War II. You do get a feeling that people we interviewed—they came home, and in many instances it was okay, you were at the Nuremberg Trials. So what? Or they're interested for five minutes, but not much more than that. And America was going about its business, and Germany now was being rehabilitated. In fact, the impact was probably not enormous, at least not immediately.

MP: You wonder, though, if there had been television then in the way it is now, how much of a difference that would have made.

LF: What's also interesting is the timing of this because as far as my generation is concerned, World War II is the last war with soldiers who came home as heroes. And it's interesting that with these interviews, we have this real sense that they're not coming back to glory. It's not that they're not heroes, it's just that there's little interest. I think that's a matter of timing. When the war was over, the tide was still high for self-congratulation, and at this point in time—

MP: It was anticlimactic.

LF: And there was the return to normalcy.

BS: This was the trial of the century probably, when you think about it, at least one of the trials of all history. And by not having quite the same kind of coverage we have in 1996, and not having television, the impact is somewhat less. Because those armed forces radio programs that I mentioned with respect to Harold Burson—he was instructed that they wanted everyone to hear about these trials. But I think the shows were 15 minutes or so. They were relatively brief, and they were on radio, and I would suspect that the hour that they were on would have been at an odd time. I don't know if they went back to America or not.

LF: The shows were taped at 9 P.M., before the shows that broadcasted in the United States.

MP: They were mainly listened to by the troops and others in Germany.

BS: So television probably would have made a very different impact. I know that in the celebration of the 50th anniversary of the Nuremberg Trials, Court TV put on 15 hours of television, using some of the film that was shot by the Army Signal Corps. They did record much of what went on, and they do have film of some of what went on. So there is a lasting record. But it's a record that could easily be forgotten. The fact between the 50 years plus since Nuremberg, and all of the wars that have occurred since then—the small wars that have occurred since then—the fact that war crime trials have not been held, except in the Bosnia situation—do you think that that tells us something about trying to implement justice as it was rendered at Nuremberg?

MP: I think what happened at Nuremberg was a very ideal moment. It was a moment almost out of time. During the recent war in Bosnia, we couldn't say that we didn't know what was happening because we have television now. And yet even so, that didn't stop any of the atrocities. If anything, a call for a Nuremberg-style trial, whether it becomes a reality or not, almost seemed to excuse the need for intervention. Maybe the day will come when the world will have Nuremberg-type trials, or, better yet, no need for those trials. It seems to be a very slow process. Nuremberg set a precedent, but it's discouraging that nothing has come of it, and I think the people that we interviewed for the most part, had that same feeling. But several of them are real crusaders, who are trying to make a world court or world peace a reality.

BS: In a sense, one of the ingredients that you need are all of those that commit the crimes have to be caught and incarcerated. And you don't always have that in the wars—or the small wars that we have had. So without having the people to try on site, it becomes practically a much more difficult thing, as the Bosnian situation has shown, with those who are not in captivity.

We used some of our interviews with photographs. We had a photo oral history exhibit, which was put on in conjunction with the opening of the Dodd Research Center. In putting together that exhibit, how did you find the correlation between the photos and the quotes, and what kind of impact do you think that had on the public that came to see the exhibit?

LF: I think it had a nice impact on the public. We got a lot of positive reviews on the exhibit. In picking out the pictures, we worked with the archives at the university, and we went through Thomas Dodd's scrapbooks and took some of the pictures that had actually been given to him and were in his possession. We used them to tell a story of Nuremberg. In many of the interviews, there's a sequence, starting from the early life, and going to how they had arrived at Nuremberg, and what they saw, and their involvement in the trials. And then what it was like for them coming back. And we tried to follow that sequence in our photo exhibit. I don't remember the exact number of photos, but we start with an image of Nuremberg in ruins and we end with an image of Robert Jackson giving an address in the courtroom. We pulled quotes from the interviews that related to the pictures. These helped develop a sense of what it was like to be in the Nuremberg community. The exhibit was well received.

MP: The other parts of the photo exhibit were contemporary photos of the oral history interviewees along with a few pictures of some of them at the time of the trials. And I think that those pictures, across the gallery space from the pictures of Nuremberg, made you realize that these were some of the people who made the other part of it—the trial itself—happen.

BS: It seemed that the impact of that—people long after the exhibit first went up—still stopped and looked at the photos and read about those who spoke. It shows, I think, the relatedness and connectedness of the oral history and photography, and what it does is make for a very good sense of trying to illustrate a point. Because you can do it graphically, and you can do it in words, and the oral history really helps spell that out, and the photos elaborate on the oral history and vice versa. So the project that we did, "Witnesses to Nuremberg" had many facets to it. It had an oral history project, it has this volume that our readers are now reading, and it had a photo/oral history exhibit. It includes archival material that will remain in the archives at the Center for Oral History at the Thomas Dodd Research Center, so that people can look at all of the original transcripts that don't appear in this volume.

At this time is there anything that you would want to add to what we have said?

MP: Just that the interest seemed to keep building on itself. As people heard about the oral history project, they contacted us, and we kept hearing from people who were not on the original list, or who knew of people who were there, or who had a fascination with the subject. I suspect that the 50th anniversary had a lot to do with it. When they see photographs of Nuremberg or hear testimony or read about it, that seems to spark their interest and revive their memories.

BS: This raises an interesting issue. Some of our interviewees have been interviewed a number of times. And some of them speak about their experience frequently, or if not very frequently, they do on occasion. Do you think that the memory of Nuremberg is different than what Nuremberg actually was?

MP: I think it would have been interesting to have been able to interview the participants at the time of the trials, and then to reinterview them 50 years later, as we're doing now, and see if there are any differences.

BS: I think this raises one of the major questions about oral history. What role does memory play? And here we're dealing with 50 years distant from the event. What I would suggest is that while we may be getting a lot of memory which is filtered over those 50 years, it is still better than not having any evidence at all—and as reliable sometimes as other kinds of sources.

LF: I don't think they make up stories for us. It's just the slant they might take in telling the stories might change because of the time that has passed or the concerns the interviewees have at this moment in time. I think we do get interesting and important stories about personal experience. I think that by reading the full interviews, you can discern for yourself people's biases. Almost any resource has some sort of bias that has to be factored out, whether you're using the written source, or whether you're using an oral source.

BS: So our "Witnesses to Nuremberg" are probably as good witnesses as witnesses in a courtroom. And maybe on that note, we'll stop.

Appendix A
International Military Tribunal (IMT) Charges, Verdicts, and Sentences, and Statistical Table of the 12 Subsequent Trials

INTERNATIONAL MILITARY TRIBUNAL (IMT) CHARGES, VERDICTS, AND SENTENCES

Defendant	Conspiracy	Crimes against Peace	War Crimes	Crimes against Humanity	Sentence
Hermann Göring	indicted and convicted	indicted and convicted	indicted and convicted	indicted and convicted	hanging
Joachim von Ribbentrop	indicted and convicted	indicted and convicted	indicted and convicted	indicted and convicted	hanging
Wilhelm Keitel	indicted and convicted	indicted and convicted	indicted and convicted	indicted and convicted	hanging
Alfred Jodl	indicted and convicted	indicted and convicted	indicted and convicted	indicted and convicted	hanging
Alfred Rosenberg	indicted and convicted	indicted and convicted	indicted and convicted	indicted and convicted	hanging
Wilhelm Frick	indicted and acquitted	indicted and convicted	indicted and convicted	indicted and convicted	hanging
Arthur Seyss-Inquart	indicted and acquitted	indicted and convicted	indicted and convicted	indicted and convicted	hanging
Fritz Sauckel	indicted and acquitted	indicted and acquitted	indicted and convicted	indicted and convicted	hanging
Martin Bormann (absent)	indicted and acquitted	*not indicted* on charge	indicted and convicted	indicted and convicted	hanging
Ernst Kaltenbrunner	indicted and acquitted	*not indicted* on charge	indicted and convicted	indicted and convicted	hanging
Hans Frank	indicted and acquitted	*not indicted* on charge	indicted and convicted	indicted and convicted	hanging
Julius Streicher	indicted and acquitted	*not indicted* on charge	*not indicted* on charge	indicted and convicted	hanging
Erich Raeder	indicted and convicted	indicted and convicted	indicted and convicted	*not indicted* on charge	life in prison
Walther Funk	indicted and acquitted	indicted and convicted	indicted and convicted	indicted and convicted	life in prison
Rudolf Hess	indicted and convicted	indicted and convicted	indicted and acquitted	indicted and acquitted	life in prison
Albert Speer	indicted and acquitted	indicted and acquitted	indicted and convicted	indicted and convicted	20 years in prison
Baldur von Schirach	indicted and acquitted	*not indicted* on charge	*not indicted* on charge	indicted and convicted	20 years in prison
Constantin von Neurath	indicted and convicted	indicted and convicted	indicted and convicted	indicted and convicted	15 years in prison
Karl Dönitz	indicted and acquitted	*not indicted* on charge	indicted and convicted	*not indicted* on charge	10 years in prison
Hans Fritzsche	indicted and acquitted	indicted and acquitted	indicted and acquitted	indicted and acquitted	acquitted
Franz von Papen	indicted and acquitted	indicted and acquitted	*not indicted* on charge	*not indicted* on charge	acquitted
Hjalmar Schacht	indicted and acquitted	indicted and acquitted	*not indicted* on charge	*not indicted* on charge	acquitted
Total Guilty	8	12	16	16	19
Total Acquitted	14	4	2	2	3

Source: John Alan Appleman, *Military Tribunals and International Crimes* (Westport, Conn.: Greenwood Press, 1971, reprint of Bobbs-Merrill, 1954) and Michael R. Marrus, *The Nuremberg War Crimes Trial, 1945–46: a Documentary History* (Boston: Bedford Books, 1997). Also see Thomas J. Dodd Papers, Archives and Special Collections Department, Thomas J. Dodd Research Center, University of Connecticut Libraries.

STATISTICAL TABLE OF THE 12 SUBSEQUENT TRIALS

Case Number	Popular Name of Case	Number Indicted	Number Tried	Death Sentences	Life Sentences	Prison Sentences	Number Acquitted	Others
1	Medical	23	23	7	5	4	7	
2	Milch	1	1		1			
3	Justice	16	14		4	6	4	1 suicide 1 severed
4	Pohl	18	18	3	3	9	3	
5	Flick	6	6			3	3	
6	Farben	24	23			13	10	1 severed
7	Hostage	12	10		2	6	2	1 suicide 1 severed
8	RuSHA	14	14		1	12	1	
9	Einsatzgruppen	24	22	14	2	6		1 suicide 1 severed
10	Krupp	12	12			11	1	
11	Ministries	21	21			19	2	
12	High Command	14	13		2	9	2	1 suicide
Total		185	177	24	20	98	35	8

Source: Trials of War Criminals before the Nuremberg Military Tribunals under Control Council Law no. 10, vol. 15, U.S. Government Printing Office, Thomas J. Dodd Papers, Archives and Special Collections Department, Thomas J. Dodd Research Center, University of Connecticut Libraries. Used with permission.

Appendix B
Transcript of American
Forces Network Broadcast
November 19, 1945

Good evening. This is Corporal Sy Bernhard talking to you from [AFN's] special booth in the courtroom at Nuremberg, Germany, the same courtroom where tomorrow one of the final chapters in the history of the Second World War will begin as 22 ranking members of the Nazi Party will be charged by the four great powers with the conspiracy that launched every major nation of the world into total war ... total war that lasted for six full years.

The courtroom tonight is empty ... darkened only slightly. It is an imposing courtroom ... a courtroom whose appointments translate themselves almost at first glance into terms of austerity, dignity, and justice. Most of the men around here tonight are GIs—GIs of the 18th and 28th Infantry ... two of the fighting regiments of the fighting First Division. These GIs are pulling guard duty—the familiar two on and four off. Inside the building they carry .45s ... outside, M-1s. They're probably the best-dressed GIs an ETO has ever seen ... razor-edged OD trousers, spotlessly white helmet liners, web belts, leggings, and gloves. And there are lots of them around, too. Most of them have their own private opinions about what's going to happen in these next several weeks at Nuremberg ... in fact, you don't have to be a GI to have an opinion of that kind. Everybody here has his own inside slant—his own rumor—cooked out of the same stuff you yourself heard just after your outfit was alerted—or just after you got on the boat.

But the most popular story is that although the trial will open tomorrow, it may adjourn for periods of time ranging from 12 days to 6 weeks ... depending, naturally, on whose hot poop you want to believe.

Note: This script was prepared by Corporal Harold Burson and Corporal Sy Bernhard. It was narrated over the American Forces Network by Corporal Sy Bernhard.

There's another good yarn that's going around this fancy latrine circuit ... a story about a bedraggled, broken-down character trying to convince the courthouse guards that he should be admitted without one of the blue pass cards—something, believe me, that just isn't done. Well, the scuttlebutt has it that this unshaven Heinie started getting browned off after his pleading did him no good. Then in complete desperation a familiar ranting began: "I demand to get into the trial. I started the whole thing. My name is Hitler." All of which, of course is a bit on the fantastic side, although you may remember the story of Otto Dietrich, the head of the Nazi Press Bureau, who unsuccessfully tried to surrender himself to a guard in the British sector some time ago. As yet, however, Hitler has not put in an appearance. But this is true: we were present when a request from the once-Admiral Raeder, one of the defendants, came over the telephone. The former admiral wanted permission to wear his red necktie in the court tomorrow. And the former admiral got his sartorial wish—he can wear his red tie.

But to bring you up to date on the more serious courthouse news: there are reports that would at least indicate the possibility, though perhaps not the probability, of a delay. Supposedly, there are four motions before the judges, any one of which could be a cause for postponement. One is that the Russian delegation is asking for a delay because their prosecutor, General R. A. Rudenko, is ill and it will be impossible for him to arrive for several days. The situation further complicates itself when it is made known that no one else on the Russian prosecution staff is authorized to represent the U.S.S.R. at trial. A motion in this effect was supposedly in discussion at an executive session of the tribunal up until a couple of hours ago. But no announcement of any decision has been made.

A second motion is said to be under way on behalf of the French delegation protesting the dropping of Gustav Krupp from the indictment because of ill health. The French are basing their move on the claim that the desire of two nations to indict a person makes it mandatory for that person to be included in the indictment. And the French, supposedly, are one of two nations interested in indicting Krupp, head of Germany's great armament works.

The third and fourth possible motions that may be considered by the tribunal are motions requesting mental examinations of Rudolf Hess, the former Hitler favorite who fled to England early in the war, and Julius Streicher, editor of the anti-Semitic newspaper, *Der Stürmer*.

But to return to Nuremberg ... and it is especially fitting that Nuremberg should be the rubbelized (sic) host to this great war crime trial. It is fitting because no other German city so symbolizes the same continuity ... the same linking theme in the long dead past, and the freshly dead yesterday of German history. For Nuremberg is the story of Germany ... the fabric of dictatorship and the culture of a military nation. Nuremberg has been the personal city of Germany's rulers since its founding in 1050 and for 800 years thereafter. Eight centuries of tradition that compelled all German rulers to take office here. So, it was only natural for Adolf Hitler to restore Nuremberg to its peculiar position in the German cavalcade. Soon after the Nazis took power in 1933, Nuremberg became the party city ... the *geheilige* city ... the holy city of National Socialism. It was here in Nuremberg that Hitler held his spectacular Nazi Party Day shindigs every year ... that is every year until April 1945, when Nuremberg gave Hitler an ironic birthday present by surrendering to the American 3rd and 45th Divisions, 91 percent of the city lying ingloriously prostrate before the conquering GIs.

Therefore it is to this shrine city that Germany's top war leaders have been brought. They have been brought here to face an international tribunal because the crimes they are charged with demand international judgment, judgment different from those others whose acts were perpetrated in a single locality or against a single nation, as, for example, the Belsen trial or the Laval trial.

Tomorrow, 20 defendants will file in to hear an indictment of documented charges, an indictment signed by the representatives of the United States, Great Britain, the U.S.S.R. and France. There are four counts presented in the indictment, but not all defendants are charged with all four counts. The first count is an all-encompassing one which claims that the defendants are guilty of conspiracy ... a common plot. The second count charges the defendants with actual crimes against the peace ... with planning, preparing, initiating, and waging wars of aggression in violation of international treaties. The third count charges them with the commission of war crimes such as the wanton destruction of towns, villages, and cities, destruction not justified by military necessity. And in the fourth count, they're charged with crimes against humanity, such crimes as extermination, enslavement, and deportation of peoples, such crimes as persecution on political, racial, and religious grounds.

Those are the charges which the prosecuting attorneys of four nations will attempt to prove in open court tomorrow, the prosecuting attorneys who represent the outstanding in legal talent in the four nations involved. Our delegation is headed by Mr. Justice Robert H. Jackson, on leave from the Supreme Court of the United States.

Mr. Justice Jackson has said repeatedly that the trial will be no cut-and-dried affair ... no mere formality to permit the winner to kill off the loser. The guilt of the defendants must be proved, for, as under our legal system, the defendants will be considered innocent until proven guilty. However, we will *not* permit a repetition of the 1921 Leipzig trials, when a *German* court tried *German* accused, accused who included a total of nine men, two of them enlisted men. The result: three and a half years' imprisonment for all nine combined.

The prosecutors will plead their cases before an International Military Tribunal, one judge, with an alternate, from each of the great powers. The Honorable Francis Biddle, former attorney general, represents the United States, and his alternate is Judge John J. Parker, a United States Circuit Court judge since 1925. Decisions of the tribunal will be by majority vote, with the president of the court, the Right Honorable Sir Geoffrey Lawrence, deciding in case of a tie. But the final verdict as to the guilt of a defendant must be agreed upon by three of the four judges. And the penalty for guilt is still an unknown element.

The defendants, who will be represented by lawyers of their own choice, fall, as players on the Nazi stage, into three categories. There are the high-ranking party members, usually government officials . . . men like Hermann Göring, Rudolf Hess, [and] von Ribbentrop. Then there are the militarists, the members of the German High Command . . . men like Alfred Jodl, Wilhelm Keitel, [and] Karl Dönitz. And third, there are the industrialists and the bankers, who, through their resources, made possible the conspiracy . . . men like Hjalmar Schacht and Walter Funk, and, until he was removed from the list of indicted because of illness, Gustav Krupp.

Twenty-four names appear in the original indictment, but only 20 men may face the tribunal at ten o'clock tomorrow morning. Robert Ley, leader of the German labor front, committed suicide last month. Martin Bormann, Hitler's deputy in the Nazi Party, has never been found and may be dead. Krupp is too ill to be moved, while only last night, Ernst Kaltenbrunner, the Nazi's top SS man, suffered a cranial hemorrhage and had to be rushed to a hospital. Although the hemorrhage was not fatal, although he showed improvement this morning, he will have to be kept hospitalized, possibly for several weeks. Kaltenbrunner retained consciousness and even remarked, "I am very sorry I cannot be in court tomorrow." Which, of course, drew quite a laugh when quoted to the press this morning.

This trial is extraordinary for many reasons. The spectacular element enters the scene because here will be assembled at one time, in one place, the remaining, living greats of the Nazi system. But the implications of the trial are deeper, far more serious. For this is the first international criminal trial . . . the first criminal trial conducted jointly by four nations, four nations which are acting outside their own countries, outside their own law.

In our travels these past weeks in connection with the coverage of these trials, GIs have had one stock question when we asked for an opinion on these proceedings. Even the combat men pulling guard here want to know, "why can't we just take them out and shoot 'em? We know they're guilty." This question and others on the legal aspects of the trial, we have discussed with members of the staff of the United States chief counsel. We had even hoped that one of the members of the prosecuting staff would be here tonight to clarify a number of involved legal questions for you. But the trial starts tomorrow . . . there is important work to be done tonight.

But to get back to our question, "what is the reason for the trial?" One of the important reasons is that the guilt of the German leaders should be carefully documented ... documented so painstakingly and with such clarity that the world could never forget. But basically, there is another reason for the trial. We of the four nations are devoted to law and order. We do not desire to employ the Nazi way ..."to take 'em out and shoot 'em" ... for our system is not lynch law. We will dispense punishment as the evidence demands.... [next pages illegible]

Suggested Additional Reading

A full accounting of the IMT trial was published in 42 volumes after the trial's conclusion. See International Military Tribunal, *Trial of the Major War Criminals before the International Military Tribunal, Nuremberg, 14 November [1945]–1 October 1946,* 42 vols. (Nuremberg: International Military Tribunal, 1947). The Thomas J. Dodd Papers at the Archives and Special Collections Department, Thomas J. Dodd Research Center, University of Connecticut, Storrs, Connecticut, contain an impressive collection of material related to the war crimes trials.

Students and general readers of this volume, however, are likely to seek more accessible sources. Joseph E. Persico provides a very readable overview in his *Nuremberg: Infamy on Trial* (New York: Penguin, 1994) and Michael R. Marrus makes documents available in his brief volume, *The Nuremberg War Crimes Trial, 1945–46: A Documentary History* (Boston: Bedford Books, 1997). Norman E. Tutorow's edited *War Crimes, War Criminals, and Source Book* (New York: Greenwood Press, 1986) is a valuable bibliographic aid, and John Alan Appleman's early *Military Tribunals and International Crimes* (Westport, Conn.: Greenwood Press, 1971), a reprint of a 1954 Bobbs-Merrill publication, offers a great deal of factual material. Telford Taylor, who played a leading role in the trials, relates his story in encyclopedic detail in *The Anatomy of the Nuremberg Trials: A Personal Memoir* (New York: Knopf, 1992). Also see his *Nuremberg and Vietnam: An American Tragedy* (Chicago: Quadrangle Books, 1970).

Another oral history of participants at the trials can be found in Hilary Gaskin, *Eyewitnesses at Nuremberg* (London: Arms & Armour Press, 1990). That book, which is organized differently than this volume, is not readily accessible in the United States.

Two helpful overviews are Ann Tusa and John Tusa's *The Nuremberg Trial* (New York: Atheneum, 1984) and Robert E. Conot's *Justice at Nuremberg* (New York: Harper & Row, 1983). William J. Bosch studied American public opinion and Nuremberg in *Judgment on Nuremberg: American Attitudes toward The Major German War-Crime Trials* (Chapel Hill, N.C.: University of North Carolina Press, 1970). The destruction and rebuilding of Nuremberg receives attention in Jeffry M. Diefendorf, *In the Wake of War: The Reconstruction of German Cities after World War II* (New York: Oxford University Press, 1993).

While the Nuremberg trials assessed the guilt of Nazi leaders, the collective and individual responsibility of rank-and-file Germans is explored in Daniel Jonah Goldhagen's controversial and important study, *Hitler's Willing Executioners: Ordinary Germans and the Holocaust* (New York: Knopf, 1996).

Index

Nuremberg reunions: Krevit and, 76; Logan and, 201; Peyser and, 148
Nuremberg stadiums: Glenny and, 54; Logan on, 195; Krevit and, 83; Peyser on, 137
Nuremberg War Crimes Trials. *See* International Military Tribunal; *specific trials*

Obercommando, 63
Obersturmbaunführer, 98
Oberursel (Germany), 96
"obeying orders" defense: Glenny on, 49, 50, 51, 52; Krevit on, 75
Oeschey, Rudolph, 161
Office of Special Investigations (OSI), 9–10
Office of Strategic Services (OSS), Presentation Branch of: directive report on purpose of trial, 26–27; documentation responsibilities, 22; Kiley in, 17–18
Office of War Crimes, 72
Office of War Information, 111, 112
Ohlendorff, Otto, 98, 102
Olmsted, Frederick Law, Sr., 16

Palace of Justice, 4; courtroom (*see* Nuremberg courthouse); design and renovation of, 21–23, 29–31; Kiley and, 33–34; King (Henry T., Jr.) and, 172; King (Robert) on, 155; Krevit's impression of, 76; security during renovations, 31
Pan American airline, 154
Papen, Franz von, 63; acquittal, 3, 224; evidence against, 199; Glenny and, 42, 43, 46
Paris: Burson in, 180–81; Kiley in, 18, 20–21, 29, 32; Pétain trials in, 29; vom Rath's assassination in, 90
Parker, John J., 145, 184, 229
Patton's Officers Club, 19
Pétain, Philippe, 29
Peyser, Joseph A., 129–30
Peyser, Max, 130
Peyser, Seymour, 3, 127–49; affidavits acquired by, 143–44; on anti-Semitism, 130; background, 127; C-47 flight to Nuremberg, 133; childhood, 127, 128–29; at Columbia Law School, 127, 130; on concentration camps, 130; on debate over defense counsel, 141–42; on defendants, 132; documentation duties and responsibilities, 138; editor of *Columbia Law Review,* 131; father, 127–28, 130; on France, 147; and German civilians, 135, 137; grandfather's migration to United States, 129–30; in Grand Hotel, 134; at Harvard, 127, 130; on Hitler, 130; on housing in Nuremberg, 134–35; on hunting Nazi criminals, 149; on IMT, 132, 141, 144–46, 147–48, 149; on international law, 146–47; interrogations conducted by, 139–40; on Jackson, 139; in Judge Advocate General's department, 131; and *Judgment at Nuremberg,* 143; on justice, 146–47, 149; on Ley, 138, 139–41; in London, 131, 132, 133; at Michigan Law School, 131; mother, 130; on Nazi Germany before WW II, 129–30; on Nazi structure, 138; on Nuremberg,

137; Nuremberg preparations, 131–33; personal impact of Nuremberg, 148; at Phillips and Nizer, 128; and reunion (1991), 148; on Russia, 147; and Russians, 144; on Sergeant Stone, 135; sisters, 128; on spectacle of Nuremberg trials, 147–48; and UNRRA camp, 135–36; on Vyshinsky, 145; on Yamashita, 142
Pforzheim (Germany), 31
Phillips and Nizer (law firm), 128
Playing for Time (documentary), 105, 106
pogroms, 129, 130
Pohl case, 225
Poland: and Guderian, 169; and Hess, 118; *pogroms* in, 129, 130
Potsdam Conference, 132
Prescott, Erma, 151
Press and Psychological Warfare Detachment (U.S.), 180
Press Wireless, 198
prison. *See* Nuremberg prison
prisoners' dock, 26, 27
prison guards: Carlow on, 66–67; Krevit on, 77. *See also* Carlow, Burton; Glenny, William H.
Project Jackson, 113
prosecutors. *See specific prosecutors*
Purdue University, 151
Pusey, Henry, 32, 76

Raeder, Erich, 42, 185, 227; sentence, 224
Rath, Ernst vom, 90
"Rat Race to the Rhine," 56
Rebdorf Prison, 169
Red Ball Express, 21
Red Division, 23, 64, 77, 80
Regnitz River, 31
Reichstag, 109
Rennan, William J., 131
revenge, 1; Glenny on, 49; Russian desire for, 4. *See also* hangings; justice; sentences
Ribbentrop, Joachim von, 63, 190, 229; Carlow and, 61; sentence, 224
Riel, Frank, 142
Rise and Fall of the Third Reich, The: A History of Nazi Germany (Shirer), 97
Rockefeller, David, 32
Rockefeller University, 32
Rogers, Sir Richard, 35
Roosevelt, Eleanor, 92
Roosevelt, Franklin D., 2, 3, 80
Root, Clark, Buchner, and Ballantine (law firm), 152
Rosenberg, Alfred, 98, 133, 148; sentence, 224
Ross, Harold, 194
Rothenberger, Kurt, 160–61
Rudenko, R. A., 20, 227
Ruffer, Gideon, 117
Rundstedt, Karl von, 44, 45–46, 49
RuSHA, 225
Russia: and debate over defense counsel, 141–42; external security for Nuremberg prison and courthouse, 57; goals for IMT, 4; Katyn massacre, 147; *pogroms* in, 130

The Authors

Bruce M. Stave is professor of History and director of the Center for Oral History at the University of Connecticut. He has served as editor of the *Oral History Review,* the journal of the Oral History Association, and is author or editor of nine books including *From the Old Country: An Oral History of European Migration to America,* which appeared in the Twayne Oral History Series and won the 1995 Homer D. Babbidge Jr. Award.

Michele Palmer is the co-author, with Bruce M. Stave, of *Mills and Meadows: A Pictorial History of Northeast Connecticut*. The former manager of Tapescribe, the transcribing service of the Center for Oral History, she also participated in the center's Connecticut Workers and Technological Change oral history project. She writes children's books under the name Malka Penn.

Leslie Frank is a doctoral student in history at the University of Connecticut. Her interests include the history of work, identity, and technology. She compiled the catalog for the Witnesses to Nuremberg oral history project.